Fundamentals of the Art of Poetry

Also by Oscar Mandel

FUNDAMENTALS

of the

ART OF POETRY

Oscar Mandel

Sheffield
Academic Press

Published by Sheffield Academic Press Ltd
Mansion House
19 Kingfield Road
Sheffield S11 9AS
England

Printed on acid-free paper in Great Britain
by Bookcraft Ltd
Midsomer Norton, Bath

British Library Cataloguing in Publication Data

A catalogue record for this book is available
from the British Library

ISBN 1-85075-852-2 cl
ISBN 1-85075-837-9 pa

Ion	I am persuaded that good poets by a divine inspiration interpret the things of the gods for us.
Socrates	And you rhapsodists are interpreters of the poets?
Ion	There again you are right.
Socrates	Then you are interpreters of interpreters?
Ion	Precisely.

Contents

Illustrations

Acknowledgments

'That poem is a splendid thing' by Richard Armour. Reprinted by kind permission of *The Writer*, Boston.

'White Paper' by John Ashbery. Copyright © by Wesleyan University Press. Reprinted by permission of University Press of New England.

'A Misunderstanding' by W.H. Auden. Copyright © 1945 by W. H. Auden. Reprinted by permission of Random House, Inc., and by kind permission of Faber & Faber Ltd.

Part of Number 16 of 'Dream Songs' by John Berryman, by kind permission of Faber & Faber Ltd. Also reprinted by permission of Farrar, Straus & Giroux, Inc.

'Poem No. 92' by Catullus, translated by L.R. Lind. Copyright © 1957 by L.R. Lind. Reprinted with permission of Houghton Mifflin Company.

'A Reason' and part of 'If You' by Robert Creeley. Reprinted by permission of the Regents of the University of California and the University of California Press.

'my sweet old etcetera', 'love is more thicker than forget', 'Buffalo Bill's' and 'un' by e.e. cummings. Reprinted from *Complete Poems, 1904–1962* by e.e. cummings, edited by George J. Firmage, by permission of W.W. Norton Company Ltd. Copyright © 1926, 1954, 1985, 1991 by the Trustees for the E.E. Cummings Trust and George James Firmage.

Parts of *The Divine Comedy* by Dante, translated by John Ciardi. Translation copyright 1954, 1957, 1959, 1960, 1961, 1965, 1967, 1970 by the Ciardi Family Publishing Trust. Reprinted by permission of W.W. Norton & Company, Inc.

Parts of *The Waste Land*, 'The Love Song of J. Alfred Prufrock', *Four Quartets* and *Murder in the Cathedral* by T.S. Eliot, by kind permission of Faber & Faber Ltd.

'In a Corner' by D.J. Enright, by permission of Oxford University Press and Watson, Little Ltd.

'The Silken Tent', part of 'Mending Wall' and part of 'After Apple-Picking' by Robert Frost. By kind permission of Random House UK Ltd, Jonathan Cape and the estate of the author.

Part of 'America' by Allen Ginsberg. Reprinted by permission of Harper Collins Publishers, Inc. from *Collected Poems 1947–1980 by Allen Ginsberg*. Copyright © 1956, 1959 by Allen Ginsberg. Copyright renewed.

Overture to Four Audiences

Amidst all the triumphs and disasters attributable to modern technology, industry and commerce, our famously materialistic world continues to hatch a vast and varied poetic life. Every year, a multitude of magazines, pamphlets and books display the poems of a myriad earnest poets; poetry is reviewed in dailies, monthlies and quarterlies; readings of poetry take place in bookshops, cafes, theaters and colleges; poets' voices are preserved on tape and disk, their owners rejoicing in any number of grants, prizes and free lodgings distributed by amiable institutions; flurries of introductory textbooks and anthologies of poetry compete for adoption in our schools; and all the while editions, commentaries, analyses and theories are printed without a hint of recession. Unmistakably, poetry is alive. Industrial fumes have done it no harm. It turns out that scrap metal can be as nourishing to the Muses as daffodils, and we can make ours, today, Charlotte Bronte's words of a century and half ago: 'Poetry is not dead, nor genius lost; nor has Mammon gained power over either.' To be sure, no one claims that the reading and writing of poetry are major preoccupations of our culture or that the nations are thirsting for hermeneutics. Poems and their theorists do not make or unmake generals and presidents. Yet the art remains a surprisingly sassy presence in the world; and I make bold to predict that posterity (though I know it often plays nasty tricks on those who speak on its behalf before it is born) will proclaim the twentieth century to have been, on the whole, and surprisingly, a silver age of and for poetry.

This then is the ground on which I am proposing a fresh inspection of the nature of poetry, its possible functions for mankind, and the special resources upon which it can draw to fulfill these functions. My book began its life as a text for an introductory junior-senior course at the California Institute of Technology, after I had ascertained (as many teachers do in similar circumstances) that the available works were not quite what I wanted. I hope it can survive and serve others in this classroom role. If it does, I take it for granted that even the most sympathetic instructors will make an argumentative triangle between themselves, their students and my propositions. My guess is that most of them will also ask their students to buy a complementary collection of poems, since those I offer make no pretence of constituting an anthology.

By and by it came to me that I had been writing all along not only a college and university textbook, but also an enchiridion—a guide-book—for lay readers of any age, in the spirit of scientists who attempt to make the essentials of their disciplines intelligible to inquisitive, intelligent audiences busy with their own specialties and occupations, yet eager to familiarize themselves with other human enterprises. These are persons who have left classrooms, syllabi, term papers, final grades behind them, and have perhaps never opened a volume of poetry since attending English Literature 206; but that tenderly half-remembered course has left them with a trace of curiosity, a wistful intention to pay poetry a visit again some day, if only for a few hours. To this non-professional yet receptive audience I also eagerly address my little book.

In addition, as a lifelong poet (among other titles to bread and consideration), I feel a natural desire to engage in a conversation about poetry with my fellow artists—those who, like myself, publish their reflections on the art, as well as those who keep their thoughts to themselves. I confess that if this were the only audience I could reach, I would be happy enough and would mope after no other.

Finally, and inevitably, I am sending this volume, with kindest regards, to my brothers and sisters in the academic world, whether or not they teach courses like my own. Professors of literature make up an amazingly large social class in the Western world, and one which produces, nowadays, wave after wave of mutually destructive 'critical theories'. These are usually broadcast in a tremendous language where phrases like 'diachronic referentiality', 'the transcendence of the great signifier', 'a set of binaries that replicate the difference between deferral and activation' can be viewed either as erecting new mansions of thought or draping Potemkin façades over flimsy shacks—observers are divided over the question.

My own view (secretly or openly shared, I am happy to say, by many of my colleagues) is that, innovative or not, all speculations on art, bar none, can be made accessible to intelligent amateurs (I use the word in its antique, noble sense of *lovers*) in words intelligible to them—and to the artists themselves—without compromising or cheapening the subject, glossing over complexities, and making childish small talk. For me, the lovely, expressive English in which poets like Sidney, Jonson, Dryden, Johnson, Coleridge, Arnold, Ransom and Eliot wrote their remembered criticism suffices, with here and there an addition and subtraction, for anything that can be thought of in any of the humanities at the close of our twentieth century. I hear good scientists complaining as well of pompous verbiage masking thin concepts; yet no one can deny that much of the esoteric language of the sciences is imposed on mankind by a universe that keeps running away from our words. My premise, I repeat, is that such is not the case for poetry, literature, the arts, and all the humanities. But to all this I am bound to add a personal note, happily borrowed from Jane Austen: 'I cannot speak well enough to be unintelligible.'

The only apology I owe the profession is that my own sometimes controversial theorizing takes place within a manual on the elements of poetry, amidst the necessary rudiments of iambs and quatrains. And yet, even there, among these simplicities, who knows but a fresh thought may crop up now and again. For the rest, if I am accused of failing to take into account some of the theories that happen to be 'in' today (and will be gone tomorrow), my answer is that I do deal with them; but I do so by indirection, stating positive doctrine and thus implying my rejection of all the negatives that are incompatible with it.

A few words about the organization and character of this volume.

It has been understood already that I have written an inquiry into the fundamentals of what poetry is and what 'makes it tick', not a historical survey of English and American poetry. This has not prevented me, however, from touching upon shifts in taste and other historical considerations wherever I thought it advisable to do so. Regarding my choice of illustrative texts, most of these are classics or else fine poems short of that status; but others, lighter in aesthetic weight (and some very light indeed) have proved equally useful as examples. However, let me repeat that this book is not and does not contain an anthology of verse. Several poems are mined and exploited again and again. And if one or two lines will do to make a point, I give no more. There are no exercises, no questions for examinations, no samples of student papers.

To make it incontrovertibly clear that I look upon the poet as an artist and not a versifying theologian, philosopher, politician or sociologist, I devote Part I to Art with a capital letter—Art-in-general—before turning my attention, in Part II, to the especial art of poetry. Even so, the other arts keep returning throughout this book, for even though the literary arts take their materials from the same supply room as do products of the human mind like political tracts and treatises on Being, their home is with the other arts; they live and die by the same 'laws' that govern symphonies and collages. I should add, however, that I concern myself very little with the artists themselves—their urges, methods, inner lives, intentions—and stick to the forms themselves—the things good or bad that have issued from the atelier.

A comment, finally, about the currently touchy issue of gender. What was I to do, in a guide-book on the art of poetry, about the problem of our male-dominated language? Oddly enough, language is more resistant to enlightened change than are laws, customs and professional opportunities. Our own, at any rate (others may be more accommodating), has a personality that blockheadedly refuses to do justice to the formerly weaker sex; and nowhere is it more mulish than in the sensitive matter of personal pronouns and words in the 'mankind' category. Justice is possible, but only at the price of clumsy writing—the 'his-or-her' sort of obstacular equity that I am at pains to avoid. Instead, I hope that my readers will silently translate every male expression, from God downward, into bisexed English, and place the guilt at the door of our intractable and, in this single respect, less than lovely and expressive language.

Part 1

About Art in General

Chapter 1

What Is Art?

Since poetry is one of the arts—Horace's *Ars Poetica* (The Art of Poetry) is our classic witness—why not attempt to find out what we mean by 'art' to begin with? 'Art' is one of those words most of us use without thinking about them very much, and it has been common currency for so long that it can no longer be held down universally to some single hard set of experiences. What we can do, however, is apply it for our purposes exclusively to situations in which the phrase 'a work of art' makes sense. Bear with me therefore for the length of an ungainly sentence, which will become more presentable when we go on to examine its parts chapter by chapter. Here then is what I propose.

> What we call a work of art is a human creation, namely a manipulation or arrangement of, or imposition upon, appropriate materials and resources resulting in a form, or a series of forms, or a set of flowing forms, which, when it stimulates our brain-centers of sight, hearing or language (singly or in combination) we admit into our consciousness as a phenomenon that we shall deem successful insofar as it produces in us a wholly or partly unmediated satisfaction, largely through the energizing of these materials and resources.

Whether valid or invalid, this definition may strike you as not only ungainly but also depressingly cold and antiseptic. Is that any way of dealing with the shivers, the perspiration, the ecstasy, the awe that take hold of a human being at the meeting point of a great work of art and a fine sensitivity? Obviously, I feel that it is.

If I were to use 'lyrical' language for my definition, I would be making—or attempting to make—literature of my own, that is to say, my explanation might be more interesting to you as a lyrical passage than as explanation. 'Poetry,' Wordsworth wrote, 'is the breath and finer spirit of all knowledge; it is the impassioned expression which is in the countenance of all science.' The sentence is so wonderfully written, so memorable, that it becomes part of that which it attempts to explain; in other words, it is itself 'poetry' or 'high literature'. Few would deny that Wordsworth is also *right*—to a certain extent. But I submit that his statement is on the whole more successful as a small literary jewel (as art, that is) than as a thesis capable of meeting the most exacting intellectual challenge. The definition I have proposed stakes all, instead, on being 'correct'. There is not the slightest danger of anyone's mistaking it for literature! The underlying idea of speaking so coldly about so warm a subject is that the explanation of the satisfaction should no more create the satisfaction than an explanation of humor should make you laugh. Or: the definition of Art should not itself be artistic.

But why, you might ask, bother to define it at all? And your question may recur when, in a later chapter, I propose to define Literature and then Poetry itself. As a matter of fact, few writers make the attempt; they probably believe that such definitions are either foredoomed or unimportant. Perhaps we can all agree that a definition of poetry never helped bring a better poem or a more sensitive reader into the world. But I am assuming that the excitement of intellectual discovery is an end sufficient unto itself. It is a satisfaction that takes human beings as far and as high above bestial life as they can go. We have all heard the reply of that intrepid mountaineer who was asked why he bothered to climb Mount Everest. 'Because it is there', he replied. If a mountain is there, somebody will sooner or later try to climb it. Somebody human; a chimp will not bother. And so it goes for the athletics of the mind. If there is something to know, there are minds that will try to know it. Perhaps the noblest words uttered by man or woman since the beginning of history were spoken by Socrates when he declared that 'the unexamined life is not worth living'. All the same, it must be confessed that noble projects are seldom meant for everybody. The truth is that most human beings find the unexamined life quite sufficiently exciting, just as most of us manage to live without scaling Mount Everest. If you are reading this book about Art and the art of poetry, I shall presume that you are one of us: those who hate to look at any vast human enterprise (and surely Art qualifies as one) without asking, 'What is it?'

Let me now, descending from these heights, offer a few preliminary explanations of my proposed definition, some of which will anticipate the detailed discussions to come.

(1) Why are the opening words of the definition 'What we call'? Because the definition is descriptive, not prescriptive. I am not saying, 'I decree that from now on a work of art shall be something that fulfills conditions A, D and W.' Rather, I am formulating the conditions—say, A, E, Q, and W—that normally appear when objects or events normally pass among human beings as works of art. This double 'normally' is inserted in order to allow for a certain fuzziness at the margin of the concept. Suppose I were trying to define the word 'house'. I would not be foolish enough to believe that I can prescribe (dictate) that the work of carpentry we generally sit on when we are at table 'is' a house. No fuzziness troubles our vision so far. But what about the four-wheeled appliance in which you drive to work every day after making sure it is filled with gasoline? Suppose someone points out to me that all too many unfortunate persons are forced to live in these vehicles? 'Where is your house, sir?' 'There'—pointing at a decayed Cadillac filled with clothing, pots and pans, etc. Should the definition of 'house' be expanded in order to take in the automobile, or should the automobile be kept out of the concept 'house' no matter how it is used? There is no way of eliminating these borderline ambiguities; nor do we want to suppress them, because they force us to keep thinking, to meet the challenges they mount, and, not infrequently, to alter our ideas.

(2) But who are the 'we' of our definition? I could with equal legitimacy have written 'I', or 'you', or 'people', or 'anyone'. Each individual makes the decision (usually subconscious and instantaneous) whether or not, as far as he is concerned, a given phenomenon qualifies as art—a decision, in our terms, whether or not to take it into his mental life as a creation whose success, for him, will be determined (at least in part) by its ability to infuse into his being an unmediated satisfaction. Similarly, each individual

decides whether, as far as he is concerned, the creation he has registered in his mind as a work of art is good art or bad art. Much more will be said on this topic in Chapter 4 and other places.

(3) The definition is *total*. This means that it provides the minimum elements that must be present in all works if we are to call them works of art; and it means that all further elements that can be imagined stand outside the definition—that is to say, they are not necessary for the thing to be called Art. This leaves open an assortment of elements and qualities and achievements that anyone can find *desirable* in art. So, by analogy, we might find it desirable in a car to have a sun-roof; and we might adamantly refuse to own one that didn't come so equipped; but the sun-roof would not become part of our definition of the species of manufactured goods known as the automobile.

(4) When the definition asserts that the work of art is a *human* act, it implies that glorious sunsets, the Rocky Mountains hooded in snow, pretty bird songs and purling brooks are none of them works of art, whether you suppose them created by God or through the chance action of complexes of molecules, and even though the satisfactions they give you can hardly be differentiated, at times, from what you might feel after looking at a painting or listening to a piece of music. Nor, in my opinion, is an attractive pebble, seashell or chunk of driftwood something that we generally call a work of art, probably because the only human work involved is that of selecting and transporting.[1]

Still, there are very reputable thinkers, and there are many ordinary people, who do call these untreated objects taken from nature, and others like them, works of art once they are selected, uplifted, distinguished and exhibited. We have reached a fuzzy border, in short.

You may also wish to dispute the human exclusivity of the definition. Might not a chimpanzee's efforts with crayons be granted

---

1.   The situation changes if, say, you clean, scrub, or lacquer the driftwood, or snip off a piece or two, before placing it on your shelf or exposing it in an art gallery, even though the passage from non-art to art may be minimal. Note, in this connection, that the Western languages—I am ignorant of the others—all speak of *works* of art; for example, *oeuvre d'art* in French or *obra de arte* in Spanish. We expect that a degree of labor be expended.

the status of works of art? Once more we stand at an uncertain border.

I admit, in the meantime, that instead of speaking of a human act, we might do better nowadays to refer to an act under human control, so as to include certain quite interesting works produced by or with the help of computers. But this is a superficial complication. Computers must be programmed, and they are programmed by human beings. If a program is programmed by a computer, still it was a human being who programmed the computer to program. Besides, it is the human being who decides what to keep and what to throw out from the welter of stuff the computers disgorge. Computers are thus but one more 'means of production' or tool for the artist.

The same principle of ultimate human control, or imposition on the materials and resources, applies to chance art (aleatory art), where, by one means or another (dripping paint onto a canvas, picking words out of a hat, etc.) the artist lets anything happen that happens to happen. But it is he who sets the operation in motion, it is he who stops it, it is he who decides what to keep and what to throw out, and—ninety times out of a hundred—it is he who touches up the results after all.

He and she and they; for, naturally, our definition blesses multiple authorships.

(5) What are the 'appropriate' materials and resources mentioned in the definition? We possess different arts because the materials and resources (or elements) that can be shaped into forms differ so widely. For example, the materials or resources proper to the art of music are the sounds produced by a vast and ever-growing array of instruments, from a couple of sticks clacked against each other to mind-boggling electronic equipment; all this plus what the human throat can produce. For a thing to be called a work of musical art, the satisfaction it gives us must be largely (not always wholly) due to what the creator of the thing has *accomplished* with these peculiar resources.

For the literary arts, the primary materials are obviously words and related signs like punctuation marks. Since these words and signs normally convey what we call meaning (even nonsense syllables can do so: they can mean nonsense), I will be talking a great deal about *propositions* as the basic material for literature in general and poetry in particular. For observe that the so-called 'music' of poetry is produced not by hitting a length of wire with a bit of felt-covered wood (for instance) but always by the appropriate resource of the art of literature: words and related signs.

(6) The resources and materials for each art are created, manipulated or arranged by the artist, or are otherwise imposed upon by him. The sounds musical instruments make are all created by mankind (out of pre-existing materials, of course; we cannot create out of nothing); the sculptor manipulates his clay and literary artists manipulate words; choreographers essentially 'arrange' the human body (often their own) and landscape artists 'arrange' plants; while art photographers impose upon their selected materials angles of vision, a choice of filters, lens openings, shutter speeds and so on.

(7) My use of the expression 'brain-centers' instead of the traditional five or six human senses allows me to align language as a power parallel to sight and hearing even though it derives from or depends upon both of these. I take it that physiologists have determined once and for all that the brain does house language areas along with visual, auditory and other specialized zones of perception and activity. If research eventually proves otherwise, our definition can be simplified and speak, more simply, of Art addressing itself to our 'functions' of sight, hearing and language.

(8) The concept of *form* is universally accepted as basic to any notion of Art. This concept remains firmly in place in our definition, but it is slightly elaborated and clarified. A poem and a painting are single (discrete) forms. A sonnet sequence, and the several panels of a medieval altarpiece (or, for that matter, the panels typical of newspaper comic strips) are series of forms. Musical compositions, dances and films ('movies', 'moving pictures') are flowing forms.

A topic worth mentioning in this connection, though I will not dwell on it, is the kinship between works of art and our countless games and sports. Students of aesthetics speak of the ludic aspect of art (*ludus* is the Latin for game); and while a close look at our definition would suggest the areas of difference between games and sports on one side and works of art on the other, it may be wise to keep in mind the fictive and playful side of art, especially if

one is reading a particularly philosophical novel or gazing at a
tragic or even macabre painting.

(9) The work of art is that special form among all the forms
created by man for which there is one and only one criterion of
success—namely the satisfaction it delivers. A successful work of
art is one that has lifted us from a near-zero level of emotion (for
instance, our normally neutral state of mind from the moment we
settle into our seats in a theater up to the beginning of the
motion picture or play) to a significantly higher level of intensity
on the plus or pleasurable side of our range of emotions. There is
no loophole from this inflexible fact of life, no escape door
opened by any theory of art. 'Please or perish!' Forgotten works of
art are those that bored, irritated or depressed. Survivors are
those that delighted.

This fact of the aesthetic life rides roughshod over any beliefs
and intentions the artist himself may cherish on the question of
what constitutes success in a work of art. Perhaps he strongly
believes that admirable art means art that promotes certain
virtues, whether personal or socio-economic-political or theologi-
cal. Perhaps it is a passionate belief of this kind that stimulates
him to create his works—so much so that, were he persuaded that
the success of a work of art consists in 'merely' giving people plea-
sure (however profound), he could not find it in himself to 'do
art' at all, and he would turn to something else, like political
activism. No matter. The world continues inflexibly to adore
works of art that give delight and to forget all the others (except
as topics in the *history* of art), no matter how praiseworthy with
respect to their positions on 'vital issues'. Of course, I am not
implying that an artist must leave his moral or political passions in
another room while he writes a poem or paints a picture. Far
from it. But his success as an artist will depend entirely on what he
has *done with* these passions.

(10) An important observation in this connection is that our
definition refuses to distinguish between a low-level satisfaction (a
mild pleasure) at one end of the spectrum and a delirium of
ecstasy at the other. Take the visual arts. They woo us a hundred
times a day, for they manifest themselves not only in the master-
pieces of the National Gallery, but also in the pattern on the rug
in my doctor's waiting room, for, as we shall see later on, art can

be art and something else as well. To use a military analogy, the term 'soldier' must be so defined as to embrace everything from a rookie to a five-star general. Our definition tolerates an elementary 'this was fun' or 'how pretty!' as it welcomes 'deeply moving' and even 'shattering' (Fig. 1).

Fig. 1. Francisco Goya (1746–1828), 'Esto es peor' (This is worse), one of the 82 etchings in the series *The Disasters of War*, provoked by Napoleon's invasion of Spain (1808–13). A victim of war is stabbed, mutilated and impaled on a tree. (By kind permission of the Norton Simon Museum, The Norton Simon Foundation, Pasadena, CA, F.1968.03.37.G. Harris 157)

Shattering? How can this be, if, in order to succeed, a work of art needs to give pleasure? It turns out (as Aristotle already knew) that, somewhat paradoxically, a creation that we call a fine work of art can beget deep pleasure even while arousing or evoking an excitement we do not care to experience in 'real life.' Thus, besides very profound but *purely* joyful feelings—such, for instance, as can be aroused by a serene landscape painting (Fig. 2) or Mozart's divinely merry *The Abduction from the Seraglio*—our satisfaction can be a compound or composite one. The satisfaction (if any) that results from tragic or shocking art—like those 'relentless portrayals of human depravity' favored by many contemporary artists or the discordant scores produced by most serious composers today—is compounded of several emotional elements, *some of which may not be pleasurable.* At the end of the emotional line, however, our experience must be positive. Otherwise the work of art has failed. Our fact-of-life remains inflexible. Indeed, we *call* the thing 'art' because, among all human creations, it is that which, in order to avoid falling into contempt, must offer an unmediated satisfaction.

Fig. 2. John Constable (1776–1837), 'Dedham Mill' (c. 1817). Pencil drawing. (By kind permission of the Henry E. Huntington Library and Art Gallery)

(11) What is this 'unmediated' satisfaction? Mediation is brokerage, that is to say a person or agency or force that transmits an action from its origin to its destination. If you wish to buy stock on Wall Street, you employ the mediation of a broker. Abstractly: in

order to go from A to K, you need to be helped along by C. And here is an example from the arts. In order to be thrilled by his newly acquired Cézanne, a certain tycoon needs to feel that it will rise 20 percent a year in market value. His pleasure in the Cézanne is thus mediated. If, however, he finds himself in love with the Cézanne after its value has dropped (and the other tycoons are laughing at him), his pleasure in it is unmediated: the painting acts for him as a true work of art.

But the concept of mediation, or brokerage, goes much deeper. Note that our definition says nothing whatsoever about improving our morals, altering our political views, supplying knowledge or deepening our wisdom as a necessary condition for successful art. For each one of these moral or spiritual accomplishments constitutes brokerage as surely as more dollars or yen for the Cézanne. A sermon is successful if it makes us better human beings. A technical article is successful if it gives us true information. A meditative essay is successful if it makes us wiser. An editorial is successful if it persuades us that a given attitude to a hot issue of the time is commendable. But a work of art is that one form created by human beings that can be successful even if it makes us worse than we were before, even if it misinforms us about life, and even if it leaves us with precisely the degree of wisdom (were such things measurable) we possessed before we enjoyed it. We can ardently desire that art make us better or wiser. But whether we like it or not, the incontrovertible fact of life remains that forms that are universally qualified as works of art have been successful (loved, admired, rewarded with fame, etc.) without detectably dispensing wisdom or decency in some, many, or any of their admirers. We wrongly idealize Art when we dream of it as always and necessarily a guiding light for mankind.

(12) The definition makes no distinction between an ephemeral and an 'eternal' work of art. It is indifferent to the absence or presence of duration. This applies to the reputation of a work of art, inasmuch as our definition does not care whether it shone for a day or ten centuries. And it applies to the work of art as a physical entity: we admit forms that last for a long time, but we also admit forms that come and go, whether their coming and going proved memorable or not. A piece of music, a dance, a play might be shown to the world only once. For that matter, there are

visual or 'mixed-media' artists today who positively take pride in the fact that their works 'self-destruct' at a rapid rate. One of them likes to drape sheets for a week or two across canyons or over bridges. All this, our definition patiently embraces.

(13) While the definition uses words as clearly as possible, a number of synonyms or near-synonyms can readily be found for most of them; the ones I have chosen were not delivered to me on Mount Sinai. For instance, instead of 'successful' you might choose 'admired'. Then again, perhaps 'satisfaction' sounds too neutral or general; do you prefer 'thrill'? Or 'pleasurable excitement'? Or should we keep saying '*aesthetic* satisfaction' instead of 'satisfaction' all by itself? The definition easily accomodates itself to an improved and refined vocabulary.

(14) 'Energizing' is another one of the terms for which you are free to find substitutes, provided they catch the fundamental meaning I intend. Whatever resources or materials an artist uses—from pigments on his brush to deep philosophical considerations at the keyboard of his word-processor—he must 'excite' in much the same way an incoming impulse excites an atom. Not so much what he has, but what he does to what he has, is the nub of the matter. And it is a matter that will require our best thinking later in this book.

(15) This brings me to *failed* works of art. It is no secret that in this business as in all others, many are called, but few are chosen. The attics of the world are crammed with lumber no one wants—works of art that were inert from the start, or became so after their day in the sun. Our definition is good-natured, however, and does not snatch the name of Art from them because they failed to give pleasure. They too were and are deemed successful insofar as they produced pleasure. In short: to call something a work of art is not, in itself, a compliment.

(16) Finally for these preliminary considerations, you may have noticed the absence of the word 'beauty' from our definition—the beauty of a vase, for instance, or of a symphony. 'Beauty' is as hard to define as Art itself; but fortunately for us, we can dodge this particular task, for beauty, however defined, cannot be part of the strict overall definition of Art. The created form that succeeds in thrilling can be as beautiful as a Greek temple or as ugly as a cathedral gargoyle. In both cases it is art. Creating beauty, it turns

out, is but one of the many ways in which an artist can energize his raw materials.[2]

2.   This should not prevent us from asking the fascinating question where, why and how the sense of beauty is born in mankind. As is true for Art itself, we must look for the answer or answers not only in the feelings and activities of primitive man, but in our animal ancestors before him. A physiological component should not be ignored. That which is physiologically most comfortable and easy to apprehend: the smooth, the regular, the gradual, the complete—all this surely underlies, together with moral approval, our modern concept of beauty. In this light, the evenly spaced columns of a Greek temple (one 'error' of five inches would have made no *structural* difference) are beautiful, ultimately, because rhythmic regularity is physiologically more comfortable than irregularity; and women wear high heels because the eye is more comfortable following an easy obtuse angle than brutally re-routed by a right angle!

Chapter 2

Three Brain-Centers

Why does my definition of Art limit this term to forms that access and must satisfy the three brain-centers, or human faculties, I have named? Why does it lock out such 'arts' as fine cooking ('the culinary art'), the making of cigars, the creation of perfumes, the 'art' of love and so many others? To be sure, no one can prohibit or compel opinions in this republic of lively but harmless discussion; every man, woman and child may call Art anything he pleases—the work of a house painter, the juggler's skill, the 'art' of travelling or choosing fine hotels and even the art of enjoying art[1]—the list has no limits. The truth is that our word has a long and variegated history. In drastic summary, we can speak of an undifferentiated and a differentiated application, both of which have legitimacy and tradition to support them. The undifferentiated tradition (combining what used to be called the 'mechanical' and 'liberal' arts) allows us to apply the term not only to poems, symphonies and the like, but also to any remarkable or professional skill, whether the skill concerns the creation of objects or a human activity, say the 'art' of bargain hunting. Compare, for instance, Horace's *Art of Poetry*, already mentioned, where the word is used in its strict, differentiated sense, with Ovid's *Art of Love*, where the poet obviously draws on the undifferentiated tradition. Here is John Dryden's translation of Ovid's third and fourth lines:

---

1. 'L'arte di goder l'arte'—the phrase is by Gabriele d'Annunzio (1863–1938).

> Seamen with sailing Arts their Vessels move;
> Art guides the Chariot; Art instructs to Love.[2]

This gives, in addition to our own examples, the arts of sailing and of driving chariots—the Roman version of racing cars. Note that in this undifferentiated mode, the *activity* of art does not necessarily result in the creation of a form to be known as a *work* of art. The 'art' of sailing is to sail efficiently, not to make beautiful sailboats. The word is readily replaced by another like 'skill' or 'craft'.

When the artist in this loose sense does create forms, these are apt to be concerned with the pots and pans of existence: the objects we need for our daily lives. Here we readily exchange the term 'artist' for names like 'artisan' or 'craftsman'.

Furthermore, because our three-letter word is a prestigious one, it tends to become attached to an ever-growing list of phenomena as interested parties recruit it for activities they wish to promote.[3] So be it. Language is not to be ordered about. However, our own severely differentiated application of the word stands pretty firm at the heart of this hubbub of designations, so that even when we make free with it (and in reality we all do) we keep somewhere in our minds the sense of an important distinction between arts like poetry, sculpture or music and the 'art' of starting a weekend (Fig. 3).

So too I am drawing a relatively small circle around the word 'artist'. Since this term naturally enjoys the same prestige as its progenitor, all those who should be called 'performers' lay claim to it: a magician is called an artist, and so is an actor, an electronic guitar player and even a clever crook (a 'con artist'). It is true that certain branches of art imperatively require performers or managers in order to manifest themselves, and this symbiotic arrangement makes it a trifle painful to deny the name of artist to one of the partners. Our language comes to the rescue now and

2.   The *Ars poetica* was probably written late in Horace's life (65–8 BC); Ovid's *Ars amatoria* dates from before AD 8, and probably brought about, or helped bring about, the poet's exile from Rome. Dryden's translation appeared in 1700.

3.   The word 'beautiful' has suffered, or enjoyed, the same fate and for the same reason: witness 'a beautiful mathematical solution', 'a beauty of a deal', 'a beautifully managed company', and so forth.

Fig. 3. Banner at the Los Angeles County Museum of Art, 1993. Were the museum's officials aware of the humor of juxtaposing the art of Degas and Matisse with the art of starting one's weekend?

then by calling a violinist (for instance) a 'performing artist'. This seems like a fair compromise. Indeed, actors and musicians rightly claim that they do not mechanically reproduce or exhibit works of art (in this instance, plays and musical scores); they *interpret* them, and as such they are perhaps once-removed artists, whose materials and resources are the works of art of others. Nevertheless, for us here and now the person who composes a violin concerto is so significantly different from the person who plays and interprets it that we persist in giving the original creator of the form his own separate designation. Let us bear in mind, however, that an artist in our strict sense of the word can also be his own interpreter. Shakespeare and Molière were actors in their own plays, and many composers perform their own scores for the public.

Be that as it may, in the realm of poetry, which is our special concern, the distinction between artist and performing artist is of minor importance. It comes into play only when poetry is recited in public. There was of course a time when all poetry, indeed all literature was delivered by oral recitation or chant. This means that professional literary performers (for example, the rhapsodes who recited Homeric and other epics in the Greek cities) provided the same essential service for the poetic artists as the singers and instrumentalists who serve our composers of musical scores. Poetry is still recited or otherwise performed in public today; but, unlike musical scores, most of the time it reaches the public without an intermediary 'performing artist'.

Now, while you might agree to despatch the 'arts' of fine living, politics, making profitable deals and the like to their undifferentiated territory, you may protest that I am going too far in barring the gate to the culinary 'art'. You may even wish to request admittance for the 'art' of making perfumes. Why not five or more brain-centers instead of three?

But if I counter with the question whether, in all honesty, you yourself do not feel that 'somehow' there is a leap of some sort from an exquisite dinner, a delicious wine or an enticing perfume to a great painting or piano sonata, a very long tradition will surely nudge you into replying that indeed something or other seems to separate these phenomena. You will inevitably smile if someone tries to equate a 'sublime' pot roast with the 'sublimity' of a painting by Raphael or a symphony by Beethoven. And the reason is not that the gastronomic masterpiece is short-lived. A Raphael would not have lost its sublimity if it had been destroyed in a fire an hour after it was finished.

In what then does this something or other consist? My speculative answer is that the circle we 'instinctively' draw around the notion of Art is due to the overwhelming importance of sight, hearing and language to man's understanding and control of the world—the understanding and control without which mankind cannot thrive nor even live. In Darwinian shorthand, human beings depended on the especially acute development of these particular faculties for the information/knowledge that made survival, and then dominion, possible for them. This seems to be the biological foundation for the notion, perhaps I should say intuition, that sight, hearing and language are our 'higher' or 'nobler' faculties. If I am right so far, I can deduce that this notion or intuition has led to the unconscious judgment that the realm of Art is to be confined, in our thinking, to forms which excite ('satisfy') these and only these 'higher' or 'nobler' or 'spiritual' faculties. For many animals, of course, a different hierarchy obtains, and if a dog were commissioning works of art, his collection would include interesting arrangements of smells, since sniffing is a vital tool for the doggy acquisition of essential understanding and control. For us, however, taste and smell remain secondary tools for knowing and coping with the world; accordingly, what we produce to satisfy these senses is generally felt (though dimly) to stand outside the privileged circle of true Art.

All in all, then, even though opening the door to cooking, wine-making and perfume-manufacturing would not impose any alterations upon our definition of Art, I will continue, in this little treatise on the facts of aesthetic life, to regard the beautiful flask that holds the perfume, and the exquisitely designed dish (Fig. 4) or the table arrangement that preludes a dinner, as works of art (minor ones, to be sure),[4] even if the perfume itself is foul and the dinner inedible; and to deny the term to the perfume and the dinner, even if both are superb.

Fig. 4. 'Show-off pie for distinguished marriages', an illustration in the *Neues saltzburgisches Koch-Buch* (New Salzburg Cookbook), published in Augsburg in 1719

If created (or 'prepared') forms appealing to our taste-buds and our olfactory sense are politely excluded from the club, so, oddly

---

4. For of course our culture recognizes arts that it qualifies as 'minor'. We will call an art minor if, even at its best, it cannot give us the richest thrill possible to art; if it cannot, as one usually puts it, touch our inner depths.

enough, are products affecting the sense of touch. To a blind man, touch is all-important; but all-important precisely because he has been compelled to find a replacement for the eyesight others employ to take hold of the world.

> Then I did as they do who go about
> With something on their head unknown to them
> Save that from others' gestures they suspect,
> And so the hand is called on to explore,
> And seeks and finds, fulfilling thus the charge
> Which cannot be accomplished by the sight.[5]

Normally, mankind uses the sense of touch—insofar, I repeat, as understanding and control are concerned—rather to confirm information than to receive it.

You might object that sculpture is an art—a certified art!—that calls for touch. Do not sculptors and art critics rhapsodize about tactile values? And, for that matter, is not 'texture' a basic term in the painter's art? The most direct response comes from the gallery owners and the museum directors themselves, presumably with the artists' blessing. They never hesitate to place large 'Do Not Touch' signs in front of all those touch-inviting forms and textures. Imagine replacing them with 'Do Not Look' signs! It turns out that, even though it is pleasant and instructive to run one's hand over a sculpture, the tactile values are already so well suggested to our sense of sight that we do not grumble when we are asked to keep our hands off it. By the same token, no painter wants us to run our fingers over the texture of his canvas. Here too, our touch confirms what our eyes have guessed.

We can well imagine an art, or 'art', that would directly please our sense of touch. We would close our eyes and allow the 'performing artist' to caress our cheeks (or other parts of our bodies) with furs, brushes, warm cotton, dabs of ice, etc. For the time being, no such art, or 'art', exists.

However, we will rightly call a created form a work of art if it *also* titillates one of the brain-centers other than those for sight, hearing and language. Works of art can easily do several things at

---

5. Dante Alighieri, *Purgatory*, Canto 12, lines 127-32, written in the early years of the fourteenth century. Translation in blank verse by Thomas G. Bergin in *The Divine Comedy* (New York: Appleton-Century-Crofts, 1955).

the same time—a theme to which I will be returning more than once, and especially in the next chapter. A prettily molded piece of marzipan, whose essential function is the non-aesthetic one (by our definition) of satisfying our lust for sweets, *also* functions as a modest—an extremely modest—work of ephemeral visual art. But creations that interest our 'erogenous zones' provide a far more powerful illustration of the 'also principle.' Most discussions of Art coyly skirt this territory—an unhelpful intellectual maneuver, considering that Eros is the uncontested lord of an infinite number of poems, novels, plays, motion pictures, paintings, sculptures, songs, operas, dances and mixed media events. If we are honest with ourselves, we will be obliged to admit that many works can and often do excite *both* our so-called nobler senses and our sexual instincts. This might happen when we admire an enticing Venus painted by Titian, or upon reading a lascivious narrative poem like Shakespeare's *Venus and Adonis*, or a daring novel like D.H. Lawrence's *Lady Chatterley's Lover* (once upon a time the subject of a major scandal and trial), or while we enjoy one of those 'explicit' motion pictures that aspire to high artistic stature.

And what is pornography? Or rather: What do people choose to call pornography? The simple answer is: Whatever erotically charged art shocks their moral sense. This answer has the virtue of accounting for the tremendous variations we find as we go from person to person, from group to group, from culture to culture, and for all these from epoch to epoch. However, let us look at this vexed and vexing question from the point of view of our definition of Art by recalling to the witness box, of all things, our piece of nicely shaped marzipan. Shall we agree that it owes (loosely speaking, of course) 95 percent of its success to its ability to satisfy our hunger for a sweet, and a mere 5 percent to its pretty shape? If we do, it follows that the marzipan functions very slightly indeed as a work of art. And this is equally true for a motion picture (for instance) that is 'deemed successful' by any given viewer to a 95 percent extent (loosely speaking again) if it satisfies his craving for sexual titillation, and to an insignificant 5 percent extent for its dramatic qualities, the quality of its photography, etc. as far as these are *not* sexually arousing. In other words, for creations of this kind, art is an 'also function', utterly subordinated to the main success (if any success at all, for pornography can fail too!) of gratifying sexual lust; whereas in the Titian we evoked a moment ago, the situation is reversed, with the erotic playing (for most admirers) the subordinate/accompanying also-role.

But we must not forget the moral shock aspect of the matter. Whether the person we are questioning receives the erotic pleasure in himself, or observes it in others, or fears to have it appear in others than himself, he is likely to use the intensely negative term 'pornographic' only if he is also morally repelled by the situation—not infrequently, as we know, to the extent of trying to summon the police to suppress the offending works. Note, in this connection, that no one asks the authorities to prohibit marzipans or chocolate cakes on the ground that they make our digestive juices flow when we look at them or smell them. In the absence of moral outrage, our language has not bothered to create a word equivalent to 'pornographic' for these attractive created forms.

Chapter 3

Mediated and Unmediated Pleasures

Here we pursue in some detail the topic of mediation we began to discuss in section (10) of Chapter 1.

The satisfaction or thrill of pleasure that is the centerpiece of our definition of Art is produced *wholly or partly* without mediation. Words of the kind I have italicized often look like throwaways, or low-key exercises in caution. These, however, happen to be very important. They imply that works of art exist that will do nothing else for some of us than excite (mildly or powerfully) our faculties of vision, hearing or language. And that is an irreproachable success. But other works of art will *do something else* we like along with—perhaps I should say in fusion with—the power they possess of thrilling us *without* any such help. Making money with a Cézanne was the example I gave in Chapter 1.

Furthermore, it needs to be said that many human creations do not come to us posing as works of art at all, or else (as with our piece of marzipan) as things that are not *primarily* works of art; and yet there is art in them, sometimes incidentally, sometimes even accidentally, inasmuch as, besides doing what they are principally good at doing, they also enter into our field of experience as creations that can deliver a thrill of pleasure unmediated by the success of their chief function. An industrial plant, for instance, or the pylons stretching across a landscape, can be incidentally or accidentally beautiful, even though being beautiful is hardly what they are mainly about. To the extent that we admire them as shapes in the world, they have procured for us—for some of us, at any rate—an unmediated satisfaction and are therefore partly works of art, however inadvertently. The proof is that if they happen to fall into disuse, the persons who found them beautiful while they were fully functional will continue to admire them.

Let me repeat. Many human creations are partly art and partly something else, or even mostly something else and partly art. Interestingly too, some succeed (give satisfaction) in one aspect but fail in the other—and not necessarily as expected or intended. A nuclear plant might fail as a desired or effective deliverer of energy, and yet remain standing as an awesome presence in the landscape. However, if an object is both satisfying in itself, directly, *and* satisfying in its other capacity (e.g. educating, enriching, empowering, and so on) then of course the effect is synergetic: pleasure becomes PLEASURE.

Imagine, as another convenient witness, some prehistoric ancestor of ours who has been handed an amulet by his reliable witch doctor. If he takes pleasure in it exclusively, or 'for all practical purposes', because he is sure that it is going to scare away the fiend that has been haunting his hut, his pleasure in the amulet is wholly mediated and aesthetically inert. It is purely *functional.*

If the carving has failed to intimidate the fiend; if our ancestor has been obliged to resort to certain powerful incantations that *have* done the job; and yet if, perhaps to his own surprise, he decides to keep the ineffectual little wood carving in his hut after all—why? because 'it is so finely wrought'; we conclude that his pleasure in the carving is wholly unmediated. He loves the carving 'for itself'. It need not *do* anything other than be there and 'radiate'. In short, the object is now a work of art for him. His pleasure is wholly aesthetic. And this is so despite the fact that the concepts 'art' and 'aesthetic' are unknown to him as concepts.

This illustration shows you, by the way, why aesthetic pleasure is often called 'disinterested'.

But now, suppose that the amulet has been highly effective in frightening the demon away once and for all; and in addition, our good ancestor thinks it is the finest little sculpture he has seen in many a day—so fine, he tells his friends, that he would have kept it in a place of honor even if it had failed to impress his ghostly enemy. In that case, his pleasure is both mediated and unmediated. It is a greater pleasure than either pleasure by itself. The work of art is (for him, at any rate) more than a work of art and yet still a work of art.

To recapitulate. Man-made forms—from pencils or aspirin tablets to Bach partitas—can be purely functional, that is to say, give pleasure only if and when they can do something for us; they can be purely aesthetic, that is to say, give pleasure simply by being there; or they can be both, giving us pleasure (as our definition tells us) by energizing the appropriate materials *and* by doing something else for us besides—like fetching millions of dollars at an auction.

Incidentally, we sometimes blame a non-art object—say an oil refinery or a philosophical treatise—for being a *failed* work of art ('bad art') when it never aspired to be a work of art to begin with. When we complain that a factory is a blot on the landscape, or that a history of the Byzantine empire is poorly written, we are in effect compelling these objects to appear before our consciousness as candidates for perception as works of art, and then reproaching them for not doing better. This amounts to a *moral* judgment that certain objects, created to be purely functional, *should* have been so formed as to be good art as well.

But now that philosophy and history have been mentioned, let us inspect certain possible other functions of art that we usually consider nobler and subtler than earning money by selling Cézannes or producing oil; I mean making us better informed or wiser, or improving the world we live in. These are intellectual and moral functions, and under the heading 'moral' we include political, economic and sociological ideals: power to the masses, fair distribution of wealth, equality of the races, justice for women, the right to abortion, fairness to homosexuals, the opposite of these—yes! pros and cons are both moral causes, however hateful they look from the other side—and innumerable other causes that have inflamed this or that portion of mankind: all these are as much moral forces as are the ideals of personal honesty, courage, generosity and taking care of your old mother. So then, we boldly place intellectual growth and moral improvement side by side with such possible functions of art as making money, acquiring prestige or curing a depression.[1]

---

1.   One kind of information, understanding, or wisdom that a work of art can provide refers to its own making, or, in general, to the nature of art itself.

At an even more exalted level, works of art, besides thrilling us without 'brokerage', can appear to us as endowed with the power to help save souls—our own or other people's. In other words, they can play a religious role that fuses with their aesthetic power and thus proceed, synergistically, to satisfy 'twice as much' (loosely speaking, of course) as they would if they were, for us, *only* works of art or *only* aids to salvation.

In short, functionality—doing something for us—can be what our culture has called 'spiritual' as well as what we normally call 'material': anything from making money or curing a headache to making us as wise as King Solomon.

Here are three important corollaries.

(1) A given man-made object can play a different one of the three roles (purely functional, purely aesthetic, or a fusing of the two) for different people. Robert Browning has a humorous example for us in 'Fra Lippo Lippi', where Filippo Lippi (a painter/friar of the early Renaissance) complains that an admirable Saint Lawrence it took him six months to paint for his monastery was applauded by the other friars, not because it was beautiful, but because it so impressed the worshippers that they 'scratched and prodded' the painted rogues busy roasting the depicted saint until they destroyed the painting. Thus the success of the painting consisted in its ceasing to exist! A proof of strict functionality if there ever was one.

> 'How looks my painting, now the scaffold's down?'
> I ask a brother. 'Hugely,' he returns—
> 'Already not one phiz of your three slaves
> Who turn the Deacon off his toasted side,
> But's scratched and prodded to our heart's content,
> The pious people have so eased their own
> With coming to say prayers there in a rage;
> We get on fast to see the bricks beneath.
> Expect another job this time next year,
> For pity and religion grow i'the crowd—
> Your painting serves its purpose!' Hang the fools![2]

This self-referential possibility of intellectual growth is a possible mediating force like all the others—a function—and non-aesthetic in itself.

2. Lines 325-35. Browning's poem appeared in 1855. 'Phiz' = face; St Lawrence was a third-century deacon in Rome, martyred (according to tradition) by being roasted on a grid. For 'so eased their own' in the sixth

'Serves its purpose' is the telltale formula. To which the painter snorts an indignant rebuke. The rest of the poem shows that for Lippo himself, the work of art fuses an aesthetic *being* with a moral and religious *doing.*

(2) The work of art can play one of these roles for any of us today and another role next year, as our minds and emotions develop.

(3) And it can move historically, for most people, from one of these roles to another. For example: a teapot useful long ago to a Chinese mandarin can become a museum piece locked up in a glass cage; advertising posters can lose their marketing function and wind up as admired works of art;[3] shoes can quit walking and rest as museum pieces (Fig. 5); a warlord's stronghold can turn into a beautiful tourist attraction, and then combine its new aesthetic role with good service as a hotel. Or in reverse: a temple that was revered for its beauty can be turned by a conqueror into a stable.

But beauty, remember, is not a required player in the aesthetic game. Early in the twentieth century the iconoclastic French artist Marcel Duchamp (1887–1968) brought into the artworld not a beautifully designed teapot, table or telephone, but a plain bicycle wheel, and then, a little later, something more shocking, a urinal that he called *Fountain* (for indeed, urinals resemble those modest and charming little fountains that are built into many an Italian wall). This was extremely disconcerting, but the principle remained the same: a human creation can lose its functionality and be offered to the world as an object capable of giving pleasure by 'just being there'—beautiful, but if not beautiful, then intellectually provocative, funny, satirical, amusingly shocking,

line, see Chapter 10 section (8), where this passage is discussed again.

3.   The publicity posters made by Henri de Toulouse-Lautrec (1864–1901) are now admired (and priced!) as masterpieces; but numberless other posters have lost their practical function over time as well and are collected for their beauty or other expressive qualities—lesser art than that of Toulouse-Lautrec, but art nonetheless. Posters are of course but one category of the correctly named 'advertising arts', any of which can produce instances of works that eventually lose their double status as commercial propaganda fused with pure art and remain alive as pure, 'useless' art, whether of high or low value, whether lasting or ephemeral.

Fig. 5. A Salvatore Ferragamo shoe. Exhibit: 'The Art of the Shoe',
Los Angeles County Museum of Art, 1992

bizarre, monstrous (we often like monsters) or anything else you
can think of, including the quality (short-lived, to be sure) of
being new. Thus I might use a paint pot to paint a paint pot on a
canvas and afterward exhibit the real paint pot, now bereft of its
function, in a museum—or simply on my own shelf at home—as a
'stimulating' piece of art.[4]

Shall we keep in mind, while talking about bicycle wheels, uri-
nals and paint pots as works of art, that our definition includes
works of art that *fail* to satisfy, whether at once or, as often hap-
pens, in the long run? A most important warning!

Our present topic, namely the evolution of objects from one
condition to another, gives me occasion to remark that the basic
concept of a work of art playing a purely aesthetic role, without any
other function attached, is a relatively recent one. Art remained
for many centuries a handmaiden to religion, politics, oratory and

4.   Remember that the pieces of driftwood etc. mentioned in Chapter 1
differ in that they are not man-made; they are bits of non-human Nature.

morality. It was conceived, in effect, as a tool. Obviously it is as a tool that Browning's fictitious friars saw Lippo's painting. In the twentieth century the Soviet and Chinese Marxist leadership consciously asserted the propaganda function of Art—that is to say its duty to advertise and promote a supposedly good or holy cause. But even in the Western world, many artists and critics demand that works of art serve a specific cause (e.g. criticizing the white, phallocratic bourgeoisie) before they can be praised.[5] Still, the main tendency of artists and critics in our 'free world' has been, since the mid-nineteenth century, to disentangle and disengage the especial pleasure Art affords from the various functions assigned to it by and in the world. Gradually, then, Art came to be seen, and practiced, as an *autonomous* human activity, parallel with rather than serviceable to other human enterprises. This is what nineteenth-century thinkers called 'Art for Art's sake'.

The truth of the matter, however, is that Art for Art's sake, or the purely aesthetic power of works of art, was never more than a possibility, a desideratum, or a permission; it could never be an obligation. *Homo sapiens* did not undergo a mutation in some moral and aesthetic gene when French theorists proclaimed that art is useless. The theorists had discovered that, at this late stage in our civilization, art *can* be useless. However, no theory can prevent our tycoon from loving his Cézanne in part because it is a splendid investment; nor the Bolsheviks, in their decades of power, from admiring a statue in part because it promoted hard work and loyalty to Communism; nor a student from enjoying *War and Peace* in part because it teaches him a great deal about Napoleon's retreat from Russia. Art is no longer compelled to be more than art; but very often it continues all the same to be more than art.

Now, instead of our fictive ancestor's ineffectual yet lovely amulet, let us examine a real candidate for the position of unmediated, autonomous work of art, and one that probably played that role even in its own time, when the *theory* of autonomous art had not yet been invented.

5.   Examples are best given in parentheses, because rapid shifts occur in our times in the specific social and political passions that affect the appreciation of works of art.

> Under the greenwood tree,
>   Who loves to lie with me,
> And turn his merry note
>   Unto the sweet bird's throat,
> Come hither, come hither, come hither.
>   Here shall he see
>   No enemy,
> But winter and rough weather.[6]

I have a couple of good reasons for choosing such a modest poem as my model. You will recall that the satisfaction demanded by our definition can be a minor one; and I am going to assume, for the sake of argument, that the reader is in fact *very* mildly thrilled by this little lyric. On the other hand, inasmuch as it was composed by the nonpareil Shakespeare (in *As You Like It*), I can pretty safely assume that you do admit it as a true work of art.

Furthermore, I am going to imagine that my reader, at this point, is a fifty-year-old lover of literature who has read more poems in his lifetime than he can number, including, quite often, 'Under the Greenwood Tree'. Now he is reading it again, and experiencing the same mild pleasure as before. The modesty of the poem, the age of our reader, and the circumstance that he has read the poem many times and probably knows it by heart—all these, working together, guarantee for us that his pleasure this particular time is not due to any increase in his fund of knowledge or wisdom. His pleasure has been renewed, hence the poem has been gently successful for him once again, but it has been of no help in improving his 'understanding of life'. I could probably make the same affirmations for an 18-year-old novice reading the poem for the first time; but our thought experiment becomes more convincing with the experienced reader who has surely sipped all the intellectual nectar the poem is capable of offering.

Since intellectual growth is but one of the possible mediating forces we have discussed, I inquire next whether the pleasure this experienced reader has felt might have been caused by his discovery that 'Under the Greenwood Tree' could help him secure a place in heaven. That is very doubtful. Is he happy, then, because

6.   If, in the second line, you read 'Who' as 'Whoever', the little poem will become crystal clear, and the absence of a question mark at the end will be accounted for. Matters of this sort will be discussed in Chapters 9 and 10.

I am paying him a modest fee as a consultant for my book? Because he feels a surge of pride at being the only person alive who has read the poem so often? Because it solves a linguistic problem he has been struggling with as a student of Early Modern English? Because he feels he has emerged from his reading a kinder, more generous person than before? Because it occurs to him that the poem paves the way for a future sexual revolution? If we reply to all these silly questions in the negative, and yet hold on to the fact that still, still he has enjoyed the poem, we are bound to conclude that his pleasure has been unmediated. It has done nothing for him except function as a provider of pleasure: but that is not a brokered event. The verbal form in question has needed nothing but its own energy to achieve its minor success. It is, for this imagined reader, a pure work of art.

In Chapter 11 we will revisit the intellectual and moral dimensions of art—specifically, by then, of the art of poetry—for it should not be concluded, on the basis of what I have said here, that we are indifferent, even in an absolutely pure work of art, to its intellectual and moral qualities. But that is anticipating; and right now, after having looked at a modest example of such purity—a charming lyric devoid of any power (as far as our seasoned reader is concerned) except the power to charm—we should evoke some 'impure' works of art in which the aesthetic and non-aesthetic can synergize.

We approach a majestic cathedral crowded all year round with awe-struck tourists. At the entrance we read a notice requesting visitors not to circulate in the church during services. Why do the worried clergymen feel the need to post such a notice? Clearly, because they know that for some of the people who will be visiting the church, the latter counts *purely* as a wonderful work of art. They will walk around in the edifice gazing and admiring as in a museum, perhaps disturbing those for whom a church counts *only* as a place of worship. Here then is our cathedral operating for one group aesthetically and for the other functionally. The first group, largely indifferent to religion, love the church because it is magnificent and feel a little irritated when their visit coincides with Mass and the faithful compel visitors to stay in a corner. The second, indifferent to the beauty of the cathedral, love it because it is the house of God and resent being disturbed in their prayers by 'insensitive' tourists. A third group, however, is both religious *and* sensitive to beauty. Those who make up this group love the cathedral for both reasons, and experience (all other things being equal) a greater satisfaction than the other two. This is again a plain fact of the aesthetic life. Take two supreme art historians of equal intelligence, erudition, professional rank, sensitivity to the arts and emotional capability. Make one of them a practicing Catholic who never forgets that a church is where his and the other worshippers' souls are launched toward salvation, and the other an atheist for whom such a thought is an absurdity. Place both in our cathedral. Their *understanding* of the cathedral, which, in theory, we can assess by reading the monographs they have devoted to it, may well be equal. But find a measuring instrument that registers degrees of elation. Implant it in our two subjects. The needle will register higher for the Catholic than for the atheist. And finally, allow for the facetiousness of my experiment, yet retain the essential principle it teaches.

There is, by the way, no theoretical limit to the number of mediated pleasures in fusion with aesthetic pleasure that people can extract from a man-made form. What about the beggar, sensitive to beauty and religion, who *also* loves the cathedral as a refuge from the heat of summer and the cold of winter?

Incidentally, the art of architecture is the ideal one to draw upon for our present theme, for architecture is hardly conceivable as 'pure' art, that is to say as art that turns its back (like our Shakespearean lyric) on any non-aesthetic source of pleasure. A beautiful house, office building, city hall or church is called upon to perform one or more very distinct extra-aesthetic functions if it is to be built at all.

Another particularly instructive case is that of philosophical texts. A treatise in one of the branches of philosophy might open for us a view on questions of Being or Knowing that is deeply impressive, even though we recognize that the author's style is harsh and dry. Another, however, could dispense its wisdom but also be 'poetic' or 'dramatic'—so much so that we gladly read it over and over, long after we have absorbed all it had to say to us in the way of philosophy, for the sheer elation we feel over the poetry or the drama.

Among ancient philosophers, for instance, Aristotle has always struck his readers as a no-nonsense philosopher: a methodical, thoroughgoing thinker and not at all a literary artist (even though he wrote importantly *on* literature); while Plato is celebrated as both an illustrious philosopher and a powerful artist (even though he wrote importantly *against* literature!). Much closer to us, we might contrast the technical-philosopher Kant with the poet-philosopher Nietzsche. Plato and Nietzsche illustrate at a very high level the potential ability of a human work to play two roles (or more) at the same time: to *do* for us what philosophy exists to do for us, and at the same time to *be* for us, beyond its instructive nature, a pure source of delight and begetter of enthusiasm.

A postscript. While non-aesthetic (mediated) pleasures can return upon the aesthetic and synergistically reinforce it, the same process can be observed in reverse order. If some non-aesthetic feeling—religious fervor, for instance—is what chiefly matters to us, we will note that aesthetic pleasure usefully reinforces that more important bliss. Such was certainly the intention of every known priesthood in patronizing the best architects, painters and musicians for their temples and churches. They did not intend spiritual elevation to enrich the aesthetic satisfaction of their congregations, but on the contrary, they sought to enlist aesthetic delight as a means of encouraging spiritual elevation.

Chapter 4

Art and its Publics

The Constituencies for Art

The twenty-one sections hereunder are to be regarded as ruthlessly condensed statements of ideas and principles, each of which could easily spread into a whole chapter and even a book.

(1) When we return—always with a touch of humor—to our fanciful vision of a primitive tribe, and imagine the assembled 'public' listening to a tale or a song, or looking at someone's new carving, we do not imagine a select few members of the tribe understanding the tale or song or carving while the rest of the group remain in the dark and report to one another that it was all 'above their heads'. Not that, in those days, every member of the tribe admired or approved of any particular product of the local artistic mind. Not everyone enjoyed, and not everyone enjoyed equally, but everyone understood. One public, one art in those (perhaps) idyllic times.

Matters are very different in the vast and complicated societies into which mankind has grown. You will remember that our definition of Art does not tell us who has the privilege of deciding for the rest of the world whether a given human creation qualifies as a work of art by owing its success to its power of begetting an unmediated pleasure; nor does it tell us whose business it is to decide for anyone else whether or not a work of art is successful, or how good or awful it is. In principle, each one of us decides these matters by and for himself; in principle, we could all live in separate and unique mental worlds. But in reality, of course, we all fall willy-nilly into groups, and these groups can be more or less accurately described. Primitive tribes form in many cultural respects single, coherent groups. In our worlds, instead, we hear about cultured and uncultured people, art movie houses and commercial movie houses, highbrows, lowbrows and middle-brows, avant-garde and experimental art, Broadway, off-Broadway and off-off-Broadway, commercial and non-commercial television, and so on. Indeed, the lowest lowbrow is aware of these distinctions, for the popular media trumpet them for all to hear. On top of this, our societies are composed of many religions, races, ethnic groups, factions of every kind, and to some extent each of these groups forms a special constituency with respect to the arts. But the constituencies we are going to discuss in this chapter are differentiated by degrees of what I will simply call sophistication—sophistication with respect either to a given art, or to several arts, or to all the arts. In other words, even if we were to inquire into, let us say, music with a strong Jewish appeal, we would still confine our attention to significant differences in sophistication in the audiences especially receptive to this species of music, and corresponding differences in the music itself.

And what is to be understood by 'sophistication'? The meaning we attach nowadays to this word has only recently come into use, although the concept, as we shall see, has a long history. As far as the arts are concerned, when we speak of a sophisticated reader, viewer or listener, we have in mind, I believe, three elements, singly or (at best) in combination: (a) an innate gift or flair for the basic materials (e.g. language) of the art under consideration; (b) experience or training in the art under consideration; (c) high general intelligence. If we imagine works of art as imposing barriers to access, we can say that the sophisticated can clamber over high barriers while the unsophisticated can vault only over low ones. Keep in mind, however, that the ability to access a given work of art does not imply that it will be enjoyed—in our terms, that it will be successful with any given person who has been able to grasp it. We are discussing the strictly focused subject of *availability to aesthetic satisfaction*.

(2) What are these barriers? We are ignoring those which are created by differences in religion, race, ethnicity and the like, as we are by-passing the barriers that tend to keep out children, the subnormal, the insane, *et al.* Looking broadly at the general,

normal, adult social scene, we notice at once that the barriers are not altogether the same for the different arts. In music, for instance, dissonant harshness debars access for many people—not people who hate music to begin with, but even people who think of themselves as music lovers. Ugliness and lack of meaning have acted as obstacles in many works of visual art since the advent of non-representational art. In literature, such factors as intricateness of structure, grammar and thought, subtlety and indirection, remoteness (sometimes extreme) from common experience, distortions of common language, erudite concepts and references or allusions to matters of which relatively few persons are informed (historical events, other works of art, philosophical ideas, and so forth) tend to demand high sophistication from the audience.

(3) The fact that the unsophisticated cannot climb or leap over high barriers in the arts does not mean, paradoxical as it may seem, that they are unable to enjoy works of high complexity. The paradox is quickly resolved if we take into account that many sophisticated works of art—think of *Hamlet* or the frescoes of the Sistine Chapel in the Vatican—open themselves partially to anyone who cares to read or look, while in part they make themselves hard of access to the naive. They could be compared to mountains that can be scaled to a degree by almost anyone, but whose peaks are for the few to reach. Or to mansions in which many but not all rooms are open to the general public. I will say more about this in a little while. Right now we want to round out this topic by noting that, conversely, many works of art whose chief constituency lies among the unsophisticated are thoroughly enjoyed by many sophisticated persons as well. In short, works that reach most powerfully a special constituency often extend their power well beyond it, until we can speak, somewhat loosely of course, of their 'universal appeal'. Take for instance William Wordsworth's famous lyric poem about the daffodils:

> I wandered lonely as a cloud
> That floats on high o'er vales and hills,
> When all at once I saw a crowd,
> A host, of golden daffodils;
> Beside the lake, beneath the trees,
> Fluttering and dancing in the breeze.

Continuous as the stars that shine
The waves beside them danced; but they
Out-did the sparkling waves in glee:
A poet could not but be gay,
In such a jocund company:
I gazed—and gazed—but little thought
What wealth the show to me had brought:

For oft, when on my couch I lie
In vacant or in pensive mood,
They flash upon that inward eye
Which is the bliss of solitude;
And then my heart with pleasure fills,
And dances with the daffodils.[1]

Such a poem is so widely 'available for aesthetic satisfaction' that, along with numberless other works of art, it deserves to be called universally appealing.

It remains true, nevertheless, that many works of art do have limited and concentrated appeal, with little or no spillover. Many creations lack the easier particulars that make them available to the unsophisticated, while at the other end of the gradient, many pieces are too flatly simple-minded to interest the sophisticated public. The following poem by Edgar A. Guest (1881–1959) may serve as an example of a simplicity that sophisticated readers are sure to dismiss:

DEPARTED FRIENDS

The dead friends live and always will;
Their presence hovers round us still.
It seems to me they come to share
Each joy or sorrow that we bear.
Among the living I can feel
The sweet departed spirits steal,
And whether it be weal or woe,
I walk with those I used to know.
I can recall them to my side

---

1.   Published in the two-volume *Poems* of 1807. Since one needs to know English in order to read this poem, 'general' or 'universal' becomes limited to a given linguistic group. Literary works need to be laboriously translated before they can reach outsiders. The other arts leap much more easily across boundaries.

Whenever I am struggle-tied;
I've but to wish for them, and they
Come trooping gayly down the way,
And I can tell to them my grief
And from their presence find relief.
In sacred memories below
Still live the friends of long ago.[2]

(4) As mentioned before, the idea of different levels of sophistication is an old one. Shakespeare, for instance, expressed it in the third act of *Hamlet*. The prince of Denmark is lecturing the touring company of actors visiting Elsinore on the right and wrong way of performing a play. Beware, he tells them, of strutting or bellowing, for this, 'though it make the unskilful laugh, cannot but make the judicious grieve; the censure of which one [i.e. the judicious] must in your allowance o'erweigh a whole theatre of others'. To be sure, Hamlet/Shakespeare is talking about acting and not about the text being acted; but he is merely extending to live performance a distinction between an elite and an ignorant public for the arts that was hoary with age even in his time.[3]

Now, however, we add that this difference subsists even when we deal with 'universally' admired works of art—like *Hamlet*. When a naive and a well-trained person are enjoying a work of art together, they seldom apprehend it in the same way. Training changes not only what we like, but also how we like what we like. 'Everybody' loves French Impressionist art; but this does not mean that the average viewer detects the same features in this art as the well-informed art lover, let alone the specialist in French Impressionist art. The unskilful (the unsophisticated in our own less attractive English) see the work in their way, the judicious in theirs—with a good overlap between them, one must add in all fairness.

2. In *A Heap o' Livin'* (Chicago: Reilly & Britton, 1916). We will analyze the shortcomings of this poem in Chapter 11.

3. Plato, for instance, has the playwright Agathon make a distinction between the 'small number of intelligent people' and the 'large number of unintelligent people' in an audience; whereupon Socrates comments: 'I'm well aware that you'd take more notice of those of your acquaintances you regard as clever than you would of the general populace' (*Symposium* 194b-194c).

Lest this separation between the 'judicious' and the 'unskilful' sound insufferably elitist and snobbish to the modern reader, I suggest a partial analogy with the realm of sports that arouses no resentment. The way a naive spectator (like the present author) looks at a tennis or boxing match, or a baseball game, or a bull-fight, is obviously quite different from the appraisal of an expert, yet these games are available as sources of satisfaction to one and all. Why should it be otherwise in the arts?

(5) We have already seen that the popular media have made most people aware of three rather than Shakespeare's two categories, namely by coining the humorous terms highbrows, middle-brows and lowbrows—the last one *truly* insulting and unjustified, inasmuch as it implies that if my tastes in music run to pop tunes (for example) I have remained at the *australopithecus* level of intellectual development. One can, in fact, be very intelligent and very gifted in dozens of ways and yet remain a primitive with respect to any given art, or all of them. This much certified, we can confirm the neutral, uninsulting concept itself, namely, that although the two traditional categories of sophisticated (judicious) and unsophisticated (unskilful) publics sufficed for many centuries, this division is clearly too crude for our own age. In order to obtain a more precise view of the realities of the aesthetic life today, we name an intermediate public of lovers of a given art (sometimes of all the arts) who are enlightened amateurs ('amateur' *means* lover) but for whom certain creations impose barriers they are not trained to surmount, though they may be perfectly *capable* of being so trained. In the world of music, for instance, basic masterpieces like Beethoven's Fifth Symphony and Tchaikovsky's Piano Concerto in B Flat, which may well delight the most sophisticated listeners on one side and the butcher and baker, to some extent, on the other, draw their widest and most enthusiastic support from that middle public, which often consists of professional people, leaders of society and the like whose expertise lies in other regions of human activity. Many members of this set fail to buy tickets when more complex, unfamiliar or subtler musical pieces are presented—say, a mass by Palestrina or the chamber music of Béla Bartok. In sheer numbers this group is well ahead of the connoisseurs of any given art, though it is in turn outnumbered by the mass public. Moreover, these in-between lovers play

a vital role as material supporters of the arts. Some are backers of opera, others fund museums, still others finance theaters, and some endow foundations that send checks to starving poets. We can hardly deny them a place and dignity of their own as a major constituency.

(6) So far, then, we discern for any given art a very large 'naive' public; a still very large yet smaller group of enlightened lovers; followed by a yet smaller sophisticated group of connoisseurs. Upon further reflection, however, it turns out that our cultures have evolved so far (for better or for worse) that three defined constituencies still do not suffice. Four are required. This is because in the second half of the nineteenth century there began to appear in the Western world a large enough number of works of art so *very* narrowly accessible—accessible to even fewer than the few—that a modern, baffled Hamlet is obliged to name one more set of 'receivers'. Once again, the popular media have recognized this phenomenon, and they have familiarized even the mass public with the phenomenon of 'avant-garde' or 'experimental' works of art, works that prove to be too barbed-wired for many members even of the cultural elite. Fringe art (as I propose to call such works) was unknown to our forefathers. Had you lived in Shakespeare's London, you would have looked in vain for some equivalent to our off-off-Broadway theaters, our exhibits of esoteric collages or our evenings devoted to dissonant music.

(7) Just as a military avant-garde (vanguard) can be successful enough to draw the main body of soldiers after it, so it happens that certain works, or certain types of work, that appealed only to a few initiates at the start, gradually acquire a larger, and possibly a very large audience. This occurs especially if the impediment consisted only or largely in the novelty of what was presented to the public. People, like animals, distrust novelty. But it may happen that after unfamiliarity wears off, the public finds the art very much to its taste. We can visit the French again for a famous example. When they showed their first works, the Impressionists were met with derision not only by the average public, but also by many of the supposedly judicious. But the novelties they introduced were quickly absorbed. The cultural elite began to applaud. And so did an ever larger public, until these painters became

perhaps the most popular group of artists ever seen in the Western world.

Many avant-garde works of art succeed less broadly, though no less profoundly—their audiences growing from a few enthusiasts at the fringe to a larger but still limited group of admirers. Thus the deeply puzzling poems of Stéphane Mallarmé (1842–98)—the chief 'inventor' of fringe poetry—have become classics, read and studied even in French high schools, but their success can never approach—quantitatively speaking—that of the Impressionist painters. Here, bereft of the music that made, or helped make it a classic, is a translation of the bare verbal bones of a sonnet Mallarmé wrote in 1886—a highly tentative translation, in that several words (including the prepositions) in this unpunctuated and grammatically perplexing text are capable of being translated in several different ways:

> To enter into your story
> It is as a hero alarmed
> If with his naked heel he has touched
> Some lawn of territory
>
> To glaciers prejudicial
> I don't know the naive sin
> That you will not have kept
> From laughing aloud its victory
>
> Tell me if I am not joyous
> Thunder and ruby at the hubs
> To see in the air which this fire pierces
>
> With scattered kingdoms
> How dying purples the wheel
> Of the sole vesperal[4] of my chariots.

Against these and other success stories, we must weigh the many works produced since the days of Mallarmé that seem to be rooted at the fringe, and may indeed have no ambition to attract

---

4. 'Vespéral' is either the book of evening prayers, or simply dusk, sundown. Commenting on the enigmatic poems of Georg Trakl (1887–1914), the enigmatic philosopher Ludwig Wittgenstein remarked, 'I do not understand them, but their *tone* makes me happy.' He could as readily have addressed this remark to Mallarmé's poetry, which remains as obscure as ever yet continues to charm ear and mind—in the original.

other constituencies. I will cite a minor instance in the second part of this chapter. A massive example is James Joyce's *Finnegans Wake* (1939). It is safe to say that this hugely experimental 'novel' will never be read—much less enjoyed—by more than a few specialists at a time. The crowds that flock to Monet will never besiege bookstores for their copies of Joyce's mastodon of a text.

(8) Fringe art is as vulnerable to oblivion, of course, as every other kind. Most of it washes down the drain along with most other artistic creations. But some of it remains alive (in print, on exhibit, in the curriculum, etc.) for a variety of reasons. One is that the initiates of any given art tend to be very influential in determining what will be read, studied, reprinted, exhibited, played and discussed. Another is that the 'satisfaction' that is so fundamental a component of our definition of art consists, on rare occasions, of an admiration, even a reverence, more or less bereft of sheer enjoyment. A third is that the artist may have produced works at other times that were both admired *and* truly enjoyed, an achievement that insures his fringe works against oblivion.[5] Finally, fringe works of art can remain alive chiefly for historical or biographical reasons. We do not love them; we consult them. But of course, in these functions they do not differ from the failed works that have addressed themselves to wider publics.

(9) It is high time now that we should note, and insist, that the categories or constituencies into which one divides the potential public, and the levels to which one assigns works of art, are nothing but convenient markers on a continuum. We know that sexy and sentimental paperbacks sell by the hundreds of thousand or millions of copies, and that the audiences for chamber music are limited. So it is convenient and realistic to define broad areas to which names can be given. But it would be an exercise in vain quibbling to argue whether Mrs Jane Doe is a middlebrow or a highbrow with respect to the visual arts, or whether Poem X is a fringe work or one available to any sophisticated lover of poetry. What we want to retain is that a variety of publics do exist in modern societies, that certain works of art have quasi-universal appeal, that others appeal to fairly definable constituencies and that,

5.   As well as his non-fringe minor and insignificant work. We might call this the law of Picasso's doodles.

finally, the sociology of reception in complex societies is itself extremely complex.

(10) At several points I have spoken of the individual's relative sophistication with regard to 'any given art'. Why this limiting phrase? Because it typically happens that a person's enthusiasm for, and insight into, one art fails to spill over into his receptivity to some of the other arts. The connoisseur of extremely sophisticated motion pictures might be very naive with regard to literature, and the expert in literature may confine his musical tastes to pop tunes. On the other hand, there are persons of wide aesthetic culture who occupy roughly the same place on our continuum with respect to two, several or even all the arts.

(11) To which works of art should we give the highest honor? Those, as some theorists have demanded, capable of reaching the whole people, educated and uneducated alike? Those that demand some expertise, that is to say a more powerful functioning of our faculties? Or those that explore the limits and try to push into the unknown? The answer to this question has to be grounded in a moral or political axiom, and neither morality nor political ideology is our business in this book, which therefore leaves you perfectly free to pronounce your verdict, should you feel the need to do so.

(12) Have I anywhere stated or implied that, if enjoyment could be measured by means of electrodes and a convenient recording device, it would be found that the connoisseur enjoys his *Hamlet* more than the ordinary groundling, or that the teenager at a rock festival feels less thrilled than the exquisitely refined reader of Mallarmé? I have not. But if no such claim can be made, on what ground can anyone urge the neophyte—say, a college sophomore, or else an older person who has never grappled with demanding art—to go to the mighty trouble of joining the ranks of the enlightened lovers? For the purely intellectual gains to be had? These gains are incontrovertible, yet wisdom is to be found in large supply elsewhere than in poetry and the other arts. Because sophisticated lovers of the arts are morally superior to naive folk? Anything but! Why then give up rock and roll for *The Well-Tempered Clavicord?*

I confess that I can find no truly solid ground for urging or recommending. I describe what can and does happen, not what I happen to feel should happen. So then: it may happen that we simply *wear out* the pleasures we have received from the easier works of art; or, if we do not absolutely wear them out, they seem no longer to satisfy all our needs; and then we bestir ourselves and move on, cost what it may. We realize that we long to use more of our powers of imagination and intellect—our 'mental muscle', by analogy with a tennis player who decides that he wants to exercise his unused muscular resources, though he will have to pay the price in buckets of perspiration. Weary of easy pleasures, bored by facile art, we decide to do what it takes to master the sensations of sophisticated, complex, profound and even disturbing art.

Thus, to begin with there must be the desire—a strong inner pressure—to move onward to new and more complex pleasures. And for the rest, the first section of this chapter has already covered the situation. A basic, perhaps innate, aptitude is called for—in the case of literature, an aptitude for and with language. For it would be one more lie to assert that anyone can become skilful in anything and everything just by trying long and hard. Plain intelligence is useful as well, insofar as it is different from special aptitude (for instance, a gift of the gab is not the same thing as intelligent talk). And after that: mental perspiration, training and more training. With tennis and any other sport, the training, obviously, is largely physical. For literature, training means reading, reading, reading, and organizing our reading, and thinking about our reading. Luckily, most of us enjoy hard training, and take the pain of it in our stride.

As we move into more complex pleasures, we also extend the sheer range of these pleasures. The intelligentsia's choices include much more of the 'exotic' than we are likely to find in the body of works admired by the naive. For if the intellectual has a single virtue that characterizes him (he is also afflicted with some vices in a more generous serving than is common), surely it is his restless curiosity—and I do not mean about his neighbor's affairs, but about the whole elusive world. Our growing connoiseur will be reaching backward into the past of his own culture and, unlike the 'unskilful', he will be reading (say) Catullus; but he will also march outward into faraway cultures, past and present, and leaf through (say) Li Po—in translation or even in the original.

With all the hard work come heady rewards. At almost every step of the way geniuses of the past and present gratify us with the powerful, amazing, gentle, delicate, beautiful, grinding, rough, joyful, bitter, pretty, austere, generous forms they have created. It cannot be said that our intellects will expand more than if we had spent the time studying the philosophers or the scientists; nor that we will emerge more virtuous than we were before; nor that we will be filled with greater happiness than what the adolescent feels at the jukebox. But because we could no longer be adolescents, forward we marched.

(13) The works of art—and in particular the works of literature—that the lovers who gather in the sophisticated range of the continuum have admired, more or less, and by and large, for a substantial number of years constitute what is called the 'canon'. This is a word appropriated—I am tempted to write misappropriated—from its homestead in religion, where it signifies (I am quoting from an old Webster) 'the collection or list of books which are received as genuine and inspired Holy Scripture'. Secularized, the term has come to be applied to the body of literary works considered at any given moment by the cultural elite—or, more precisely, that part of the elite interested in literature—as worthy of being loved, admired, preserved and transmitted.[6]

The differences between this laymen's canon and the various theological canons are evident. The canon of sacred texts for a given religion (or for a given branch of a religion) is named and imposed by a clearly identifiable authority or series of authorities—a Council of the Roman Church, for example, or a congregation of rabbis. The intelligentsia, instead, is not an identifiable body, and has no institution in which it vests decisions, so that we have to look for evidence here and there in order to venture the supposition that Work Z is by now canonical. Furthermore, the religious canon is a simple yes-or-no affair. The disputes are long since settled, and for each community a text is either in or out of the canon; and if it is in, it is wholly in. In the literary world,

---

6.   The 'canon' also refers to the body of literary texts that is proposed, or widely accepted, as being authentically from the hand of a given author. In music, 'canon'—from the Greek meaning 'rule'—refers to a type of contrapuntal imitation. In the sense under discussion here, the word seems to be infrequently used for arts other than literary.

instead, a work can be thought of as securely settled at the center
of the canon, or floating at some distance from the center, or in
some danger of being extruded altogether, or of not belonging
there to begin with. Furthermore, as we have seen, works are
often preserved and transmitted without being loved and admired.
I have before me, for instance, an aging anthology of eighteenth-
century English poetry that displays the authors all literate
persons recognize at once, among them Jonathan Swift, Alexan-
der Pope, Thomas Gray, Samuel Johnson, Robert Burns and
William Blake.[7] Relying on their best works, these writers seem to
dwell securely near the center of our English literary canon.
Another group represented in the anthology consists of poets like
Matthew Prior, John Gay, William Collins and William Cowper,
who are widely recognized as minor yet estimable talents. They
may well continue for a long time to be mildly loved and modestly
admired. Finally, however, the anthology reprints a clutch of
poems by artists like William Walsh, John Byrom and William
Julius Mickle, who are as forgotten as any poets can be. Are they
canonical as well? The editor does not pretend that they are. He
wisely informs us in his preface that

> a few poems have been admitted primarily because of their
> autobiographical value; others, a larger number, because of their
> importance as indications of significant tendencies. I have had in
> mind the need of students who will use the material of the book as
> the basis for an historical study of the period.

Such works, then, are not canonical in our sense of the term, for
their preservation and transmission is determined on non-aes-
thetic grounds. Similarly, by the way, museums act as repositories
not only of acknowledged masterpieces, but also of works—often
very bad works—that are useful witnesses to, and sometimes sig-
nificant movers in, the history of art.

The final and perhaps most important difference between the
literary and the religious canon is that while the latter is as fixed
and permanent as anything human can be, the one we are con-
cerned with evolves in time by a kind of aesthetic voting that takes
place under a myriad influences. More about this presently.

7. *English Poetry of the Eighteenth Century* (ed. Cecil A. Moore; New York:
Henry Holt, 1935).

(14) Wordsworth's poem about the daffodils is undoubtedly a classic; and in a work about the fundamentals of art we need to ask, if only for a moment, what seems to be generally understood by that word. It too, of course, is a word that serves many masters. Classical music is opposed to popular music as the sort of music which is too difficult to appeal to youngsters or the masses. And yet, we hear of 'popular classics', with reference to songs and tunes that have lasted beyond a single generation. Then again, in literature 'the classics' encompass anything whatever preserved from the writings of the Greeks and Romans. We even read about 'instant classics' of any art at any level from enthusiasts who settle the future for the rest of us before it happens.

Perhaps we come close to a classic use of 'classic' if we think of it as a verbal medal pinned on canonical works that have been in the canon for a long time *and* are very widely known, loved and admired. How long is long and how wide is widely are questions we can allow to hang in the air; observing only that while works of art can become canonical almost at birth—so immediately and powerfully are they admired that they enter at once into university curricula and become 'hot' subjects of discourse at conferences, in journals, and so on—they seem to need maturing for some years before they are generally spoken of as classics.

As we have seen already, many works are canonical without ranking among the supreme masterpieces. By the same token, a number of classics are routinely called 'minor'. It would appear, therefore, that a work of less than supreme value receives the enviable medal alongside the divinities if, besides having lasted a while in the canon, it is also very widely known. 'Everybody' knows *Hamlet*; but 'everybody' also knows *The Christmas Carol*—obviously a minor classic.

Now it is true that canons and classics are concepts and realities made up and nurtured by the intelligentsia, who are the vocal cords of nations. But the sophisticated not only enjoy a multitude of works of art created by or for the naive—they are also quite capable of escorting some of them into the canon and even making classics out of them as time goes by. This became true of many popular ballads that had been sung by humble folk since the Middle Ages, and of folktales not written down until the eighteenth century. As for our own times, who knows what popular tune, or what billboard, or what comic strip may survive as a classic into the far-flung future thanks to those who work at making their culture visible and audible to itself and to other cultures?

(15) Popular or 'serious', every new work of art shown to the public is, in effect, a candidate for canonization—even the 'performance' or 'happening' that boastfully proclaims its ephemeral life, since it is apt to be conscientiously recorded, photographed and filmed from every angle. As far as belles lettres are concerned, open any ten survey anthologies of poetry in English, and you will see that they all dutifully reprint a major selection of the classic poems in our language. Hence the overlap among them will be very extensive. No such anthology can permit itself to exclude Keats's 'Ode to a Nightingale', for instance. But in their selection of recent poems, the editors will be seen to diverge considerably, and ever more so the closer they come to the present they share. What we are witnessing is the 'aesthetic voting' that is always taking place, with editors acting as especially influential advocates. Most of the very recent poets and poems they choose for inclusion will eventually vanish from view. However, it may happen that one of those very-much-alive poets pleases beyond the single editor who printed three or four of his poems in his college text. Others ask for his poems, perhaps because he has been favorably reviewed in a few journals. Critics begin to talk about him. Someone organizes a conference about his work at the Modern Language Association, the cathedral of the professionals of literature in America. A book by one of its members refers to our happy poet as 'one of the freshest voices we have heard in a generation'. The poet is well on his way to acquiring a place in the canon—unless the critical fire goes out, the boiling water cools, and our poet reenters obscurity or even reaches oblivion. It seems therefore that the fate of a living artist bears some resemblance to that of a politician. To be sure, aesthetic voting does not occur on given dates by means of bits of paper stuffed into a box. It is done all year long, spontaneously, in numerous, widespread gestures of acceptance or rejection. But all the same, some artists are so to speak elected, some remain in office, some are defeated, some are re-elected, and some are never heard from again.

(16) To a large extent, the additions and deletions from the canon, as well as the promotions and demotions within the canon,

are due to the movement of what we vaguely call cultural tides; but we can often detect well-identified individuals and common-interest groups pushing and pulling these tides quite visibly and audibly. The editors I mentioned above illustrate the point. Along with teachers, critics, journalists and many other individuals and groups, they are the advocates who agitate or act for changes in our tastes. Here, for instance, are the words of Professor Terry Eagleton, whose high reputation in the literary world (as these words are written) makes him a very influential advocate:

> The canon is inconsistent even by its own criteria: some of what it excludes should, by rights, be there, and some of what is there should not be. Stanislav Lem's *Solaris* is better than [Wordsworth's] *The Excursion*, but science fiction happens at the moment not to be a canonical genre, whereas epic, even a botched one, is.[8]

Such words represent, in brief of course, an effort to alter the canon—or, in our other terms, to change our 'aesthetic votes'. Some of us who are unacquainted with Mr Lem's novel may now make a point of reading it, and reading it under the impression of the influential advocate's strong feeling about it. And, if it is true that *The Excursion* dwells in the canon (it does so, I suspect, barely and by basking in the reputation of Wordsworth's best-loved poems), there might also be started a movement now for pushing it into outer darkness as a mere document in the life and art of a great poet.

(17) Tastes change not only with regard to individual works of art, but also with respect to types, periods and other groupings of art—as Professor Eagleton's remarks make clear. Indeed, the history of practical criticism (what is 'in' and what is 'out') is a sobering one. Perhaps comical is the better word. More often than they care to advertise, the intellectual elite have reversed the judgments of their predecessors, and even heaped abuse and ridicule on them—only to come in for the same treatment by their own successors. Here is an astonishing instance concerning a period and type. For several centuries, the sophisticates of Europe disdained the cathedrals built in the Middle Ages, and saw

---

8.   In 1992, when he wrote these words, Terry Eagleton was the Thomas Warton Professor in English Literature at Oxford. The passage quoted is in the *Times Literary Supplement*, 18 December 1992, p. 5.

them crumble without raising their voices—let alone their hands. The adjective 'Gothic' was used in derision. The reversal, when it came, was swift and complete. The sophisticates turned around, 'Gothic' became a high compliment, and we have learned to adore what was once despised.[9]

(18) So then, changes can be quick and dramatic. Normally, however, the canon's motion and fluidity are relatively slow. Furthermore, the favorites are more likely to experience ebbs and flows within the canon than outright expulsion and dramatic reversal of expulsion. John Donne's poetry, for instance, suffered a period of anemic regard, but was never expelled from the canon before it grew sensationally in esteem early in the twentieth century. Many tales of this sort can be told, whether about large groups of works, or the works of single artists, or individual works of art. Much therefore as we may chuckle over the fads and fashions, the retractions, the fulminations, the self-assurances mocked by later self-assurances, it would be unwise to succumb to a facile cynicism: fluidity is not chaos. Overall, the love and admiration that the sophisticated feel for numberless works of art tend to be deep and lasting: the classics stand firm. *King Lear* and the *Mona Lisa* are unlikely to fade from our regard. Eavesdrop through a crack in the door on a group of poets and critics; listen to them as they quarrel over the merits of Shelley's poetry (for instance); and after several persons have declared their contempt for its overblown, sentimental, incoherent rhetoric, walk in and boldly recite 'Departed Friends', affirming that you agree with Shelley's disparagers, claiming that 'Departed Friends' is superior to the Romantic poet's typical work, and urging that it be required for study at our universities. You will be reassured at once. Everyone looks embarrassed. Are you joking or serious? Of course you are joking. Your friends are relieved that your brain hasn't softened. It is true that they used rather strong words about poor Shelley; but they did not mean to equate him with an Eddie Guest. In other words, they were not advocating expulsion from the canon,

9. And here is a notable individual instance: the elite almost unanimously condemned the Eiffel Tower when it was built. Then they learned to admire and love it along with the rest of the population, and it became a work of engineering art whose appeal comes as close to being literally universal as anything mankind has ever devised.

but a more modest place within it. Since, however, fundamental harmonies of this kind beget no discussion, they tend to be ignored in favor of the drama of apparent anarchy.

(19) Now we turn to the sensitive subject of *false canons*. The editor who included several untalented poets in his anthology of eighteenth-century poetry disclaimed any attempt to secure even a modest place in the canon for them, so we have no quarrel with him. Nor with the advocate who suggested that we change our tastes in literature by bestowing less admiration on Wordsworth's interminable poem and more on a novel of science fiction. But a problem arises for us when powerful individuals or groups manage to *enforce* or *prohibit* given types of art, or certain specific works of art, or the works of certain artists. They may claim that the art for which they seek preference is aesthetically superior to the art favored before. Their critics may retort that this is a lie; that in truth they are pushing to impose and enforce their favored art on the public for mostly political, social, economic, theological reasons (and the like). Standing outside as neutrals, we, on our side, will assert only that the imposed canon is false if it fails to alter our tastes, our standards, our aesthetic voting in the long run, and therefore collapses if and when it loses the backing that enforced it.

We do not need to turn the clock back very far in order to locate some illustrations. Both Joseph Stalin and Adolf Hitler imposed on their subjects the kind of art they favored and excluded the kind they thought unfriendly to their views. Open resistance was impossible. Practitioners of disallowed forms and styles of art were exiled, imprisoned or murdered. The official canons were clamped on the schools and made manifest by public commissions, as well as in theaters, movie houses and concert halls. Now, it would be incorrect to say that the whole population resisted, either silently or overtly. This was not the case at all. Many people agreed with the tastes and distastes of these dictators. But most of the 'judicious'—the cultural elite, that is—did not. As a result, as soon as these empires collapsed, normal aesthetic life picked up where it had left off, and the old canons were reinstated without a dissenting murmur. This proved that for the sophisticated public at any rate, the Communist and Nazi canons were false.

I do not mean, however, that a canon supported or even imposed by totalitarian regimes is *necessarily* false in our sense of the word. We cherish and have canonized countless works of art created under more or less strict censorship and control. Dictatorial taste, more or less stringently enforced, is not incompatible with great art. In the *Aeneid* Virgil trumpeted the glory of Rome and its emperor, and could not have chosen to debunk them. The best as well as the worst painters of the Middle Ages and Renaissance worked largely in obedience to the Roman Catholic Church. England's best and worst poets and playwrights dared not attack the policies or persons of their sovereigns. Under Louis XIV every French artist, good or bad, did obeisance to his Majesty. Since we have not, by and large, overthrown these canons, the inevitable conclusion is that many of the tyrants of the past had better taste than the thugs who ran the Soviet Union and Germany in the twentieth century. Or more precisely: their tastes tended to be in harmony with those of the intelligentsia; largely, indeed, because they had been tutored by the intelligentsia, something that has seldom been true for the dictators of our own era. In all these instances, therefore, we are dealing with authentic canons.

Dictatorships are quietly thorough; democracies are vociferously inefficient. No one among us has the power to enforce unloved works as masterpieces or turn masterpieces into unloved works. What we do see, however, is the occasional pressure group that acquires enough power to influence such centers of canon formation as curricula, textbooks, museums, concert halls, and so on. The influence is sporadic, manifesting itself in strenuous agitation here and there, and resulting in a number of successes, some temporary, some durable. Here is a minor but representative example. In the fifth edition of the *Heath Introduction to Poetry*, edited by Professor Joseph DeRoche (1996), the reader discovers, wedged between several poems by Byron and Shelley, three lyrics by a certain Lydia Sigourney (1791–1865). 'The Mother of Washington: On the Laying of the Corner-stone of her Monument at Fredericksburg, Virginia' begins as follows:

> Long hast thou slept unnoted. Nature stole
> In her soft ministry around thy bed,
> Spreading her vernal tissue, violet-gemmed,
> And pearled with dew;

and continues in the same vein for 51 lines.[10] No one can doubt that the professor has seated Sigourney between two male members of the traditional canon in deference to feminist pressure on the latter; but I want this small victory of a pressure group to stand for any and all such victories, small or great, obtained by groups demanding the canonization of works by Indians, Blacks, Latinos, the homeless, the working class, or, at the other side of the ideological fence, fundamentalist Christians, white supremacists, anti-gay activists, *et al.*; and of course we bear in mind that other countries will be blessed with other such groups, each hoping for enough clout to revise textbooks (and other media) to suit its program.

Let me make it clear at this point that our business in this study of the art of poetry is not to argue for or against demands for social justice, political progress or compensation for historic wrongs. The sole and limited question we need to address here is whether the forced imposition of a Sigourney into a revised canon—through changes in texts, curricula, patronage, funding, discussion, and so forth—would sooner or later so modify ('improve') the tastes of the elite that from being pushed for ideological reasons she would take her place between Byron and Shelley as the result of our free aesthetic voting. If, upon being successfully pushed, she kept her place only by force, her canonization would be false in that it would be annulled if the pressure were off. But if, after a generation or so of dwelling on her poetry perforce, most of us were to become true Sigourney lovers after all, eager to keep her poems alive between those of Byron and Shelley even after the force had been evacuated, then her entry into the canon must needs be called true and authentic.

(20) Each country's educational system constitutes a dictatorship, more or less strict and detailed, that imposes the 'official' canon on its defenceless student populations, from the first grade all the way to the doctorate. How can we determine whether these

10. Professor DeRoche does not give the lady her full name, nor does he in any way identify her. She was Lydia Huntley Sigourney, known as 'The Sweet Singer of Hartford'. Besides her many humanitarian activities (including support for the temperance movement), she was the author of 67 volumes of poetry (!), and the most popular American bard of her generation.

'required reading' canons are fundamentally authentic? There is in fact an easy test, because everyone finishes school on a certain happy day, at which time the school's dictatorship comes to an end, the pressure is off, and then we can observe what happens— not to the entire student body, but to the intelligentsia interested in a given art (or several, or all the arts) whose conscious or unconscious 'mission' will be to patronize, preserve and pass to the next generation the works it admires and loves. It appears from this test that in a general way the canons of the 'free' countries we know about are authentic. *King Lear* and the *Mona Lisa* are safe. You may call this efficient brainwashing or gentle formation of taste. But the fact remains that the force has been removed, as is proved by the circumstance that the mass public, which has sat in the classrooms too, wiggles away from the classics without penalty, while the brainwashed, or educated, youngsters set about preserving and transmitting Milton and Handel in their turn.

(21) Nevertheless, we all remain free to wiggle out and shape our own canon as private heretics from the 'official' one, or as active advocates, whether ideologically motivated or not, of the works *we* love and admire. No one would conform exactly to any list a student of the arts might, for instance, draw up of the thousand-and-one most favored works of literature in a given country in a given year. In short, the canon is a statistical concept that does not care if I curl up with a book I am the only one left in the world to love. Here again, and finally, the art canon breaks company with the canon as understood in our religions.

Illustrations

After offering Wordsworth's lyric as a broadly appealing poem— one that can delight, I think, the very naive as well as the most sophisticated English-speaking reader—we might do well to examine a few texts whose constituencies are probably concentrated in some particular zone along the slope of sophistication.[11] 'Departed Friends', by the once very popular Eddie Guest, is a fair instance of a work of art whose power is concentrated at the naive

11. If any of my examples seem inappropriate, you are invited to think of others while trying to preserve the concept being illustrated.

end. In another chapter I will try to give the reason or reasons for this; because however obviously dreadful this poem will seem to readers in the trained and experienced reaches of the gradient, an analysis of the obvious can be extremely illuminating. Be that as it may, we remind ourselves that concentration in a given area of the gradient does not mean that everyone who lodges in that area will be a fellow-admirer; and, more significantly, that some persons who are highly sophisticated with respect to other arts or other human activities may remain naive with respect to poetry and as a result be favorably impressed by Guest's poem. And again: the same observations apply to all the arts.

Elizabeth Barrett Browning's famous sonnet to her husband Robert probably receives the most, and the most enthusiastic, votes from the large middle audience:

> How do I love thee? Let me count the ways.
> I love thee to the depth and breadth and height
> My soul can reach, when feeling out of sight
> For the ends of Being and ideal Grace.
> I love thee to the level of everyday's
> Most quiet need, by sun and candle-light.
> I love thee freely, as men strive for Right;
> I love thee purely, as they turn from Praise.
> I love thee with the passion put to use
> In my old griefs, and with my childhood's faith.
> I love thee with a love I seemed to lose
> With my lost saints—I love thee with the breath,
> Smiles, tears, of all my life!—and, if God choose,
> I shall but love thee better after death.[12]

It might be a good exercise to inquire why this poem would be, in places, 'a bit hard' for the mass audience, and why, for many sophisticated connoisseurs of poetry, its success falls somewhat short of matching its fine intentions. In spite of this caveat, however, the sonnet seems to be securely entrenched as one of our minor classics.

Shakespeare wrote love sonnets too, as everyone knows; but some or even many of his are truly out of the range of the mass audience, have a limited hold on the middle audience of poetry

---

12. *Sonnets from the Portuguese*, number 43. This sonnet sequence was published in 1850. The third and fourth lines are anything but clear.

lovers and reserve their power chiefly for an elite of connoisseurs. Centuries after they were written, the obstacles they pose are in part lexical: Shakespeare's language needs to be 'translated' into modern English in more places than one could wish. But even in their own time, most of these sonnets were refined dishes meant for connoisseurs' palates. Here is the infrequently anthologized number 100 of the sequence:

> Where art thou, Muse, that thou forget'st so long
> To speak of that which gives thee all thy might?
> Spends't thou thy fury on some worthless song,
> Dark'ning thy power to lend base subjects light?
> Return, forgetful Muse, and straight redeem
> In gentle numbers time so idly spent;
> Sing to the ear that doth thy lays esteem
> And gives thy pen both skill and argument.
> Rise, resty Muse: my love's sweet face survey
> If Time have any wrinkle graven there;
> If any, be a satire to decay
> And make Time's spoils despisèd everywhere:
>> Give my love fame faster than Time wastes life;
>> So thou prevent'st his scythe and crooked knife.[13]

The difficulties of this and many other poems do not derive at all from an intellectual dimension that places them beyond the middle audience. What, after all, is intellectually difficult about a call to one's own poetry to give up base subjects, return to singing the girl who inspires and appreciates one's poems, and praise her so well that her growing old will cease to matter? Thoughts like these are accessible to everybody. But for the mass and middle

---

13. The sonnets (most of them, at any rate) were privately circulated long before they appeared in print in 1609. 'Numbers' (line 6) means 'verses' in this context, that is to say lines of poetry. This meaning, derived from the regular numbering of beats (accents) in a line, is no longer alive. 'Lays' (line 7) are songs or poems; 'resty' (line 9) means indolent—the only word in the poem that has disappeared from the language; 'prevent' in the last line is to forestall or foil—and this is a more dangerous trap for the modern reader than an obviously archaic word, for the reader might not think it necessary to look up a word he recognizes and one that seems to make sense. *Seems* to make sense, for in fact it would be absurd for a poet to assert that poetry (the Muse) can prevent aging in the modern meaning of the word 'prevent'.

audiences problems arise with some of the expressions (like 'Spend'st thou thy fury'), the drastic compressions (e.g. 'be a satire to decay'), the allusive indirection of the first two lines— Shakespeare's poetic manners, we might say, and those of his times.

In order to remove the obstacle of archaic or time-altered words, I give a more recent poem for which the chief audience is probably the same as that which thrills to Shakespeare's sonnet. It is William Butler Yeats's 'The Mother of God', published in a collection in 1933.

> The three-fold terror of love; a fallen flare
> Through the hollow of an ear;
> Wings beating about the room;
> The terror of all terrors that I bore
> The Heavens in my womb.
>
> Had I not found content among the shows
> Every common woman knows,
> Chimney corner, garden walk,
> Or rocky cistern where we tread the clothes
> And gather all the talk?
>
> What is this flesh I purchased with my pains,
> This fallen star my milk sustains,
> This love that makes my heart's blood stop
> Or strikes a sudden chill into my bone
> And bids my hair stand up?[14]

Once again, the difficulty here is not caused by some abstruse idea accessible only to a handful of geniuses. Far from it! But the middle audience tends to be put out by indirections like 'a fallen flare through the hollow of an ear', unexpected ideas like the fearfulness of the Nativity (an old idea indeed, yet one that runs counter to our modern jollification of this event), or shocking juxtapositions like the birth of Christ with hair standing on end.

It is no secret, of course, that much of the poetry written in the twentieth century requires the reader to face the unexpected and the disturbing. Ideas not esoteric in themselves seem again and again so enigmatically expressed as to require the intervention of

---

14. *The Poems of W.B. Yeats* (ed. R.J. Finneran; New York: Macmillan, 1983). The 'three-fold' of line 1 refers to the Trinity.

professional interpreters. A little-known short poem by Wallace Stevens illustrates this point and takes us still farther from the naive and middle publics:

THE SURPRISES OF THE SUPERHUMAN

The palais de justice of chambermaids
Tops the horizon with its colonnades.

If it were lost in Uebermenschlichkeit,
Perhaps our wretched state would soon come right.

For somehow the brave dicta of its kings
Makes more awry our faulty human things.[15]

Such a poem—one among thousands—wrenches us decisively away from the middle audience. All who read Stevens admire him, but few read him. We are quickly sliding toward the far end of the gradient.

Still, Stevens is not the most forbidding of poets. He has always charmed a literate intelligentsia that remains unsympathetic to many an extreme maneuver in poetry or in the other arts. For such extreme maneuvers we can turn to innumerable poems composed, so to speak, in the ever-lengthening tail of Mallarmé's comet. Here, for instance, is Jackson Mac Low's cryptically titled 'Poe and Psychoanalysis':

Point, out effect
A not dreams
Point, stables young child, hand out a not let young stranger invites stranger.

Palace, on emotion.
Are now door.
Palace, sleeper.[16]

For the time being, such poems, which perpetuate the Mallarmean strategy (although they may claim quite different poetic philosophies and kinships), are unable to spread their glow beyond a clan of *aficionados*—and it should be stressed that their authors may not want it any other way. Still, we can ask whether

15. From *Harmonium*, published in 1923 (*The Collected Poems of Wallace Stevens* [New York: Alfred A. Knopf, 1957]). See further discussion on pp. 138 and 292-93.

16. Written in 1960, this poem first appeared in *Stanzas for Iris Lezak* (Barton, Vermont: Something Else, 1972).

some of these works will gradually elicit so much admiration, and even enjoyment, from the broader elite that they will become part of the canon. If so, they will have earned the right to be called 'avant-garde' rather than 'fringe', since it will turn out that they made up a true vanguard in the process of canon formation. Otherwise, any such work will either continue as an object of admiration for the extremely few and special, or else it will become, like the poems of William Walsh, John Byrom and William Julius Mickle, an inert element in the history of poetry.

Part II

The Art of Poetry

Chapter 5

What Is Poetry?

So far we have concerned ourselves with Art as a whole, but I hope we have never forgotten that our especial subject matter is the particular art of poetry. Now that we are narrowing our attention down to this special art, let us bear the reverse in mind; much that will be said about poetry can be transferred and applied to most or all of the other arts.

Why not begin by re-reading the general definition?

> What we call a work of art is a human creation, namely a manipulation or arrangement of, or imposition upon, appropriate materials and resources resulting in a form, or a series of forms, or a set of flowing forms, which, when it stimulates our brain centers of sight, hearing or language (singly or in combination) we admit into our consciousness as a phenomenon that we shall deem successful insofar as it produces in us a wholly or partly unmediated satisfaction, largely through the energizing of these materials and resources.

This definition is ready-made for the particular art of Literature. Our only task is to specify that the 'appropriate materials and resources' of this art are words and related signs. 'Related signs' include other elements with linguistic import, most notably punctuation marks, but also, for instance, the spacing around the words. Since in poetry these signs and spaces tend to play significant roles more frequently than in other literary forms, I propose that we look right away at a couple of instances before returning to language as such. The first is a frothy yet by no means trivial little piece by Richard Armour (1906–89):

> That poem is a splendid thing.
> I love to hear you quote it.
> I like the thought, I like the swing.
> I like it all. (I wrote it).[1]

The parentheses are obviously essential to the meaning, the fun, and even the profundity of Armour's jingle. Parentheses mean 'not very important', or 'not the main point at all', and Armour utilizes that meaning to play an ironical game with us, since in fact 'I wrote it' is very much the main point.

And here is a poem that displays some of the significant maneuvers involving spacing, capitalization and punctuation characteristic of a great deal of twentieth-century poetry:

> Buffalo Bill's
> defunct
>   who used to
>   ride a watersmooth-silver
>   stallion
> and break onetwothreefourfive pigeonsjustlikethat
>   Jesus
> he was a handsome man
>   and what i want to know is
> how do you like your blueeyed boy
> Mister Death[2]

Through the squeezing together of words, the shooting of the pigeons is now felt to be a real feat of pistol-packing rapidity; the speaker, in lower case, effaces himself modestly before his hero, Death, and Jesus; the latter is isolated, more perhaps to emphasize the exclamation than to honor the Lord; the omission of punctuation helps the overall speed already suggested by the stallion and the pigeon killing; and the unleashing of the lines from the

---

1. In *Writing Light Verse and Prose Humor* (Boston: The Writer Inc., 1971).
2. 'Portrait' by E.E. Cummings (1894–1963), published in 1923. In *Complete Poems* (ed. George J. Firmage; New York: Liveright, 1991). Cummings was one of the pioneers of these maneuvers. These truly avant-garde experiments succeeded (see our previous chapter): they have become part of the poetic language; they are no longer avant-garde; the main body has joined up and absorbed the vanguard.

customary discipline of marching off from the left margin takes us from decorum to headlong agitation and 'lets the air in'. Such, at any rate, are possible and legitimate reactions to the poet's energizing of his materials through those 'related signs.'

Still, no one can take away from words, words, and more words their central position: words are what the related signs are applied to, after all. Sometimes—not very often—the words are created ('Jabberwocky' is an instance), but normally they are selected from the immense available repertory, and always arranged in some *form* or other. On occasion they are both created and selected from the available data bank, as when (for instance) a noun is wrenched into an unprecedented verbal function, like 'I nouned him out of his habit of adjectivating all over the page,' or a known word is partially modified into something semi-new, like 'modifried'. By definition, of course, words stimulate the language-center or centers of the brain, reaching the latter through the eyes or ears or both. And, as our definition records, the energized words and related signs are deemed successful insofar as they please 'on their own', whether or not they have also *added* to our information, intelligence, wisdom, virtue or socio-political awareness. Thus what distinguishes literature from all other verbal texts (e.g. grocery lists) is the particular fact that literary and *only* literary texts owe their success to the unmediated delight they have created, and *only* literary texts need to provide such unmediated delight if they are not to 'die'.

Language is for a man of letters what such phenomena as lines, colors and textures are for the painter and created sounds for the composer. This means, obviously but portentously, that literature shares its materials and resources—all the words and signs in the language—with almost every human activity other than art, and thus brings it closer to non-art domains of human thought and activity than the arts that use wordless media. Dangerously closer at times. A piano sonata is normally neither Christian nor Muslim, neither Democratic nor Fascist, neither Black nor White. But the artist who uses words trespasses, in a sense, on the territories occupied by politicians, lawyers, priests, businessmen, philosophers, journalists—nearly everybody! And does so, very often, because he passionately wants to. Many literary artists are so deeply committed to a non-art Cause that they even chafe at the idea of practicing an art instead of 'manning the barricades'. Not that painters, composers and dancers are necessarily indifferent to non-art causes. Far from it. But the very medium used by literary artists predisposes them for participation in the numberless struggles of mankind carried out through words before blows are exchanged. All this notwithstanding, the immovable fact remains that the literary work of art, like a piano sonata or an abstract painting, succeeds with mankind only by delivering an unmediated satisfaction, whatever else it may also provide the reader in the realms of theology, ethics, politics, his pocket-book, and what have you. It shares its materials and resources with everybody, but the degree of its success is measured by a yardstick all its own.

Let us proceed to the standard division of the realm of Literature into its traditional sub-species of Narrative Fiction, Drama, the Essay and Poetry, without haggling over details, overlaps, and mini-confusions. Then, without further ado, we can ask whether Poetry is at all susceptible of a definition of its own. This is a touchy issue, for it is often claimed that poetry is undefinable. I suspect that certain poets and some writers on the art of poetry enjoy this idea, since it sets the enterprise of poetry apart in a prestigiously mysterious domain all by itself. The guides to poetry used as college texts in the United States commonly duck the problem, or else wave it off by means of a few easy phrases.[3] And yet it would be surpassingly strange if something that human beings have been doing with language 'forever and everywhere' (the exaggeration, if any, is minimal) could escape definition. So then,

---

3. A recent textbook opens with the question 'What is poetry?' and answers as follows: 'The gift of language is what makes us human, and poets make the fullest use of it. They often seem to write with a heightened sense of awareness, with a special intensity—"in a fine frenzy," in Shakespeare's words.' Continuing: 'Poets are in love with words. One way to define poetry is to call it language at its best: Poets use its full potential, using more of it and using it to better advantage than we usually do. Poets mobilize to the fullest the image-making capacity of language... Poetry has the ability to delight the ear and the power to stir our emotions. It has the potential, if we let it, of making us more responsive and thoughtful human beings' (H.P. Guth and G.L. Rico, *Discovering Poetry* [Englewood Cliffs, NJ: Prentice–Hall, 1993]). Some of these statements apply to poetry plus any number of texts no one would call poetry, and some of them apply to some but not to other texts that everyone does call poetry.

after defining Art, and then, under Art, the Art of Literature, we shall bravely go on to define, under the Art of Literature, the Art of Poetry.

> Poetry is the branch of Literature whose words and related signs are preponderantly delivered (when written down or printed) in premeditated limited quanta.

Like our overall definition of Art, the definition of Poetry attempts to be accurate and not itself a display of fine writing. An 'unromantic' description of this sort stands unapologetically at the opposite pole of Shelley's 'A poem is the very image of life expressed in its eternal truth...Poetry is the record of the best and happiest moments of the happiest and best minds'—words that appear in the famous *Defence of Poetry* of 1821. Enthusiastic outbursts of this kind are common in the vast literature on poetry, but they work better as propaganda for the art than they do as philosophical explication of it.

A few notes on my definition:

(1) A 'limited quantum' is nothing more than the old-fashioned 'verse', for which it is here both a substitute and a definition. Poetry, in short, is literature in verse form, verse being a unit of verbal energy delivered as a burst, a spurt, a bundle. Once the burst is over, the text *turns*, a word I use here to indicate that the word 'verse' derives from the Latin *vertere*, which is 'to turn'. But the point is that a burst is of limited duration. A line of poetry cannot go on and on indefinitely. One might compare it to 'a single breath', and, instead of speaking of quantum, spurt, etc., call the duration in question the 'breadth of a breath'. To be sure, we can stretch our breath considerably (as in underwater swimming); but there is a human limit. Accordingly, while artists often give us *very* limited quanta (short lines) like Archibald MacLeish's often-quoted

> A poem should not mean
> But be[4]

—where 'But be' is a full line of poetry (begging, incidentally, for a great deal of qualifying commentary!); we also find extended

4.   Archibald MacLeish, from 'Ars Poetica', in *Poems 1924–1933* (New York: Houghton Mifflin, 1933).

quanta that give us the literary sensation of holding out under-
water until we come up for another gulp—as is the case with Walt
Whitman's single line:

> I pass death with the dying and birth with the new-wash'd babe, and am
> not contain'd between my hat and boots.[5]

However, at a certain point, or rather across a certain grey area,
the length becomes so long that the feeling and idea of a quan-
tum is lost, and we cross over into the prose territory of the
paragraph. More about this by and by.

(2) 'Preponderantly delivered': in other words, a prose passage
embedded in a poetic text does not affect the latter's status as a
poem. By the same token, a literary work of prose like a novel may
well resort on occasion to the special power of a short line, acting
as a full paragraph—a line that, were the likes of it used prepon-
derantly, would turn the novel into a long narrative poem.

(3) 'When written down and printed': oral delivery is as valid a
way of reaching an audience as print. A spoken poem is simply
that which will appear in verse form if and when it is faithfully
transcribed. Prime examples: the *Iliad* and *Odyssey*, and folk bal-
lads throughout the world.

(4) 'Premeditated', in order to preclude accidental arrange-
ments. We are describing a human act that has been thought over
with a degree—usually a high degree—of care.[6]

(5) Until the twentieth century, it could be sensibly argued that
rhythmic patterning (rhyme being a special and relatively late
invention in our world), is *the* defining element for poetry. Edgar
Allen Poe called poetry 'The Rhythmical Creation of Beauty'. But
by the second half of the nineteenth century, some of the best
poets had demonstrated that something no one ceased to call
poetry could triumphantly survive though shorn of any system of
rhythmical recurrences. A new definition, one that absorbed this
revolution, was needed.

5.   Walt Whitman, from 'Song of Myself' No. 7, first published in the
Leaves of Grass edition of 1855.
6.   If there is an artist somewhere who lets chance decide where the line
will turn, our definition still embraces him, for it is he who launches and
oversees the process (see Chapter 1, [3]).

Could we say, however, that *if* a text exhibits rhythm through-
out, we are bound to call it a poem? Not so. If it is given to the
public in the shape of a story or an essay, it will inevitably be
thought of as a piece of prose, though written in an unpleasantly
mannered style.

(6) The grammatical structure of the limited quanta is not rele-
vant to our definition. It is safe to say that in the typical poem
some, many, most or all of the verbal 'spurts' come to a close
without an end-stop, that is to say a period, question mark or
exclamation point, like the first of the two lines by MacLeish
quoted above. But poems have been written in which every single
verse does come to a full syntactical stop—where, in other words,
the premeditated decision has been to turn each time at the end
of a sentence.[7] And, as might be expected, we come across single
lines of authentic poetry that consist of more than one complete
sentence; for example,

Ask of the Learn'd the way? The Learned are blind.[8]

II

Limiting the bursts of verbal energy remains poetry's very own
means of energizing language, whether the poet chooses to cut
off and *turn* after so many syllables, or so many beats, or after
rhyming words, or goes the commonly seen newer way, where the
decision is to cut off irregularly, according to any principle that
pleases the artist line by line. Poetry has to share with the other
literary categories all other sources of effective energy. Now, how-
ever, the question can be asked whether 'limited quanta' is a
trivial or a vital factor in producing the thrill of a literary work. In
other words, was it worth while for mankind to invent the separate
literary category called 'poetry' on the basis of this one differenti-
ating element?

Re-read the Buffalo Bill poem quoted in this chapter. I think
that the issue is not in doubt. Its presentation as 'bursts of energy'
is not dismissable as a trivial gimmick. Poetry as a set of limited

7.   For a couple of examples see, below, the poems by Allen Ginsberg
and Galway Kinnell.
8.   Alexander Pope, *An Essay on Man* (1733–34), Canto IV, line 19 .

units of verbal energy possesses, by virtue of this method, its own especial powers to strike hard, to make music, to insinuate meanings, to focus attention and to heighten our daily contacts with language. Hence, when I write a poem, the line-breaks I choose, which limit the 'breadth of my breath', are sacred to me; I do not allow my editor or his printshop to tamper with them; they are an essential and unique way of energizing my text. And this is certainly not true of a prose work like the present one, where it is a matter of indifference to me at which point a given sentence or line will stop and turn.

I shall now imagine that I am writing from a farmhouse to a friend and colleague in the city who is deeply involved in social and political movements. We cut into the middle of my imaginary letter. '...I suppose we two will never see eye to eye. Those five or six *isms* that agitate you all year round and make you write pamphlets, ring doorbells, circulate petitions, and all but throw bombs at your enemies—I can't help having my doubts about them, especially here, looking out over an ample and peaceful wheatfield. You tell me that so much depends upon your activities. And I look around, and I say, so much depends upon the brown stain on that peach; so much depends upon that mud-brown hoe leaning against the cracked barn-wall; so much depends upon a red wheelbarrow glazed with rain water beside the white chickens...'

Those of you who are familiar with the established (or being established) canon of twentieth-century American poetry will at once have recognized William Carlos Williams's most anthologized poem, 'The Red Wheelbarrow', infiltrated into my imaginary letter. But if you are unacquainted with it, you will probably not have guessed that a poem was embedded in my text at all. If I had tipped you off to the presence of a famous poem, you would not necessarily have found precisely the right place where it occurs. And if you had, still you would probably not have arranged the words in quanta exactly as Williams did:

> so much depends
> upon
>
> a red wheel
> barrow
>
> glazed with rainwater

beside the white
chickens.[9]

The poet must have supposed that his quantized arrangement
of words was a more skilful and therefore thrilling manipulation
of the resources available to the art of literature than the
arrangement that, in my imaginary letter, made them part of a
paragraph that far exceeded the 'breadth of a breath'. What did
Williams gain by alternating four times a relatively long line with
four times a two-syllable word? What did he gain by isolating
'upon' from 'depends', 'barrow' from 'wheel', and so on? It might
be suggested that the poet's technique forces us to attend—lov-
ingly attend—to each element of the picture he is drawing; even
to the extent of making us separate for our tighter attention the
wheel from the wheelbarrow, the rain (in general) from the
water, the whiteness from its chickens; while at the same time
throwing in, so to speak, the traditional pleasure of symmetry in
the line lengths. Such a separation-for-attention is conspicuously
absent from the prose letter into which I lodged Williams's text.

You are not obliged to 'buy' this reading. You may dislike the
poem. You may dislike the poet's choices for making his turns.
But liking and disliking are not the issue here. What we recognize
is that for a text of this sort, the act of turning is a non-trivial,
indeed a vital, move by the literary strategist we call a poet.

That the act of turning, or delivering limited quanta, is the cen-
tral and defining poetic act becomes even clearer when we read a
poem like the following:

five princes
buried their
father divid
ed his subjec
ts forgot his
advice separ
ated from eac
h other and w
andered in qu
est of fortun
e[10]

9.   In *Collected Earlier Poems* (New York: New Directions, 1938).
10. In *Hinge Picture* by Susan Howe (Cherry Valley, NY: Cherry Valley Edi-

Breaking a line *within* a word was something our forefathers never thought of! And yet, has not the poet most ingeniously suggested by means of her crumbling form that the princes are headed for failure and chaos? This reading does not imply that the poet absolutely needed to cut the word 'wandered' (for instance) where she did. She could have disarrayed the poem in some other manner, except perhaps for that haplessly pathetic final 'e'—a full line of poetry, of course. But we can admire the energized meaning created by the disarray as such.[11] Be that as it may, the more extreme the experiment, the clearer our two basic points: one, that poetry is defined by its limited quanta, and two, that this element is of high significance.

Does the paragraph I am writing at this point become poetry— bad poetry but still poetry—if I cut it up in order to present it as a series of limited quanta? Let us look at a better example, however, furnished by an advertisement for a fancy housing development in Los Angeles (Fig. 6).[12] The typesetter, no doubt following precise instructions by the copy-writer for the advertising agency, has displayed the materials in limited quanta very much like a typical free verse poem of our time. Can we therefore call this the work, not of a great artist of course, but at least of a poetaster writing doggerel? And if not, then on what ground can we refuse even the lowly name of doggerel to this advertisement? And why, for that matter, is a laundry list not a poem?

The answer is that neither the present paragraph cut up to look like a Cummings poem, nor a laundry list, nor the advertisement for Mulholland Estates is 'deemed successful' if and when it begets an unmediated thrill. The advertisement is deemed suc- cessful if and when it sells 'estates'; the laundry list is successful if it tallies with the items returned to me; and my paragraph is suc- cessful if it adds to your store of knowledge, or at least challenges you to think. In short, we fall back again on the concept of the unmediated satisfaction. And we restore the copy-writer to his

tions, 1974). The poem can also be found in Ron Silliman (ed.), *In the American Tree* (Orono, ME: National Poetry Foundation, 1986).

11. In 'emblem' poetry, line lengths are shortened and lengthened so as to form a visual representation (e.g. a wing, a strand of DNA) of the subject treated in the poem.

12. In *Angeles,* June 1989 issue.

dignity as a brilliant employee of his agency, instead of berating him as a wretched artist.

More importantly—and, I admit, more controversially—the proposed definition firmly excludes the so-called 'prose poem,' much practiced since the late nineteenth century and showing no sign of exhaustion. Neither authors nor critics are violating any law by using this prestigious label for the products in question (it is an odd fact of modern life that 'poem' and 'poetic' are prestigious words in a culture that pays almost no attention to the thing itself)—except the much-battered law of philological sanity. A prose poem is like a well-dressed nude, a square circle, or a 41-line sonnet. Language, at best a fragile creature, disintegrates. Here is a brief and (incidentally) very fine example—an up-to-date view of our progenitors in the Garden of Eden, behind which we find the theme of trying to undo what has been guiltily done:

IN A CORNER

> Hunched in a corner of the garden, behind an innocent tree, the two of them tickling the back of their throats with blades of grass. Both of them bent over, side by side, retching, heaving, hoping, despairing. It is the eleventh hour, they must clear themselves of the deed. Coughing, spluttering, hiccuping. Trying to disgorge their last meal, trying to spew up the apple.[13]

We have seen that the quantum, or verse, or breath, can be fairly lengthy—as it is, typically, in Walt Whitman's and in much of Algernon Swinburne's poetry. But the 'prose poem' clearly exceeds the limit. We are 'breathed out' long before it decides to turn. To be sure, many works of undeniable prose, and almost all 'prose poems', exhibit elements we loosely call poetic, among them rhythm, alliteration, rich metaphors and high intensity of emotion. This loose usage (similar to the undifferentiated uses to which we put the word Art itself) allows us to speak of the 'poetic prose' of some very long novels, for instance. But that is very different from formalizing a species of literature as 'prose poems'.

---

13. The second of 'Two Poems' by D.J. Enright, *Times Literary Supplement*, 15-21 December, 1989; yet categorized as a prose work in his *Under the Circumstances: Poems and Proses* (Oxford: Oxford University Press, 1991).

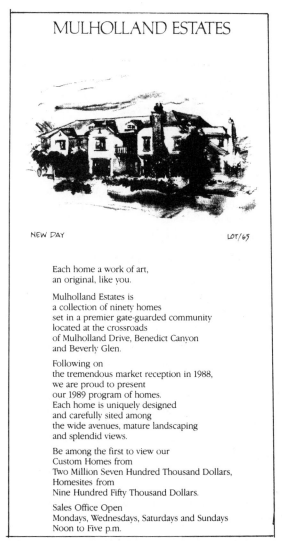

Fig. 6. Advertisement for Mulholland Estates in *Angeles*, June 1989

To sum up, 'prose poems' are brief prose works that, had some-
one called them *cameos* (for instance) at the time they originated,
would have filled a concluding chapter in a text on the novel,
story and essay without dreaming of become part of the realm of
poetry.

Cameos are discrete works of literature. But in a significant
number of twentieth century poems we find prose chunks (if I
may be allowed the unlovely word) embedded in what is other-

wise, and on the whole, indubitably poetic work. Consider the fol-
lowing two examples of poetic texts, each with its prose block. The
first consists of six lines from Allen Ginsberg's 73-line 'America':

> America save the Spanish Loyalists
> America Sacco and Vanzetti must not die
> America I am the Scottsboro boys.
> America when I was seven momma took me to Communist Cell meetings
> they sold us garbanzos a handful per ticket a ticket cost a nickel and the
> speeches were free everybody was angelic and sentimental about the
> workers it was all so sincere you have no idea what a good thing the
> party was in 1935 Scott Nearing was a grand old man a real mensch
> Mother Bloor made me cry I once saw Israel Amter plain. Everybody
> must have been a spy.
> America you don't really want to go to war.

And so on.[14] Our second illustration is a poem by Galway
Kinnell titled 'The Biting Insects':

> The biting insects don't like the blood of people who dread dying.
> They prefer the blood of people who can imagine themselves entering
> other life-forms.
> These are the ones the mosquito sings to in the dark and the deer fly
> orbits and studies with yellow eyes.
> In the other animals the desire to die comes when existing wears out
> existence.
> In us this desire can come too early, and we kill ourselves, or it may
> never come, and we have to be dragged away.
> Not many are able to die well, not even Jesus going back to his father.
> And yet dying gets done—and Eddie Jewell coming up the road with
> his tractor on a flatbed truck and seeing an owl lifting its wings
> as it alights on the ridgepole of this red house, Galway, will
> know that now it is you being accepted back into the family
> of mortals.[15]

14. In *The Collected Poems 1947–1980* (New York: Viking Books, 1985).
Note that what I consider as a prose area in a poem is normally counted as a
single line. The names in our excerpt refer to leaders or martyrs of various
radical movements. The Spanish Loyalists were the defeated leftists in the
Spanish Civil War of the 1930s. See Chapter 9 for a discussion of allusions in
poetry. 'I once saw Israel Amter plain' is an indirect allusion (see Chapter 9
again)—namely to a lyric by Robert Browning that starts, 'Ah, did you once
see Shelley plain?' 'Mensch' is German for human being, but Yiddish for
what we call a *real* human being.

15. In *Imperfect Thirst* (Boston: Houghton Mifflin, 1994). Unlike the allu-
sions in Ginsberg's poem, which are public, the reference to one Eddie

Both examples contain one or more long lines that most of us will feel as 'limited quanta'. But both include chunks that will surely be felt as a temporary switch to prose. I would argue that the two feelings are quite dissimilar—dissimilar, but not, *a priori*, superior or inferior to each other. Hence there is nothing unacceptable, per se, in the alternation. A work of art can hold dual citizenship, just like a human being.

Indeed, 'mixed media' works are very much in fashion, for the traditional barriers separating genres have been widely felt to be tyrannical and stifling to the creative imagination. Either the artist mingles two or more very different arts within a single work—combining, for instance, a poem with a painting on his canvas or wiring sound effects into a sculpted piece; or else he marries two or more sub-types of a single type of art—for instance, painting with sculpture, or, to come home to our subject, poetry with prose. On the other hand, we shouldn't think that hybridizing the arts is a new idea. Greek and medieval sculptors happily painted their statues, and if you listen to an opera like Beethoven's *Fidelio*, you will find that between the musical stretches a plain spoken drama is taking place. Songs, of course, nearly always combine poetry with music. Why then should a poet hesitate to switch to prose in the middle of his poem?

Notwithstanding the increased appeal in our times of mixed-media experiments, the mix of poetry and prose exemplified by 'America' remains a minor presence in modern literature. Most poems still occupy a separate room in the house of literature, and it is enough to bear in mind that the door leading to the other rooms is ajar, not locked, and now and then it opens just wide enough to allow an interesting sharing of furniture.

Of course, what truly matters in the end is not what we label a work, but how successful it is. Do you insist on calling your cameo a prose poem? And do you see that 20-line paragraph inside your poem as very much part of your poetry? So be it. Let us move to the tough question: Have you succeeded in creating out of your imagination a work of art we can cherish?

Jewell is a private one. Do we need to know who this person is in order to make sense of Kinnell's enigmatic poem? Or in order to admire it—even if it doesn't quite make sense for us? I will return to this problem in Chapter 9.

III

If we look into the more or less 'private room' of poetry, we discover that quite a few of the objects that furnish it carry identifying labels—labels that are never, or almost never, applied to prose texts. Many of these labels identify rhyme, number of lines per stanza and metrical patterns: *couplet* and *iambic pentameter* and even *free verse* (an un-pattern) are good examples. Other labels name whole poems composed according to given patterns and rules of external form—for instance *sonnet* and *sestina*.

More will be said on these topics in later chapters, because external form remains an important energizing agent in poetry. But I will be returning hardly at all to another kind of label—still exclusive to poetry, or nearly so—namely, that which points more or less distinctly to types of subject matter rather than (or as well as) external form. The *epic*, for instance, is a very long poem (external form) on a grand and heroic subject that is important to the whole of a community. The *ballad* is a narrative poem with a strong folk element. The *ode* is a lofty, lyrical poem in several stanzas composed in a variety of meters and rhyme schemes. The *elegy* is a poem of mourning. An *epigram* is a brief witty poem whose wit delivers a sting. A label like *eclogue* differs a little in that it usually refers to a setting, a scenic background, namely a pastoral one, but we can still list it here. Some of these labels, I repeat, do include a prescription concerning external form, yet the more significant indication they give is non-formal—'a grand national theme' rather than 'to be expressed in rhyming iambic pentameter'.

There are also vaguer labels we find attached to poetry, but now no longer exclusively so. A *lyric* or *lyrical* poem is one whose verbal music (insofar as unsung words make music) is particularly evident. A *narrative* poem is one that shares a piece of territory with the novel or short story. A *dramatic* poem obeys our definition of poetry but is also a dialogue or monologue. The trouble is that a given poem could be lyrical *and* narrative *and* dramatic (since plays narrate a story). And of course there is no lack of lyrical prose calling out for our admiration.

All the terms I have listed, and similar ones not listed here, are useful in their places. Naming things is almost an obsession with human beings, as the writers of Genesis already knew. Our own way will be to treat labels lightly, and evoke them only where they are relevant to our concern with aesthetic energy.

Chapter 6

The Poem's Propositions

Stated and Implied Propositions

Words and their related signs are to literature in general, and to poetry in particular, what sounds are to music and what shapes and colors are to painting. To be sure, just as words can be part of a musical experience (songs and operas) and also of a visual experience (text within a painting) so musical and visual elements can play significant roles in the literary experience. Nevertheless, words and their related signs continue to constitute the fundamental 'materials and resources' of all the literary arts.

Materials, of course, must be used. Something must be constructed out of them. In the literary arts the words and related signs are collocated so as to form *meanings*. As we have seen already, at the fringe of literature, and especially at the fringe of poetry, we run into an occasional denial or avoidance of meaning, and in such instances we are obliged to return to our building blocks of words and their related signs—or even to the fundamental individual sounds—instead of rising to our next base, as we are doing now: meaning. But even the fringe writers would allow us to proceed, in a general manual of poetics such as this one, upon the premise that the words of literature are normally assembled into units and wholes of meaning. This is worth encapsulating and memorizing: LITERATURE ENERGIZES MEANING (in order to satisfy), whether such meanings are single and simple or multiple and difficult to master, whether you agree with them or not, whether you feel they are true, false, self-contradictory or uncertain.

In this and several following chapters we will be concentrating our attention on the meanings that are being energized. Afterwards we will study the acts of energizing these meanings. And then we will consider the limitations of this tantalizingly neat division.

From now on I shall be using the term *proposition* for any unit of meaning that exhibits, or to which, after some thought, we can ascribe a subject and a predicate. In a proposition, something is said about something or someone. A proposition might consist in no more than a single word, like 'Agreed' (i.e. 'We are agreed'). Even a lone punctuation mark like '!' might suffice in an appropriate context (the context might make it mean 'Imagine that!'). And of course a proposition need not be an idea (like 'The child is father of the man')—it can be a pure sensory statement (like 'I saw a crowd, / A host, of golden daffodils').

Behind the openly stated propositions of a poem or other literary work we are usually invited to look for implied ones. Implied or inferred propositions make up an immense realm of meanings, for language is seldom self-limiting or univocal. And since we so often 'read between the lines' in everyday situations, it is hardly surprising that in literary texts too there is often 'more than meets the eye'. Language *can* be self-limiting; but typically it 'radiates' meanings, and these we are calling implied propositions. However, implications are created not only by the discrete stated propositions, but also, crucially, by what the latter look like in the presence of their fellow-propositions in the poem—in short, the context. An analogy: dressed in a certain way, a person could look rich among beggars but beggarly among the rich. Similarly, a proposition may emit others by virtue of the company it keeps. Here is a remarkable instance where the mere fact that one element in the poem is very brief in the context of the whole yields a supremely important implied proposition:

THE COLLAR

I struck the board and cried, 'No more;
I will abroad!
What? Shall I ever sigh and pine?

My lines and life are free, free as the road,
  Loose as the wind, as large as store.
        Shall I be still in suit?
Have I no harvest but a thorn
To let me blood, and not restore
What I have lost with cordial fruit?
        Sure there was wine
Before my sighs did dry it; there was corn
  Before my tears did drown it.
Is the year only lost to me?
  Have I no bays to crown it,
No flowers, no garlands gay? all blasted?
        All wasted?
  Not so, my heart; but there is fruit,
        And thou hast hands.
Recover all thy sigh-blown age
On double pleasure: leave thy cold dispute
Of what is fit and not. Forsake thy cage,
        Thy rope of sands,
Which petty thoughts have made, and made to thee
  Good cable, to enforce and draw,
        And be thy law,
While thou didst wink and wouldst not see.
        Away! take heed;
        I will abroad.
Call in thy death's-head there; tie up thy fears.
        He that forbears
  To suit and serve his need,
        Deserves his load.'
But as I raved and grew more fierce and wild
        At every word,
Methought I heard one calling, *Child!*
And I replied, *My Lord.*[1]

The mere fact that the act of submission takes two lines while the act of rebellion roils over 34 of them yields the proposition that God's power and grandeur are so great that he need not indulge in a debate with the rebel: one word suffices to bring him to heel. A splendid idea is conveyed without a statement; simply

---

1. George Herbert (1593–1633), who, as the reader may have guessed, was a minister. His one volume of poems, *The Temple*, was published shortly after his death. The bays of line 14 make up the wreath won by a poet victorious in a poetic contest.

by a structural maneuver. In this instance the maneuver was to apply relative brevity, but the possibilities for a poet are well-nigh endless. Here, for one more example, is a poet who uses the structural maneuver of running two contrasting propositions together in the same line. We are reading the second stanza of a poem describing rifle drill in basic training:

> This is the lower sling swivel. And this
> Is the upper sling swivel, whose use you will see,
> When you are given your slings. And this is the piling swivel
> Which in your case you have not got. The branches
> Hold in the gardens their silent, eloquent gestures,
> Which in our case we have not got.[2]

Each of the five stanzas of this poem repeats the maneuver of physically juxtaposing the words concerning the mechanical-murderous drill with those addressed to the sweet natural scene. The mere act of juxtaposition—in a single flowing line of poetry—emphasizes, on the physical level, that the drill is taking place amidst 'neighboring gardens' (first stanza); but, more importantly, on the philosophical level, it implies the proposition that good and evil, ugliness and beauty, occur, not in separate worlds, as morally speaking they ought to, but side by side, in a daily continuum.[3] Such, at any rate, is my particular phrasing of the implied proposition; you may formulate it better; but the point is that implied propositions can radiate not only from stated ones, but from *any* element contained in the text, including the manner in which the latter is laid out.

We will see later that the music (or lack of it) in a poem can also suggest propositions that the poet has not stated. Nor must

2.   Henry Reed (1917–1985), 'Naming of Parts', from *A Map of Verona and Other Poems* (London: Jonathan Cape, n.d.). The contrast between nasty 'civilized' mankind and wonderful innocent nature is a literary *topos* that goes back to Antiquity, was given new vigor during what we call the Romantic Age, and flourishes today more than ever.

3.   Characteristically for the poetry written since World War I, the poem does not *tell us* what our emotional response to the propositions, stated and implied, should be. It does not have an 'oh, I shudder' sort of passage anywhere. It presents only what T.S. Eliot has famously called 'the objective correlative' (of the emotion).

we forget the 'related signs' of our basic definition: remember Armour's parentheses and Cummings's squeezing of words together. Of course, when all is said and done, most implied propositions are radiated by stated ones as such. Herbert's concluding 'My Lord' implies 'I surrender, submit and obey,' with or without any other structural, rhetorical or musical maneuver. Be that as it may, a world of ideas—and feelings, of course—can be suggested by means other than direct statement.

What Meaning Means

What is understood by the 'meaning' of words and sentences?[4] The position taken here is that language, far from referring endlessly and hopelessly to yet more language (as some extreme skeptics hold), emerges from and stays rooted in or linked to our pre-verbal and continuing non-verbal physiological experiences— experiences like those lived by animals and infants. This language-less state is represented by the circle shown in Diagram A.

Diagram A

This is to be regarded as the *core* made up of all our pre-verbal and non-verbal perceptions and emotions, our recollections (accurate or inaccurate) of these perceptions and emotions, and, in addition, all the things we are capable of imagining visually, audially, tactilely and so on without language—altogether a huge world of experiences that precedes language and later continues to co-exist with language. In the normal human adult this core is in many ways more highly developed than that of even the highest animals, but its essential reality is one we share with all living things, and with our own baby selves—before we learned to experience speech as something more than noise signals emitted or received.

4.   I am leaving out the 'related signs' at this point in order to simplify the discussion. Nothing essential is affected by doing so.

It may not be amiss to add, by the way, that billions of years of evolution have seen to it that these non-verbal experiences are duly responsive to the stubborn realities of the universe. Language is the final, and dramatic, refinement of this process of adaptation. Rain is wet, wet is disagreeable, cave protects from disagreeable wet—all such realities of Nature are meaningful long before words shape them into speech-propositions.

Around the core we could now draw a first concentric ring made up of innumerable 'beads' representing all our individual words. I show a single one of these in Diagram B.

Diagram B

This bead could stand for bicycle, ride, fast, above, two, like, because—all the words, in fact, that are so directly 'threaded' (as the figure shows) to our non-lexicated core that we can readily imagine ourselves understanding what they stand for even if, like the lower animals, we did not have access to language at all. Imagine a dog (Fido will represent the animal world for us in this chapter) who is showing signs of anxiety as his master returns. Let us translate his unverbalized meanings into words: 'If I hear my master coming through the door, I will promptly hide, because I tore up his pillow a while ago.'[5] Not only are the non-verbal equivalents (and roots) of 'I' and 'hear' and 'master' and 'through' and 'door' and 'promptly' (and so on) accessible as meanings to the dog, but so are subtler ones of causation, time, similarity and difference, and many others that we symbolize through prepositions, conjunctions, adverbs, as well as time-nouns, space-nouns and verbs.

Unlike animals, however—as far as we know, at any rate—human beings can invent, imagine, or deduce the existence, or

5. Obviously in any language a great number of short phrases function like individual words.

the possible existence, of core phenomena to which they apply language similar to table and chair: thus God, centaur, electron, nanosecond, invisible. These are still first-ring beads, and, as you can see, they are of great importance to mankind.

Diagram C shows a few first-ring beads glued to each other and threaded as a unit to the core. Any such group represents what we are calling propositions. They are, if you will, words grammaticized—like the ones I put together just now for our dog.

Diagram C

I have drawn four beads in the figure in order not to clutter it up, but the following sentence would take about ten: 'All our townspeople, standing under the three o'clock sun, shouted their "aye" of approval.' Remarkably, our dog has access even to fairly sophisticated propositions of this sort. Fido has a sufficient notion of 'all', of 'our' (as in 'us dogs'), of 'townspeople' (they dress differently from the country folk), of the afternoon sun and the hands of the steeple clock, of shouting in general, of 'aye' in particular, and of approval (petting versus beating). There is no doubt, therefore, that the meaning of this proposition emerges from and returns for verification to our own core of pre-verbal and non-verbal experiences.

Our first-ring language corresponds by and large to the 'imagery' so often discussed in books on poetry. 'Imagery' is a useful word, and applying it in this way is a tribute to our most significant sense (see Chapter 2); but we must keep remembering, every time we find it in connection with poetry, that it covers *all* the senses. I have already given an instance of noise. Let me add these lines by Walt Whitman:

Houses and rooms are full of perfumes, the shelves are crowded with
     perfumes,
I breathe the fragrance myself and know it and like it.[6]

Here too is 'imagery', but you can see why this is a deceptive term, and why I will be trying to keep my distance from it. To return to our present theme, however: Whitman's lines are very clearly made up of first-ring notions, and no one would know it better than our sniff-happy dog![7]

In Diagram D we return to our dog's wordless meanings and verbalize them for him again: 'If I hear my master coming through the door, I will promptly hide, because I tore up his pillow a while ago.'

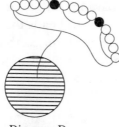

Diagram D

The black beads represent the logical linkages among propositions made possible by words like 'if,' 'because,' 'and,' 'but,' 'when,' and a mass of others. We might call such words (or phrases) the articulators. We have noted already that they too live in the first ring, where we share them with 'dumb' animals.

Meaningful verbal propositions or series of propositions are created out of, sanctioned by, and linked to our core experiences. On the other hand, Diagram E shows us two conditions of absence of meaning, or the presence of unintelligibility.

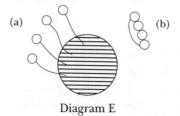

Diagram E

6. Lines 1-2 of *Song of Myself* No. 2, first published (without section numbers) in 1855.

7. Who might well remind us, if he could, that each species has its own *type* of core. A dog's world of meanings is heavily committed to odors, that of deer to sounds, and so on.

The four separate beads of 11a might represent 'Lungs gathered seen Mercury.' Each individual bead is threaded to the core in a perfectly normal way. But now, unlike the beads of Figure 10, they do not glue to each other and thread to the core as a unit: the 'sentence' is unintelligible. In poetic practice, as we saw in Chapter 4, this type of unintelligibility is dear to writers of what I called fringe poetry. Infinitely more common, however, is the type figured in 11b, where the beads do stick together, but fail to thread into our core—they float free and unconnected, until 'interpretation' or 'paraphrase' comes to the rescue and substitutes an equivalent series of beads that does connect to the core, as well as to many other such series, that is to say propositions.

This topic is important enough to warrant an immediate illustration. Here is a short poem by William Butler Yeats (1865–1939):

THE MAGI

Now as at all times I can see in the mind's eye,
In their stiff, painted clothes, the pale unsatisfied ones
Appear and disappear in the blue depth of the sky
With all their ancient faces like rain-beaten stones,
And all their helms of silver hovering side by side,
And all their eyes still fixed, hoping to find once more,
Being by Calvary's turbulence unsatisfied,
The uncontrollable mystery on the bestial floor.[8]

Assuming that you can identify the Magi and Calvary, and setting aside for a moment the puzzling textual fact that these Magi, presumably on their way to witness the birth of Christ, are 'unsatisfied' by the drama of his *death*, let us look at the last two words of the poem. In terms of our Diagram E, we can say that 'bestial' and 'floor' thread separately to the core without any difficulty. But when Yeats couples them as part of the full sentence, they fail to thread into the core as a unit. What on earth is a bestial floor on which an uncontrollable mystery is sitting or standing? We can at any rate imagine a cow flying over the moon; but

8. Published in 1914. From *W.B. Yeats: The Poems, New Edition* (ed. R.J. Finneran; New York: Macmillan, 1983). The three Magi appear in Matthew 2.1-12 as 'wise men'—astrologers from the East guided by a star to witness the birth of Christ. But Yeats's 'helms of silver' (line 5) suggests that the poet adopted the much later, curious tradition that the three were kings.

what is to be done with a bestial floor? Fortunately, when an editor comes to our rescue with a translation of the line as 'Christ's miraculous birth in the stable at Bethlehem', and we replace our two free-floating beads with the sufficiently equivalent series of beads 'the floor of the stable where Christ was born surrounded by beasts', the new group immediately sends out a reassuring thread to the core. We may be less than grateful to the famous poet for his questionable compression, but at any rate the phrase becomes as meaningful as, for instance, 'I rode your bicycle.' Both can be schematized as in Diagram C.

But what about the baffling idea that the Magi are trying to find 'once more' the birth of Christ, because Calvary—the death of Christ—has left them unsatisfied? Literally, this concept so sharply contradicts our fundamental sense of time's arrow—a sense we share with all living things—that it cannot thread to the core. It makes as little sense as saying, 'I am looking forward to last Sunday because the Sunday a month from now has left me unsatisfied.' Again, students of Yeats's poetry, after consulting his other writings, offer their help, and 'domesticate' the enigma by suggesting that Yeats is evoking *new* Magi looking for a Second Coming, because the events from Christ's birth to his Passion have failed to solve the world's problems.[9] There may be more refined formulations than this one, but the point I am making is that by introducing an explanatory equivalent proposition, we can resolve the time-impossibility that appeared to beset the poem, and thus reconnect Yeats's concept to the core.

Continuing with our diagrams: Diagram F shows an unthreaded single bead. This could represent a set of letters making up a non-word ('thmulopp'), or any word in a language we do not understand. Obviously, this is a type of obscurity which need not detain us.

Diagram F

9. Going outside the poem in order to elucidate it is a subject I shall be dealing with in Chapters 7 and 8.

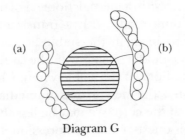

Diagram G

Let us look instead at Diagram G(a), which represents another extremely common type of obscurity. Here we find two perfectly intelligible propositions, each one solidly linked to the core, but lacking a connection between them. Here is an example in plain prose from the opening page of Anthony Trollope's *The Eustace Diamonds*, a novel published in 1873. 'We will tell the story of Lizzie Greystock from the beginning, but we will not dwell over it at great length, as we might do if we loved her. The admiral was a man who liked whist, wine,—and wickedness in general we may perhaps say, and whose ambition it was to live every day of his life up to the end of it.'

Of course, you will remember that our sets of four beads are shorthand for any number of them, with articulators between them. As such, they schematize quite efficiently the obscurity of the passage just quoted. What shall we do with it? The 'bestial floor' maneuver does not work here, because the propositions in themselves are perfectly intelligible (i.e. threaded to the core) and need not be replaced by equivalents, that is to say paraphrased, in order to make sense.

As you may have guessed, the trouble comes from the lack of an intermediary, or bridging proposition. I am sure that after a few seconds of thought, we can all devise such a proposition; however, we need not bother to do so in this instance, for you may also have guessed that I cheated. Trollope provided the bridge himself as follows: 'She was the only child of old Admiral Greystock, who in the latter years of his life was much perplexed by the possession of a daughter.' For our rather special purpose the first (main) clause of this sentence suffices. Once these beads are in our hands, we insert them between the first two sets, and suddenly, as shown in Diagram G(b), the units thread into our core as a total-ity rather than as discrete series.

My illustration is deliberately rudimentary. For a far subtler one, we might re-read Galway Kinnell's 'The Biting Insects':

> The biting insects don't like the blood of people who dread dying.
> They prefer the blood of people who can imagine themselves entering
> 　other life-forms.
> These are the ones the mosquito sings to in the dark and the deer fly
> 　orbits and studies with yellow eyes.
> In the other animals the desire to die comes when existing wears out
> 　existence.
> In us this desire can come too early, and we kill ourselves, or it may
> 　never come, and we have to be dragged away.
> Not many are able to die well, not even Jesus going back to his father.
> And yet dying gets done—and Eddie Jewell coming up the road with
> 　his tractor on a flatbed truck and seeing an owl lifting its wings
> 　as it alights on the ridgepole of this red house, Galway, will
> 　know that now it is you being accepted back into the family
> 　of mortals.

The first three lines appear to construct a self-sufficient thesis. It happens to be imaginary (like a fairy tale), but since, as we have seen, human beings are able to make up, imagine, invent core experiences, these lines pose no problem of meaning. Now, however, the poet proceeds to voice a contrast between human beings and animals other than human beings. Other animals simply allow themselves to die when their bodies wear out, whereas people sometimes kill themselves before that happens, or else, on the contrary, fight their own death every inch of the way. In light of the first line, it seems clear that the persons who 'have to be dragged away' are the same as those 'who dread dying'. And that, the poet reports, means most of us. Even Jesus rebelled—for a moment, at any rate (see Matthew 27.26). But the struggle is useless, and we die anyway, as the prose chunk informs us. At this point, a character named Eddie Jewell appears, driving a truck. We gather that he is a farmer. He sees an owl alighting on a house, and he knows (suddenly?) that the poet is 'accepted back' into the family of mortals.

Quite a few connecting or bridging propositions are wanted here. What is the connection between the fact that many persons don't like to die and the dislike insects feel for such persons? Why this strange prejudice of the insects? And of what importance is it?

Again: Why and in what sense had the family of mortals (all living beings?) rejected the speaker? And what does this presumed rejection have to do with the poet's general observations on the attitude of biting insects, and the attitudes of people toward their own death?

Again: What is the connection between the poet and the mysterious Mr Jewell?

Again: Why is the *you* of the last line given its emphatic position in the clause? (Now it is you; at other times it was somebody else?)

Etc., etc.

But we could even ask: did connecting propositions exist in the artist's mind as he wrote his poem? Or was he intentionally writing a fringe poem of sorts, and meant the several parts of his poem to remain in the condition of Diagram G(a)?

Let us suppose that this is not a fringe poem; exercise our wits in private to insert connecting propositions that will make it intelligible; and move on to our next topic.

More rings can be drawn outward from the first, as suggested in abbreviated form in Diagram H

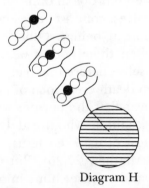

Diagram H

Now we have transcended the limits of a language that is so directly rooted in non-verbal experiences that we can imagine living without the words altogether and joining some of the higher mammals. The second ring is no longer threaded to the core, but rather to the words and propositions of the first ring which *are* so threaded. These higher propositions are no longer accessible to dogs or apes or human infants. From the town-meeting of Diagram C we now move to a proposition like 'Democracy is the best form of government.' Strictly speaking, 'best' should be placed in the first ring;[10] we know that even the humblest animals can distinguish between good, better and best, in addition to good and bad. But the proposition as a whole is 'abstract', that is to say it is abstracted (detached) from our sensory experiences. Nevertheless, all such propositions are meaningful only if and when they are threaded to words (like those of the town meeting) that are in turn threaded to the core.

As for the third and outer ring of Diagram H, it is placed there to accomodate even more abstract statements, which emerge from and are linked to other abstract statements before they can be traced 'downward' to their non-verbal roots. Thus the *very* abstract proposition: 'Order can be of a political as well as a chemical type.' Ultimately, propositions of this kind can no more exist without the non-verbal core than the most concrete ones we can devise, such as 'Bird flies!'

The words and sets of words beaded in a series of outer rings and no longer directly threaded to the core might be called *collectors*. They are usually called generalizations or abstractions; but the term I propose as a supplement reflects their function of collecting under a single verbal roof (so to speak) some, many, a great many, or innumerable core experiences and their first-ring verbalizations. But no matter how distant from the core, no matter how huge the collectors, they remain meaningful to us only insofar as we can trace them inward step by step into the core.

Multiplied by billions into a staggeringly complex mesh—but one that never departs from the rudiments of our figures—the network of all our individual and assembled beads represents our universe of meaningful verbal propositions.

In the sciences and in philosophical speculations, the more abstract propositions tend to be the ones common mortals have the most trouble understanding—'existence precedes essence' or 'a mathematical equation is a statement of equality involving two or more numbers or functions which may be known or unknown quantities'. Many poems also utter more or less difficult abstract propositions that need to be explicated by 'translating' them into

10. And so should the black beads representing articulations. It is characteristic of abstract propositions that collector words will stand side-by-side with first-ring words.

the first-ring language from which they originate. But typically, difficulty in poetry is the reverse of difficulty in science and philosophy. Typically, difficult poetry offers first-ring language that needs to be 'translated', either into a slightly different first-ring language that threads cozily to the core ('bestial floor' is a good example), or into outer-ring language (a generalization) that then returns upon the puzzling images and threads them cozily to the core.

Here, for instance, is a poem by Alfred Tennyson (1809–92):

> I will not shut me from my kind,
>   And, lest I stiffen into stone,
>   I will not eat my heart alone,
> Nor feed with sighs a passing wind;
>
> What profit lies in barren faith,
>   And vacant yearning, tho' with might
>   To scale the heaven's highest height,
> Or dive below the wells of death?
>
> What find I in the highest place,
>   But mine own phantom chanting hymns?
>   And on the depth of death there swims
> The reflex of a human face.
>
> I'll rather take what fruit may be
>   Of sorrow under human skies;
>   'Tis held that sorrow makes us wise,
> Whatever wisdom sleep with thee.[11]

Three abstract propositions can be detected here, whose nuclei are 'barren faith' (line 5), 'vacant yearning' (line 6) and the belief that 'sorrow makes us wise' (line 15). But these are easier than several of Tennyson's images; that is to say they are collectors readily linked to first-ring language and thence to the core. Fido does plenty of yearning, for example, without always getting the bone he wants. Faith is also a collector word whose first-ring components (e.g. 'God will help me recover the use of my legs') thread without trouble to the core. Instead, and typically, the

11. This is No. 108 of *In Memoriam*, the long series Tennyson wrote after the death of his friend Arthur H. Hallam, and published in 1850. 'Thee' in the last line refers to Hallam.

more difficult task for the reader consists in translating some of Tennyson's images into familiar generalizations. Thus feeding a passing wind with sighs (line 4) is translated, consciously or unconsciously, into something like 'grieving uselessly'. Lines 7-8 can be translated into something like 'metaphysical speculation', which returns us (odd though it may seem) as easily to first-ring language and the core as 'vacant yearning'. And what of the fable-like imagery of the third stanza? How shall we translate it? Perhaps into something like 'Whether we think of eternal life or of death, we find both peopled with human beings and human needs and fears.'

Very often, however, enigmatic first-ring scenes become meaningful more directly, when we exchange one or several beads for others, at which point a thread suddenly appears between the proposition taken as a unit and the core. Suppose we use our bicycle to cobble an apparently unintelligible clause: 'My bicycle rode into the pudding.' This has a surreal look; that is to say, you can now visualize something that never existed (and why not 'the centaur ate a cumulus'?) but you cannot refer this particular proposition to some useful generalization, nor mesh it with any other in your immense network. Cannot, until I slyly argue that if a fog can be compared to pea soup, which it often is, it can also be called a pudding. In short, my bicycle rode into the fog. One first-ring bead has been exchanged for another, and suddenly the proposition is ready to attach itself to a large number of other propositions (e.g. 'The result was that I ran into a tree'). Crude as my example may look, it provides the elementary model by which we try to solve many of our problems in reading poetry.

It is of course an essential feature of the core that it be roughly uniform within the species. We call this rough-and-ready, this sufficient uniformity 'normalcy'. There can be no communication without it. Hence without it, death is swift and sure. If, for two out of a hundred zebras, a lion looks like a shrub, the king of animals will soon be feeding on the two non-conformists. By the same token, language can operate only on the basis of sufficient uniformity. If my words, 'There is a lion hiding in the bushes' causes you to visualize a rabbit— if, that is to say, you misundertand me—you will presently become a lion's snack. Not suprisingly, therefore, we find the same principle at work for *meaning* that we set down for *taste* in Chapter 4. Individuality, yes; but individuality within sameness. God, electron, time, hunger, red, airplanes, liking, yesterday—thousands upon thousands of words, and propositions, cross safely from individual to individual. Granted, we seldom understand each other perfectly; but we even more rarely misunderstand each other completely; and on that basis poetry, literature and life itself manage to function.

Chapter 7

More about the Poem's Propositions

Overall Propositions: Subjects and Themes

Propositions as units of meaning (stated or implied) do not, of course, take us very far. Except for a few fringe texts, all poems are coherent *assemblies* of propositions, pieces fitted together to form a whole, and although we may take considerable pleasure in the separate pieces, we are likely to feel a want until we have grasped some totality—the thing or things the poem says as a whole. An analogy: the parts of a Greek temple are fine in them-selves, but what is finest of all is the entire temple, which corre-sponds to the poem's 'making sense' as a whole.

In Diagram I, three sets of two beads represent three articulated propositions wrapped in a super-bead (we might call it a cocoon) that is yet another proposition.

Diagram I

The three sets of white beads could stand for as many brief propositions, like 'birds fly while John gazes and Fido barks', but they are also meant as abbreviations for any number of brief and long ones. To avoid complications in the figure, I am dropping from it the distinction between first-ring and collector words—between the concrete and the abstract elements in our language. The cocoon represents the *subject* of the poem; for instance: 'The poet, having enjoyed a day among the daffodils, takes home the memory as a restorative from the pressures of city life.' There is thus a subject whenever we detect what in a novel we call an action or plot.

Diagram J shows a larger cocoon (b) enveloping the subject-cocoon (a) and other elements in the poem. This super-cocoon represents a *theme*—for example, 'The healing power of nature.'[1]

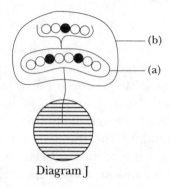

Diagram J

'Subject' and 'theme' both refer to 'what the poem is about', but the subject, stated or implied, is no more than a summation of the action of the poem, while the theme, if any, is always—whether stated or implied—a general non-trivial (substantial) concept. 'A day spent in the country' is a subject, but 'The beneficent influence of nature' is a theme.

Of course, such formulations (which we usually make in silence to ourselves) are typically neither exhaustive of the subjects and themes nor copies or imitations. They are nothing more than useful handles by means of which we seek to *take possession* of the originals—a concept I will be using frequently from now on.

While Diagram I indicates that some poems demand of us only that we grasp their overall subject, stated or implied, Diagram K

---

1.   Although I have drawn these cocoons as lines—again in order to simplify matters—they likewise consist, obviously, of 'beads' similar to those that represent the verbal units of the poems themselves.

suggests that other poems, being plotless, directly impress a theme (stated or implied) on their propositions. The drawing, accordingly, lacks the cocoon I have used to indicate a subject matter distinct from theme and thus passes directly to the theme.

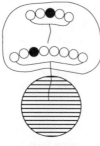

Diagram K

The many parables told by Jesus in the Gospels provide us with the neatest possible illustrations of subject-then-theme. This one, for instance:

> Listen! A sower went out to sow. And it happened that as he sowed, some seed fell along the footpath; and the birds came and ate it up. Some seed fell on rocky soil, and it sprouted quickly because it had no depth of earth; but when the sun rose the young corn was scorched, and as it had no root it withered away. Some seed fell among thistles; and the thistles shot up and choked the corn, and it yielded no crop. And some of the seed fell into good soil, where it came up and grew, and bore fruit; and the yield was thirtyfold, sixtyfold, even a hundredfold.

The subject here could be simply summarized as follows: 'Jesus narrates a parable in which a man obtains bad and good results from the seeds he sowed.' But the twelve apostles are puzzled. They know perfectly well that their Master has not appeared on earth to tell children's stories or give advice to dim-witted farmers. So they search for a theme behind the subject, or what we often call the moral of the story. However, like modern undergraduates trying to make out what Wallace Stevens means in his 'Surprises of the Superhuman', the Twelve, we are told, fail to understand the tale. Jesus, not unlike a college professor trying to 'teach poetry', manifests a touch of impatience before he explains:

You do not understand this parable? How then are you to understand any parable? The sower sows the word. Those along the footpath are people in whom the word is sown, but no sooner have they heard it than Satan comes and carries off the word which has been sown in them. It is the same with those who receive the word on rocky ground; as soon as they hear the word, they accept it with joy, but it strikes no root in them; they have no staying power; then, when there is trouble or persecution on account of the word, they fall away at once. Others again receive the seed among this-tles; they hear the word, but worldly cares and the false glamour of wealth and all kinds of evil desire come in and choke the word, and it proves barren. And there are those who receive the seed in good soil; they hear the word and welcome it; and they bear fruit thirty-fold, sixtyfold, or a hundredfold.[2]

With this, the apostles have firmly grasped the theme implied by the subject, which they can now summarize without further diffi-culty as 'The message of God is effective only for those who are truly receptive to it'—or words to the same general effect.

We turn to a poem that is mental light-years away from Gospel parables, namely a mischievous lyric by Ben Jonson, published in 1609:

> Still to be neat, still to be drest,
> As you were going to a feast;
> Still to be powdered, still perfumed:
> Lady, it is to be presumed,
> Though art's hid causes are not found,
> All is not sweet, all is not sound.
>
> Give me a look, give me a face,
> That makes simplicity a grace;
> Robes loosely flowing, hair as free:
> Such sweet neglect more taketh me,
> Than all th'adulteries of art.
> They strike mine eyes, but not my heart.[3]

Here we cannot speak of a subject (action, plot) on the one hand and a theme on the other. Jonson has simply written a poem on a certain theme, or topic. What an expert can do, if he wishes,

---

2. Mark 4.3-20, in *The New English Bible* (New York: Oxford University Press, 1970).

3. 'As' in line 2 is 'as if', and the 'adulteries' in the penultimate line are primarily if not exclusively 'adulterations'.

is to seek out a theme behind the theme, and suggest that this praise of 'sweet neglect' is not to be limited to Jonson's view of women. The expert could conceivably enrich our reading by placing the poem in a context of a number of Renaissance writings concerning what the Italians called *sprezzatura*, the nonchalance and ease that comes of true mastery. Or other large readings may be proposed. But surely we have taken very satisfying possession of this lyric if we remain content with its explicit theme.

Many poems seem to present an action without a theme, that is to say without a generalizing non-trivial concept that underlies the subject. They seem to want to limit what they say to the individual instance of the poem instead of proceeding, like Ben Jonson's lyric, to a generalization. To illustrate, we look at a sniping poem by John Donne:

THE APPARITION

When by thy scorn, O murderess, I am dead,
    And that thou think'st thee free
From all solicitation from me,
Then shall my ghost come to thy bed,
And thee, feign'd vestal, in worse arms shall see;
Then thy sick taper will begin to wink,
And he, whose thou art then, being tired before,
Will, if thou stir, or pinch to wake him, think
    Thou call'st for more,
And in false sleep will from thee shrink,
And then, poor aspen wretch, neglected thou
Bath'd in a cold quicksilver sweat wilt lie
    A verier ghost than I;
What I will say, I will not tell thee now,
Lest that preserve thee; and since my love is spent,
I'd rather thou shouldst painfully repent,
Than by my threatenings rest still innocent.[4]

Such a poem calls for no inquiry on our part into underlying themes. Its subject is obviously a lover berating his unfaithful mistress. We can take satisfying possession of the poem without forcing it to generalize about love, women, the Renaissance or Life.

In epic poetry, the story is so long that traditionally the artist

---

4.   Posthumously published in 1633. A vestal (line 5) is a Roman virgin-priestess in the temple of Vesta, goddess of the blazing hearth.

summarizes it at the outset: he presents in a few words the subject he is about to treat with many. Our earliest instance is Homer's *Iliad*, whose opening lines I give in Alexander Pope's translation:

> Achilles' wrath, to Greece the direful spring
> Of woes unnumber'd, heavenly goddess, sing!
> That wrath which hurl'd to Pluto's gloomy reign
> The souls of mighty chiefs untimely slain;
> Whose limbs unburied on the naked shore,
> Devouring dogs and hungry vultures tore,
> Since great Achilles and Atrides strove:
> Such was the sovereign doom, and such the will of Jove![5]

Observe that Homer (via Pope) announces his subject—or a substantial part of it, at any rate. No theme in our sense of the term—no overarching non-trivial concept—is in view.

When we pass from a 'folk epic' like the *Iliad* to a highly sophisticated one like Milton's *Paradise Lost* (published in 1667), we find that the poet, respectful of tradition, provides the cocooning subject; but then, conscious that subject and theme *can* be two separate though linked concerns—one lurking behind the other—he also states the theme in a proposition of its own. The subject is set forth in the first five lines:

> Of Man's First Disobedience, and the Fruit
> Of that Forbidden Tree, whose mortal taste
> Brought Death into the World, and all our woe,
> With loss of Eden, till one greater Man
> Restore us, and regain the blissful Seat,
> Sing Heav'nly Muse...

While the Muse is noble enough to inspire the great subject, a voice nobler still is invoked for the grandiose theme:

> And chiefly Thou O Spirit, that dost prefer
> Before all Temples th'upright heart and pure,
> Instruct me...

5.   Pluto is the god of the underworld; Atrides (the son of Atreus) is Agamemnon; a 'doom' is a sentence—obviously a hostile one. The *Iliad* as we have it today was probably given its near-final written-down form in the sixth century BC, but this was preceded by several centuries of both oral and written poetic activity culminating in the text that has come down to us. Pope's translation, in the idiom of his own times, was published in 1715.

That to the highth of this great Argument
I may assert Eternal Providence
And justify the ways of God to men.[6]

As though Milton were secretly teaching us how to read poetry, he grants the Muse (a merely heathen lady) the easier task of formulating the subject, the story, the plot; and then turns to the divine Spirit to define the theological theme that is to be extracted from the story. There can be no better illustration of the distinction—if and when one is present in the text.

I am far from suggesting that when a poet facilitates our task by stating his subject and theme, as Milton does, the account is necessarily closed. Other subjects, other themes may be uncovered by the reader. Furthermore, a poet may half-state as well as either state or not state at all, and thus leave it to the reader to elaborate and complete the thought. For instance, when Robert Frost wrote his famous 'Something there is that doesn't love a wall,' he was teasing us to eke out his reticent 'something'.[7]

What we need in the next place is an example of poetry in which the theme is implied and nowhere stated. Here is a memorable lyric by William Blake (1757–1827), entitled 'The Sick Rose', which he published in his *Songs of Experience* in 1794:

O Rose, thou art sick!
The invisible worm
That flies in the night,
In the howling storm,

Has found out thy bed
of crimson joy:
And his dark secret love
Does thy life destroy.

The stated individual propositions—practically in Basic English—are easily absorbed: a sick rose, a worm flying about at night in a storm, the worm landing on the rose, the worm destroying the rose. Taken together, the propositions easily form themselves into the subject, which is a grim little fable.

A child hearing this story might ask with a pout, 'Is that all?' For

6. As might be expected, Fido would be able to understand most of the terms in Milton's subject, but few in the theme.
7. This is the first line of his 'Mending Wall' (1914).

it must be admitted that the tale is *very* short and sketchy. Most adults would sympathize with the child's question. But whereas the child would typically look for more story, the adult will probably search for 'significance'—that is to say for a theme.

Why so? Why does the mere subject not fully satisfy? For one thing, the poem contains a number of highly charged words— 'howling', 'crimson joy', 'dark secret love', 'does thy life destroy'. Too much excitement, on the whole, for a worm nibbling away at a rose. But in addition, this worm is invisible: a strange worm indeed. And the rose is said to be a bed or in a bed—a bed of crimson joy: very odd and troubling—an erotic touch, perhaps? Most baffling of all: where we expect that the worm's secret *hate* should sicken and kill the rose, we are stunned to discover—perhaps on reading the poem a second time—that *love* is doing the vicious work. An invisible worm whose love destroys a rose turns out to be one of those propositions—the joined beads of our diagram—that fail to connect with our familiar meshwork. These images need to be explicated through a more abstract but familiar non-trivial proposition that will cocoon the beads of the proposition and bring the latter home into our network; and such a proposition will be a theme.

You can see that we are beginning to treat Blake's poem as a parable. But whereas Jesus promptly explained his parables, Blake remains mysterious, and requires us to extract the theme by our own efforts. The artist he was must have known that, paradoxical as it may sound, to say in so many words what he wanted to say would have diluted much of the energy of his poem through verbiage.

But what might be Blake's meaning? Normally you would be urged to read and re-read and meditate until some plausible solution manifests itself. But it may also happen that a poem will not yield its secret to us until we have made some inquiries outside of it—characteristically by reading other works (poems or prose) by the same writer, but sometimes also by becoming acquainted with his life and times. I shall be referring to these and other sources of understanding as *off-stage illumination*. The poem is like an actor performing on stage for us by the light he himself radiates. Sometimes, however, that light is not strong enough for us to discern what is precisely going on; and then we may try to locate and switch on certain spotlights in the wings. Now, I am not asserting flatly that the theme of Blake's parable is impossible to ascertain without off-stage illumination. But the difficulty is considerable. Deliverance comes when we leaf attentively through Blake's other short poems. Presently it will transpire that the poet distrusted such authority figures as parents and priests—people who preach and enforce authoritarian moral doctrines, by means of which they chain up our childlike innocent instincts. Lines like the following (from 'The Garden of Love') come to the aid of our perplexing lyric:

> And Priests in black gowns were walking their rounds,
> And binding with briars my joys & desires.

Since parents and priests and other authority figures truly *love* us (or say that they do), we begin to see what this loving but destructive worm represents (exactness is not called for). The notion that those who love us can also hurt us is a familiar one; even Fido is acquainted with its 'first-ring' meaning. The images that at first looked hopelessly obscure are now illuminated. The rose can stand for any form of beauty, innocence and even sensuality, and invisibility can signify an unspoken, hidden influence. Thus the seemingly unattached, free-floating propositions have rejoined the network and then, as always, our core.

I ask again: would the poem have been improved if Blake had added a stanza explaining his theme? Few would think so. What was impressive in Milton would have been merely cumbersome here. Furnishing maximum information is the mission of an airline time-table, not that of a poem; here it is the joy that counts. And few things spoil our delight like pontification.

Nor, as I said in a parenthesis, is exactness of interpretation called for. Not in this instance, at any rate. Part of the 'energy' (the power and beauty) of Blake's poem resides in its mysteriousness. It is a haunted poem. His own meticulous statement, or some over-precise formulation of our own, would play false to it. We do need to approach it with a thematic notion that allows us to take possession of it. But some poems invite a degree of tact. They can be brutalized by too much insistence.

You may have noticed, by the way, that even as we explore the ways in which a poem means, we keep returning to the energizing, or empowering, of meaning—including, subtly, the energy of reticence. If I am not mistaken, a poem like 'The Red Wheelbarrow' does not discourage precision in the act of formulation. It is a daylight poem. It too, of course, like 'The Sick Rose,' presents a subject that seems to cry out to us that an implied proposition should complete it: the poem surely has a theme; surely it is not *only* about a particular wheelbarrow the poet ran up against! Let us quickly read it again:

> so much depends
> upon
>
> a red wheel
> barrow
>
> glazed with rain
> water
>
> beside the white
> chickens.

If asked to find a theme without studying other poems by Williams, letters by the poet or critical discourses about him, most readers will readily suggest that the poet is celebrating simple, homely, solid, colorful objects. We may note, in addition, that these are farm objects rather than Wordsworth's daffodils or other 'beauties of Nature'—and that fact too can be incorporated into a thematic statement. As for the phrase 'so much depends', we cannot go wrong in reading it as a reminder that we need to wake up to and give thanks for such everyday country things. In a word, they are important. Of course, you may have read the poem somewhat differently; or you might wish to formulate the implied propositions some other way, *your* way. Perhaps you see something unstated in the poem that I have missed. And yet, in all likelihood you and I will be staying in the same conceptual vicinity.

Implying generalizations from one or more concrete bits of 'raw data' is hardly the exclusive privilege of poets. Everybody does it; and the more sophisticated the culture, the more frequently do its members indulge in implied statements: giving hints and letting the listener, reader or viewer deduce the rest We need to remember again and again that *every* element other than what is mentioned in our basic definition of poetry is shared by the latter with other human forms of expression.

Unthreatened by Chaos

Conceptual vicinity. The importance of this idea cannot be over-stated. Whenever, departing from the poet's very own words, we either summarize or paraphrase him in order to clarify what he seems to be saying, and whenever we search for an implied theme, we do so, by definition, with words of our own.[8] Obviously, every person's summaries and paraphrases and every person's render-ing of one or more themes will differ to a degree from everybody else's. The poet's own words are unalterably fixed; but *our* words about his words can roam with a degree of freedom. Does this mean that chaos ensues? We have asked this question before, and the answer remains the same: not in the least. Human beings do not need to communicate perfectly in order to communicate. Our interpretations work even if they are only in each others' conceptual vicinity. They are not clones. But neither are they aliens from another planet—or even from another culture. When we are interpreting poems like 'The Sick Rose' and 'The Red Wheelbarrow', we do not try to arrive at mathematically exact agreement, but at neighborly notions. When that happens, we have taken possession of the poem together.

Suppose then that, after consulting a history book, you decide that Blake's worm represents the French Revolution's armies, the sick rose a neighboring country they overran (claiming to do so for its own good, hence the mysterious 'love' in the poem) and the bed of crimson joy its happiness before they marched in. You are not alarmed by Blake's other *Songs of Innocence and Experience*. This time, you say, he decided to use some of the very images he exploited for his other themes in order to write about the French Revolution. Does a scholar produce a letter by Blake himself that contradicts your idea? So be it, you reply. To begin with (you point out), authors cannot be trusted when they comment on their own works. Furthermore, once a poem is launched into the world, it is for the world, not the artist, to interpret it. If we mock

---

8. A summary is a condensation, an 'in-a-nutshell' maneuver, while a paraphrase is a series of words that run parallel to and 'translate' words that pose a problem of interpretation. Both procedures allow us to approach, or approximate, the poem itself. See Chapter 9 for more on this subject.

you for being the only person in the world who has ever so interpreted the poem, your response is 'Delighted!' You relish being a loner. Are you a student whom an irritated instructor might fail in the course you are taking? No problem: you give your instructor the answers he wants to hear and keep your eccentric view secret until the term is over and you are rid of him.

However, eccentric interpretations are by no means confined to students and older lay readers. It must be reported here that highly innovative, startling and 'daring' interpretations emanate from the highest quarters of literary criticism—interpretations that convince some experts, but look almost as farfetched to others as the notion that 'The Sick Rose' concerns the French Revolution. The flurries of excitement such new readings cause may create the impression that chaos does prevail, after all, in the republic of letters.

And in truth, as I have said before, this particular republic is a wonderfully free one. Plenty of critical insults are exchanged in it, but no one is muzzled, no one lands in jail. Those daring new readings either convince or do not. Some survive and enter the mainstream of interpretation; most fade discreetly from view. You personally are absolutely at liberty to interpret a given text in your own way. But one of the primordial facts of the aesthetic life is that those who love poetry, have read a great deal of it, and have a certain aptitude with words, form a *de facto* family throughout the world, or at any rate within a given culture. Let me repeat: the disputes make all the noise; but, though often unnoticed, the overall agreements easily dominate the scene of interpretation. Meaningful language exists because human beings constitute a single biological species. Ours is an expandable uniformity, one that might be likened to a rubber band; we do not fly off into different spaces unreachable by a common language. As a result, although there might be some dispute as to whether a flower is a rose or a carnation, few radical revisionists would interpret it as a potato.

Multiple Themes

Themes, I said a while ago, can multiply. Even in an apparently simple Christian parable, one theme could introduce another. An epic like *Paradise Lost* can turn into an all but inexhaustible quarry of possible large meanings. And so can a brief poem like 'The Red Wheelbarrow'. Rare is the word or phrase to which we cannot, if we are clever enough, apply yet one more signification. All the same, our big moment is the first: it comes to us when the poem leaps from partial or complete darkness into bright light. We respond with a joyful 'Aha!' Yes! *That* (essentially) is what the text has been trying so beautifully to tell me! There may be more, we muse, much more, and wiser heads than ours have probably seen deeper and farther. But! We have taken possession of the text. We *have* it. And have it, we know, in communion with *most* of the other members of our cultural family.

For it is unnecessary to exhaust all the possible meanings of a text that, let us remember, does not depend for its life and survival (what I have called its success) on its truth, its moral authority or its ability to save our lives or our souls, but on its power to make us rejoice. We are talking about art, not about theology, philosophy or science. Let us be perfectly honest. We do not need poetry to provide for our daily bread, find us a mate, beget children and raise them, make money, cope with viruses and old age; and—pushing honesty to its conclusion—we do not absolutely need it to 'understand life' (whatever that means). One *loves* poetry; one is not saved by it. This principle places a decent boundary around the extensions of interpretation—at least for those who do not make interpretation their profession. In our reception of the work of art, diminishing returns *may* gradually set in as we circle outward from the center of meaning, from the 'big moment'. We should pursue and hound these meanings as long as we are convinced that an important something-else lurks behind the words, and as long as our discoveries enrich our pleasure; but we need not keep up the hunt until every possibility of language has been exhausted, assuming that such exhaustion is even possible. I hasten to add and to stress that this is not a counsel of laziness. It is counsel of tact. Life is short. The time you are spending trying to wring some ultimate secret from a poem might be better employed reading (not skimming!) twelve new ones.

Chapter 8

Still More about the Poem's Propositions

Leaving the Text in Order to Return to It

Nevertheless (continuing from our previous chapter), if a poem both puzzles and delights you, tantalizing you with the notion that you have not taken true possession of it yet, a fascinating search may begin, of the sort I mentioned in connection with 'The Sick Rose'—which is just the kind of text that is apt to both puzzle and delight, to yield meanings at the start and yet not *enough* meanings. This search for off-stage light will, or should, begin with the artist's other works. That is where you are most likely to find hints regarding his fundamental concerns, or even direct answers to your questions. Other important off-stage sources of light may be the poet's life, personality and beliefs as far as we know them through letters, reports by family and friends, documents of all sorts; then the historical situation (politics, economics, social realities, etc.) in which the poem is embedded; a political, social or metaphysical ideology underlying this situation; the artistic tradition in which the poet was or is writing; his direct literary debts (the sources); and even the circumstances of public reception, publishing methods, patronage and the like. Many critics also happily apply the tools of deep psychological analysis to works of art in order to explain them, or improve on other explanations. Any of these, or all, may suggest credible meanings (and the satisfaction that ensues) when the poem does not radiate them sufficiently on its own. This very deep principle can be exemplified by as tiny a poem as a nursery rhyme.

Little Jack Horner
Sat in a corner,
  Eating of Christmas pie;
He put in his Thumb,
And pull'd out a Plum,
  And said what a good boy was I.

Nursery rhymes are often little allegories directed against pow-
erful personages or ideologies, but playing it safe as ditties for
children. This one, for instance, is said to go back to the perilous
times of Henry VIII (king of England from 1509 to 1547), who
confiscated all the Church property he could lay his hands on.
Jack Horner, according to this off-stage elucidation, was in fact a
certain Thomas Horner, steward of a wealthy but imperiled abbey.
The unscrupulous Horner knew that the abbott had concealed
the deeds to 12 fine manors in a pie (at Christmas time?). He
extracted one of the deeds on the sly for his own benefit, and
lived—he and his descendants—happily ever after. Now read the
rhymes again and discover how transformed your understanding
and appreciation are—assuming, of course, that you credit the
information I have given you.[1]

Many contemporary American readers don't know how to han-
dle the love-and-hate poetry of the days of Queen Elizabeth and
King James I. Forgivably, they fail to catch its 'tone of voice' for
want of information regarding poetic conventions of the time or
the myriad social presuppositions the texts of any period conceal.
They are not sure whether Donne is jesting or serious in 'The
Apparition'. Sometimes they wonder, did the coldness or infi-
delity of mistresses literally kill lovers in those days? And did
people believe in ghosts? In Shakespeare's sonnets we are apt to
be startled by his declarations of love for a young man. Did our
bard have homosexual longings? Or could men express deep love
for male friends in former times without provoking in their read-
ers any such implied propositions? Many, many things said in the
poetry of other places and other times are clarified by off-stage
information about the world as it was then and the literary con-
ventions of the age, in addition to the clarifications frequently
brought in by biographical information.

1.   It is provided by W.S. and C. Baring Gould in their *Annotated Mother
Goose* (New York: Bramhall House, 1962).

The question, however, is whether a poem stimulates you to undertake searches of this sort (which, by the way, may be rewarding on their own, even if they fail to unlock the particular mysteries that baffled you in a given text). As I said before: if you feel that you have already taken satisfying possession of the text, you may well turn the page and read on. Your own curiosity and eagerness will determine whether you wish to bathe a work of art in lights whose provenance is no longer within the work itself (as far as *you* are concerned), but rather located in circumstances, reports and documents outside the text, including, always and principally, the other works of the author himself. Fortunately, in many instances we have editors by our side who have explored the off-stage sources and brought us their information in introductions and notes—like the note to Jack Horner I made use of just now.

As against 'The Sick Rose', which normally fails to yield its secrets without further search, we might recall Yeats's 'The Mother of God', which, overall, seems 'possessible' on its own terms (provided, of course, we understand the words and the allusions). And yet, like so many of Yeats's poems, it is grounded in a complicated and peculiar doctrine concerning recurrences in history, two-thousand-year cycles beginning each with a violent birth and bloody convulsions—a doctrine that undoubtedly bears on and expands the narrow meaning of which uninitiated readers can take satisfactory possession.[2] Some might advise you to read profoundly in Yeats so as to grasp this and other poems more fully. Others might suggest that the poem's essence is available to readers who do not have the time or inclination to go farther.

Consider the following rather more difficult poem:

THE HANGING MAN

By the roots of my hair some god got hold of me.
I sizzled in his blue volts like a desert prophet.

The nights snapped out of sight like a lizard's eyelid:
A world of bald white days in a shadeless socket.

---

2.   Armed with this off-stage information, we find a *second* meaning for Yeats's 'bestial floor' in 'The Magi' (see Chapter 6). Religions, he felt, begin in violence or (to use his word) turbulence.

A vulturous boredom pinned me in this tree.
If he were I, he would do what I did.[3]

Several attentive readings are required here before most read-
ers can feel they have taken at least partial possession of the
poem. And yet, even without leaving the text itself to seek help
off-stage, we can perhaps discern that someone who has commit-
ted suicide is speaking; a boredom resembling the perennial
whiteness a prophet would find in the desert seems to be respon-
sible; and the person addressed by the hanging man appears to be
another wretched candidate for self-murder. But here again, for-
aging outside the text can be of help. This time, the light does not
shine down from an impersonal theory of history but from infor-
mation we happen to possess about the poet's intimate life—
information about hospitalizations, bouts of insanity and (in
retrospect, for us) ultimate suicide. A student of mine who had
read Sylvia Plath's autobiographical novel *The Bell Jar* (1962) imme-
diately read the second line as a reference to shock treatments,
and the second stanza as a hospital scene, all white and nightless.
Note that he was 'translating' these puzzling images into familiar
ones, that is to say paraphrasing these difficult passages. Sizzling
in the blue volts of a god, for instance, is undoubtedly good
English, but the phrase floats free of that billion-fold network in
our brain that constitutes our world of meaning. Instead, the
image of shock treatment in a hospital is *in* that network, even if we
have never witnessed any such scene. No wonder, therefore, that
the rest of the class responded with a decided 'Aha!' (expressed in
varying ways), indicating a sense of taking possession.[4]

One more point. It sometimes happens that off-stage light can
lead you to love a poem (or any other work of art) that you

3.   Sylvia Plath (1932–63) in *Ariel* (London: Faber & Faber, 1965).
4.   As an autobiographical novel, *The Bell Jar* combines under one roof, so
to speak, the search for off-stage clues in a poet's life *and* in her other works.
In Chapter 11, Plath writes: 'I could see day after day glaring ahead of me
like a white, broad, infinitely desolate avenue.' In Chapter 12 she has this
evocation of shock therapy: 'Then something bent down and took hold of
me and shook me like the end of the world. Whee-ee-ee-ee-ee, it shrilled,
through an air crackling with blue light, and with each flash a great jolt
drubbed me till I thought my bones would break and the sap fly out of me
like a split plant' (New York: Houghton Mifflin, 1971).

disliked at first. It may turn out that, unbeknownst to you, your dislike is due to a gap in your fund of information—a gap that the poem itself cannot fill (Donne's poem does not tell you whether his readers believed in ghosts); information has to be brought in from outside the text; and then, perhaps (though not necessarily) your dislike melts into admiration.

Degrees of Understanding

From a theoretically imaginable condition of supreme understanding of a poetic text all the way to perfect helplessness, there are many degrees of what I have called possession of the text; and we can experience a thrill of pleasure anywhere along this gamut of understanding. Sometimes the subject is plain enough but we cannot grasp the theme behind it. Sometimes even the subject eludes us and the poem breaks down for us into a series of more or less interesting fragments of meaning—bead-clusters that do not connect. (This may well be what happens to many readers when they encounter 'The Hanging Man'.) In my opinion, it is virtually a law of aesthetics that the mental condition of partial or fragmentary grasp of the propositions of a literary text is less satisfying than the sense of thorough (if never godlike) comprehension.[5] All other things being equal, energized meaning is more thrilling than energized half-meaning. Nevertheless, fragments of meanings or incomplete meanings may be wonderfully energized for us even without completion, let alone the ideal state of supreme understanding. I have suggested already that a poem like 'The Sick Rose' can give us deep aesthetic pleasure even before yielding a plenitude of meaning. Here is a more recent example by W.H. Auden (1907–1973):

A MISUNDERSTANDING

Just as his dream foretold, he met them all:
The smiling grimy boy at the garage
Ran out before he blew his horn; the tall
Professor in the mountains with his large

---

5.   Note that I am speaking of mental states. That our sense of comprehension may prove at a later point to have been mistaken is not the issue here.

Tweed pockets full of plants addressed him hours
Before he would have dared; the deaf girl too
Seemed to expect him at the green chateau;
The meal was laid, the guest room full of flowers.

More, the talk always took the wished-for turn,
Dwelt on the need for stroking and advice;
Yet, at each meeting, he was forced to learn,
The same misunderstanding would arise.
Which was in need of help? Were they or he
The physician, bridegroom, and incendiary?[6]

This has in common with Blake's lyric the fact of being a little story, and a tantalizing one. The story is both intelligible and enigmatic—enigmatic in that most readers, perhaps all readers, find it hard to 'cocoon' its propositions into an overarching subject matter, and that, again, into a theme. Who is doing what at the 'green chateau'? Why the grimy boy? Why a deaf girl? Why the professor? What is the meaning of the strange uncertainty as to who needs help? Why are 'they' or 'he' given the strange designations they get in the last line, one of which is, in normal usage, distinctly negative while the other two are plainly positive?

We shall try to elucidate Auden's sonnet in Chapter 18. In the meantime, I am suggesting that it is a successful poem (admirable, enjoyable, beautiful, powerful, fine...) even before we solve the problems it poses; that is to say, it has the power to satisfy many of us before we grasp its subject or venture to formulate its theme, and even if we fail in our attempts to do so. Nevertheless, we will most probably be happier with it the moment we have answered, or have had credibly answered for us, the questions I have raised—perhaps, once more, by finding a switch or two commanding some off-stage illumination.

If at first all that a poem yields to you is a series of more or less interesting fragments, it will normally happen that the fragments are held together by a *drift* of meaning that we can formulate in a general way—'something about love', 'something about nature versus civilization', and so on *ad infinitum*. This is like perceiving

6. In *The Collected Poetry of W.H. Auden* (ed. Edward Mendelson; New York: Random House, 1945). Written in 1934, this poem has been variously printed without title, under the title 'Nobody Understands Me', and as presented here.

that an object in the fog is at any rate an elephant and not a
house. Indeed, there is usually enough meaning in difficult
poems to generate distinct emotional qualities. Anyone who reads
English can detect the large difference in mood between Blake's
haunted lines and the polite and temperate voice Auden adopts.

Auden's poem stands approximately midway between an open
text like 'I wandered lonely as a cloud' and poems that approach,
or definitely reach, impenetrability. Modern poetry offers us an
immense choice as we travel down that road. I select two texts at
random. First, a poem by Robert Creeley (b. 1926), somewhat
modified by the poet from an earlier version:

A REASON

Each gesture
is a common one, a
black dog, crying, a
man, crying.

All alike, people
or things grow
fixed with what
happens to them.

I throw a stone.
It hits the wall,
it hits a dog,
it hits a child—

my sentimental
names for years
and years ago, from
something I've not become.

If I look
in the mirror,
the wall, I
do the same thing.

Let me hit you.
Will it hurt.
Your face is hurt
all the same.[7]

7.   From *The Collected Poems 1945–1975* (Berkeley: University of California
Press, 1983). The more recent a poem, the less opportunity there is for

A poem of this sort leads us into the 'my bicycle rode into the pudding' world, where images need to be translated into other images, or into collector language, where the syntax requires normalization (discreetly, in the backs of our minds), and where general statements—like the significant one made in the second stanza—solicit a certain amount of commentary; all this until the entire poem rejoins, as we hope and trust it can—our vast network of meanings.[8] In the meantime, however, most of us can surely detect a drift that already satisfies—something like a sour 'the everyday little cruel acts we perform and suffer stick to us for good'. This seems to account for much of the poem, and perhaps for the title: the poem gives a reason why we are what we are. But how confident am I that this drift of meaning truly works—that is to say, truly accounts for every word and sign in the text? Not *very* confident! Hence I remain in part unsatisfied—with myself, to a degree, but mostly with the poem; perhaps because it is pleasanter to make the other party responsible...

Now examine the following poem by John Ashbery (b. 1927):

A WHITE PAPER

And if he thought that
All was foreign—
As, gas and petrol, en-
gine full of seeds, barking to hear the night
The political contaminations

Of what he spoke,
Spotted azaleas brought to meet him
Sitting next day
The judge, emotions,
The crushed paper heaps.[9]

commentary by critics, declarations, letters, diaries by the author and other off-stage sources of light to have become available. Poems that are successful (in our sense of the word) without being fully or even partly understood—and we have just seen that this is perfectly possible—will gradually attract a body of elucidating texts. Ultimately—if the poem continues to please—editions appear with introductions and notes offering these elucidations to the busy unspecialized admirer.

8.   See the Appendix to this chapter.

9.   From *The Tennis Court Oath* (Middletown, CT: Wesleyan University Press, 1962).

Exploded syntax (an 'if' clause without conclusion)—what John Berryman has picturesquely called 'crumpling a syntax with a sudden need'—leaves us with a long but aborted proposition, within which fragments meaningful in themselves, like 'all was foreign', float free. Perhaps, though, a drift can still be made out—something political, perhaps—as is, indeed, suggested by the title. But until we are inspired or given guidance in the form of an overall proposition that will suddenly cluster the beads into our web, we must catch our pleasure, if any, from the fragments of meaning and evocation ('an internal mirage created by the words themselves', Mallarmé wrote) and perhaps from the 'pure' sounds of the words.

Incidentally, I will be returning to the Creeley and Ashbery texts in the next chapter.

The most authentic fringe poetry is that which systematically and ideologically avoids any determined meaning, or (burning all bridges) denies any meaning at all, determined or indeterminate. Either way, we are now talking about dada poetry, whether prac-ticed by an originator like the Rumanian Tristan Tzara or by the stream of 'experimental' artists who have continued as the *enfants terribles* of poetry (and the other arts) in a comically bewildering variety of movements, usually accompanied by passionate mani-festos.[10] The principles behind these strategies vary. Some feel that the act of writing unmeaning poetry reflects the exhaustion of useful meaning in the modern world. Others assert that impos-ing a given, determined meaning is an act of fascist 'totalizing'; we should all be free to co-create meaning with the poet, who simply hands us the building blocks we can play with. (Such may be the intention of 'Poe and Psychoanalysis', which we read in Chapter 4).[11] Still others fall back on whatever pleasure we can derive from

10. Dada (literally, in French, a hobby-horse) is the name of a movement born in Zürich in 1916, though it had roots in late nineteenth-century France. 'Dada attacked conventional standards of aesthetics and behavior and stressed absurdity and the role of the unpredictable in artistic creation' (*The New Columbia Encyclopedia* [New York: Columbia University Press, 1975]).

11. 'Poe and Psychoanalysis' is probably an 'aleatory' poem, that is to say, a text for which the words or phrases have been selected at random, or pos-sibly by a method that produces random words or groups. An author may

the sounds of the words and the visuals of layout on the page.

Whatever the theory, the reality of the matter is that the refusal by dada (fringe) poets to energize shared meanings has kept their work from satisfying more than a few persons. This need not be a judgment. An artist may hate the very thought of being loved by more than a few soul mates. I am merely reporting a fact, but it carries an important implication, to wit, that energizing *meaning*, even if it is but a drift of meaning, remains the absolute condition for a dimension of success wider than marginal in the arts whose material is language.

Interestingly, in the visual arts, dada and its siblings and equivalents have enjoyed wide-ranging success: an extremely varied public almost all along the continuum we discussed in Chapter 4 admires, enjoys and purchases avant-garde works, and crowds into the galleries and museums where they are exhibited. There are no such successes in the literary world, where dada poets have had to keep recriminating against the narrowness of bourgeois taste. This enormous disparity in the success of two branches of art that were born together and sustained each other is extremely significant, for it shows that when visual artists abandon meaning, they fall back on the very rich fundamental resources of striking if incomprehensible pictures, or more fundamentally yet, on colors, textures, lines and shapes; all of them elements that (as infants and children could attest) delight us without further ado. But when poets give up meaning, they have, as we shall see by and by, very little to fall back on.

decide to use any words whose sounds come from one end of the alphabet, followed by any words whose sounds come from the other end. Another poet might rely on dream-connections of words, or on associations private to himself, or else decide to use only words lacking the letter *e*. The idea, mentioned in Chapter 1, of pulling words from a hat was invented by Tristan Tzara, who can be thought of as the patriarch, the Abraham of randomized texts.

APPENDIX

Using the system of diagrams introduced in Chapter 6, we can treat Creeley's first stanza as follows:

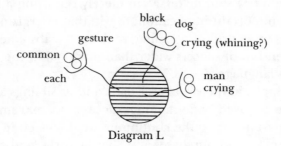

Diagram L

'Each' and 'common' are collector words that thread indirectly but easily to the non-verbal core. The other words are all first-ring beads. The three clauses are intelligible separately, but the text itself does not supply the connector beads that would enable us to make of the eight beads a single unit threading into the core.

Chapter 9

Practical Pointers for Reading Poetry

After soaring among a number of high-flying concepts, let us land on earth for the homely work of learning how to take satisfying possession of individual poems. Some poems, as we already know, are hard to enjoy yet most enjoyable after hardship; some yield their delights at lower spiritual expense. For all, however, a few tips to the reader may be helpful.

(1) To begin with, and rather obviously, you should *read a poem more than once*; the first time for an overview, and then, slowly and attentively, again, and perhaps again, and then perhaps once more. At every reading it will yield more of its intimacies. Poetry tends to be an art of compressions, of precise construction, of intense concentration on details of language and music; as a result, some of its beauties are apt to elude us at a first reading. Who would think he had exhausted a Beethoven quartet after a single hearing?

(2) *Reading poetry aloud in good company* is not only a delightful way of spending one's leisure time, it will also provoke the sort of discussion that yields a crop of ideas, some of which would certainly not have occurred to all the participants if each one had read the poem by himself.

(3) Whether it is a single passage or the entire poem (its theme, for instance) that gives you trouble, *formulate a hypothesis* as soon as possible, test it against the entire poem to see whether it makes sense, and, like a scientist, be ready to throw it out if it does not. If indeed it fails you, try a new one. You will recall that one of the pleasant difficulties that poetry, more than any other branch of

literature, is likely to raise comes of its love of first-ring language—physical language—'images'—that are very often concretizations of abstract notions. Auden's 'A Misunderstanding' affords an excellent instance, with its mysterious visitor, its castle, the guests, etc. And you will also remember that, typically, we need to 'translate' these physical things into familiar abstractions that enable us to return to the poem with a joyful sense of possessing it. That is how we proceeded in Chapter 6 with one of Tennyson's poems from *In Memoriam.* We launched our hypotheses at the problematic images, and made sure that the notions we derived from the images harmonized with the whole of the poem, whose theme also required a verifiable hypothesis. We were satisfied when it all seemed to 'hang together'.

A temptation you must overcome, while simultaneously enjoying and guessing at a poem, is to close your eyes to passages that resist or contradict your hypothesis, in the vain hope that somehow, if you had the time or took the trouble, you could make them cohere and fit. Re-read; does the troublesome passage continue to resist your hypothesis? Try a new one. For your hypotheses must account for every word and related sign of the text.

Another dangerous temptation is to formulate hypotheses that suit *your* likes and dislikes, or reflect *your* areas of familiarity, instead of adapting your reading to the poet's discourse. No one does this consciously; we never *decide* we are going to tailor a text to fit our own mental height and weight. We do it unconsciously: it is the easiest and pleasantest way; it makes the poet one of *us.* Unfortunately, for all you know, the poet may be saying odious things (from your point of view) or bring up topics you never knew existed. That cannot be helped. You must not compel him to say what *you* would have said, or what *you* would like him to have said. The curves of your reading must follow the curves traced out by the text. You must not bend the text to *your* curves.[1]

In formulating your hypothesis, you should also imitate the scientist in applying the law of parsimony. Be parsimonious with your suppositions. Do not look, as the French say, for noon at two o'clock, or, to change the metaphor, do not travel ten miles for

---

1.   'Must not' is a manner of speaking. The police is still absent. Correctly: 'must not' if you wish your interpretation to be shared by others—to be recognized by others as more or less true to the meaning of the words.

meanings you can find at your fingertips. See first if the simplest solution works. It was only because the simplest solution for 'A Sick Rose'—namely, that it was no more than a grim little story—failed to satisfy us that we began to let our minds travel. For that matter, you could briefly return to our discussion of this poem, and of Sylvia Plath's 'The Hanging Man' as well, for examples of the formulation of hypotheses. But I repeat that this imaginative act applies to single passages as well as to overarching themes.

(4) As a matter of course, all the words of a poem must be understood. Too often readers try to guess, vaguely and hopefully, at the meaning of words they do not know, or worse still, to skip over them in the lazy hope that they are not essential. This laziness may be excused when we read a newspaper, but the poet, who tends to draw every possible virtue out of the words he selects, and whose vocabulary is likely to be immense, must not be treated like a journalist. We should not be deceived by the fact that both persons use language. That is like saying that the supermarket cashier and Einstein both use numbers.

Looking up unknown words (if the editor of your text has not done it for you) is the most obvious action of all and requires no further comment. When you encounter words like clem, piaculative, concinnity, nicker or metaphrast, you must petition your everyday dictionary, and, if that fails you, proceed up the ladder until you reach the many-volumed Oxford English Dictionary (OED). Needless to say, words in foreign languages—many poets love to use them, and nowadays more than ever—make the same demand on you.

A bit more insidious are the words that seem to be familiar, but whose familiar meaning simply refuses to fit the particular poem you are reading. This problem arises most frequently in older texts, since our language has evolved considerably over the centuries. Plainly archaic words like 'soote' or 'mings' sound the alarm by simply appearing on the page. But other words are 'false friends'—they deceive you by looking familiar when in fact they have changed their meanings. 'Doom' is an example we noted in Chapter 7. 'Kindly' in an Elizabethan text may mean 'naturally' (according to its kind, or species); 'tall' can mean 'brave,' 'to affect' might mean 'to love'. Even simpler words can cheat your expectations: 'and' might mean 'if', 'on' may mean 'of', 'which' can be 'who' or 'whom', and 'that' could mean 'what' ('I am that I am' in the King James version of Exodus 3.14). In the last lines of Shakespeare's Sonnet 130 the plain 'she', which is obviously a pronoun for us, makes no sense until we treat it as a noun, a synonym for 'woman':

> My mistress, when she walks, treads on the ground.
> And yet, by heaven, I think my love as rare
> As any she belied with false compare.

The natural impulse is to treat 'she' as the subject of 'belied', with the implication that she (the mistress) told lies about other women—she belied them. But as soon as you grasp that this meaning is impossible in context, you must try other hypotheses, and keep trying until it dawns on you that the poet is saying that his sweetheart is as rare as any woman ('any she') who has been belied (by other poets, perhaps) with false comparisons—probably of the 'my mistress is like a goddess' species.

Note also in these lines the somewhat shifted meaning of 'rare' (i.e. excellent), the faintly archaic 'belied', and 'compare' for 'comparison'. More important still, a 'mistress' in the language of our forefathers might be nothing more than the woman courted by her 'lover', that is to say her suitor. Elsewhere in the poem, Shakespeare speaks of his mistress's hair as 'wires', and we must rid our minds of the unromantic modern meaning of this word.

Many editions of poets and anthologies modernize old spellings; but some do not; and then, of course, we must cope with an unfamiliar and sometimes quite strange orthography, emanating from a past which, in any case, took more liberties with spelling than we do today. We will see a couple of examples presently.

In sum, when we wish to open our minds to the experiences of our forefathers in *any* field, a small but rewarding effort of mental adjustment is required.

(5) The words 'mistress' and 'lover' were in fact ambiguous in Shakespeare's own time. One could not tell, without further hints, whether the couple had or had not 'made love' already. Besides, 'making love' could mean, in all innocence, nothing more strenuous than flirting. With this I introduce *the problem of ambiguity*, a condition many modern critics delight in, especially when a second meaning of a word or phrase pulls the reader in a direction

opposite to the obvious one, so that the poet appears to undercut his own ostensible statement. The result is irony, perplexity, undecidability—the mental states that happen to be in vogue in one epoch (like ours) and cease to be admired in another. In reality, the multiplicity of possible meanings of many if not most of our words is both an opportunity and a nuisance for the poet. He can deliberately invite several meanings, or be happy (posthumously, very often!) if readers discover some that he himself had not suspected; but on the other hand, he has no foolproof way of locking out meanings he doesn't want. Meanings exist whether he likes them or not. Ultimately it is up to us, the readers, to filter an overload of meaning out of our readings. We do this especially when the text itself, or something we know about the artist, suggests to our judgments that the poet truly did not want additional or contrary meanings to blur his message. And indeed, just as too many guests can spoil a party, so too many available meanings can disperse and muddle the effect of a text and consequently dilute our pleasure.

A minor instance of desirable exclusion can be found in Donne's 'The Apparition':

> When by thy scorn, O murderess, I am dead,
>   And that thou think'st thee free
> From all solicitation from me,
> Then shall my ghost come to thy bed,
> And thee, feign'd vestal, in worse arms shall see;
> Then thy sick taper will begin to wink,

and so on. 'To wink' means to flash fitfully, but it can also mean to give a discreet and friendly tip. For most of us, this second meaning, if allowed to pass through the filter, would disperse and diffuse the strongly focused meaning that works best. And I trust that John Donne would have agreed. Nor, I think, would Allen Ginsberg rejoice if, in his 'America', a portion of which we read in Chapter 5, we allowed 'party' to mean, not only the Socialist or Communist bodies he clearly had in mind, but also what we understand when we say, 'I'm throwing a party next Sunday, and you're invited.' To do so would create a sharp edge of irony, undercut the text—and ruin it aesthetically.

Pick up the word 'mind' in Anne Sexton's 'Ringing the Bells':

> And this is the way they ring
> the bells in Bedlam
> and this is the bell-lady
> who comes each Tuesday morning
> to give us a music lesson
> and because the attendants make you go
> and because we mind by instinct,
> like bees caught in the wrong hive,
> we are the circle of the crazy ladies
> who sit in the lounge of the mental house
> and smile at the smiling woman
> who passes us each a bell...[2]

There may be a strong temptation for some readers to undercut the meaning of meek obedience ('mind your mother now!') that the context requires, by sneaking in the meaning of rebellion— the ladies both obeying and objecting to the music lesson; and the critics of our time tend to jump at such an opportunity for 'ambivalence' and 'deconstruction'. No one can force you one way or the other; not even Sexton herself (1928–74), were she among us to encourage the ironical reading or, on the contrary, chide us for misrepresenting her. A text is a text; the poet has written 'mind' and must take the lexical consequences, no matter what we may discover in her own letters, articles and whatever. But if the text fails to signal to us that more than one meaning is called for, why should we favor the dilution of ambiguity over the power of focus?

This might be a good time to re-read 'The Surprises of the Superhuman':

> The palais de justice of chambermaids
> Tops the horizon with its colonnades.
>
> If it were lost in Uebermenschlichkeit,
> Perhaps our wretched state would soon come right.
>
> For somehow the brave dicta of its kings
> Makes more awry our faulty human things.[3]

---

2.   This 30-line poem was published in 1960. I take it from Sexton's *The Complete Poems* (New York: Houghton Mifflin, 1981). While the subject matter of harmless insanity is of course stated in the poem, it is also implied and strongly supported by the simple, repetitive, childlike syntax. Remember that *anything* whatever in a poem can imply propositions and feelings.

3.   'Palais de justice' is the French for hall (palace) of justice, and the German word in line 3 is the 'superhuman' in the title.

When Stevens writes that the *palais de justice* might do more good if it were 'lost in' *Uebermenschlichkeit*, should 'lost in' be read as something desirable or undesirable? When we say 'the mountain-top is lost in the clouds', the meaning is grand; and there is nothing wrong with being 'lost in thought'. But in 'I am lost in the woods' the meaning is negative. Surely the ambiguity—indeed, the contradiction—is undesirable at this point. The poem solicits the first meaning, since it seems to inquire into the possible result of an elevation of human institutions to something all but divine, where their weaknesses would be happily lost.

Nevertheless, in many instances texts do appear to send signals to many or most readers that certain words should be read with more than one meaning in mind. In 'God's Grandeur', for instance, Gerard Manley Hopkins (1844–89) speaks in his usual fervent tones of the desecrations wrought by man on Nature. Still, he writes, 'nature is never spent'. And why not?

> There lives the dearest freshness deep down things;
> And though the last lights off the black West went
>   Oh, morning, at the brown brink eastward, springs—
> Because the Holy Ghost over the bent
>   World broods with warm breast and with ah! bright wings.

Why is the world bent? Is it bent in the sense of loaded down by the trade and toil that Hopkins has been lamenting ('All is seared with trade; bleared, smeared with toil')? Is it bent with adoration of God? Or is it bent geographically speaking (the horizon's arc)? The two first meanings might appear to be as incompatible as the two meanings of Stevens's 'lost in' where I firmly selected one and excluded the other. But if we look again, we find that the opposites are supported by the whole poem: the world is bent with trade and toil *and yet* (by the grace of God) also bent in adoration of God. The third meaning, less important, adds itself without disturbing Hopkins's paradox.

The word 'broods' is also susceptible of more than one interpretation. The idea of a mother-hen is clearly suggested in the line, and so is the more philosophical meaning of a rather anxious meditation. Since a mother naturally broods a great deal over her offspring's future, we see that both meanings—God as parent and God as worrier—cooperate to good effect.

If these readings appear to you unforced, untouched by eccentricity and clean of ideological preconceptions, you could take them as models of how to deal with multiple meanings in a tactful, civilized manner that safeguards your pleasure while nursing the sense that you are accepting the poet's guidance rather than imposing on him the all too abundant possibilities of language.

My final tip about multiplicity of meanings is: watch those connective words! Language displays man's inertia as evidently as it proves his inventiveness. This laziness shows itself particularly in those little 'articulators' that I have represented with black beads. Whether the words are prepositions, conjunctions or adverbs does not matter here. What matters is that many of them carry two or more possible meanings, and may constitute a serious obtacle to comprehension, especially because they are so modest and so familiar that we may not suspect them of being troublemakers. Later in this chapter you will find instances concerning 'since', 'from' and 'to.'

(6) Owning a small library of reference works, in addition to a few English and foreign-language dictionaries, is an obvious help when it comes to *identifying the unfamiliar names and places* you are bound to encounter in the course of your extensive reading of the poets. We have already met with a few of the standard characters of our culture, among them the Greek ones for Pope's version of the *Iliad* and the biblical ones for Milton's invocation in *Paradise Lost*. But of course, the sky, as they say, is the limit. Poets can name or refer to anything they have ever read or anyone and anything they have ever known or imagined. And whatever it is they name—a tribe in Zimbabwe, a language spoken along the Amazon, an ancient Mesopotamian inscription, a character in a Bulgarian epic—is part of the poem's vocabulary.

Once again, twentieth-century poets frequently tax our fund of information well beyond what was the norm in times past. It must be reported that many of them do not scruple to refer to private experiences no one can look up in works of reference. When this happens, their assumption, it must be supposed, is that the *drift* I have discussed suffices—the reader need not know precisely who and what is meant. Ezra Pound (1885–1972) is always convenient for an illustration of this poetic maneuver. Here are the opening lines of Canto XXVIII of *A Draft of XXX Cantos*, published in 1930:

And God the Father Eternal (Boja d'un Dio!)
Having made all things he cd
think of, felt yet
That something was lacking, and thought
Still more, and reflected that
The Romagnolo was lacking, and
Stamped with his foot in the mud and
Up comes the Romagnolo:
   'Gard, yeh bloudy 'angman! It's me!
Aso iqua me. All Esimo Dottor Aldo Wallushnig
Who with the force of his intellect
With art and assiduous care
 Has snatched from death by a most perilous operation
The classical Caesarian cut
Marotti, Virginia, in Senni of San Giorgio
At the same time saving her son.
May there move to his laud the applause of all men
And the gratitude of the family.
      S. Giorgio, 23d May. A.D. 1925.[4]

For those who are attracted to this sort of poetry, the two-volume *Companion to the Cantos of Ezra Pound*, with its 12,000 entries, provides the information that 'boja d'un Dio!' means 'hangman of a God!'— an oath in the dialect of the north-central Italian region called the Romagna. The other phrase, in the same dialect (line 10), is sufficiently translated by Pound himself as 'It's me!'— although the innocent reader may not be aware of this. 'All Esimo', though slightly wrong, returns us, at any rate, to standard Italian, and is a respectful mode of address in a letter ('To the excellent Doctor'). Whether 'the Romagnolo' refers to any youngster of the region leaping from the womb or to Cesare Borgia who was duke of Romagna in the sixteenth century remains unascertained. As for Doctor Wallushnig and Virginia Marotti, the 12,000 entries can only inform us naively that the first is 'probably an Austrian doctor in Venice, ca. 1925', and the second 'a Venetian woman'. Senni, says the two-volume crusher, 'seems to be the name of a hospital', while San Giorgio, we are told, is an island and a church in Venice.[5] The reader, faced with allusions even

---

4. In *The Cantos 1–95* (New York: New Directions, 1965).
5. The *Companion* is by C.F. Terrell; it was published in 1980 by the University of Maine Press. Any of the hundreds of other Pound studies might

specialists boggle at, has a choice between rejecting the work so riddled as a failure (it fails to thrill) or enjoying its drift (here, obviously, something to do with childbirth) in the belief that the drift and not the precise meaning is of the essence.

Allusions can be indirect. In 'The Surprises of the Superhuman', for instance, Stevens clearly wishes us to think of Nietzsche's doctrine of the Superman, but he does not say so outright. The title of Sylvia Plath's poem, 'The Hanging Man', alludes to one of the figures in the tarot pack of cards.[6] Or else, poets can quote the works of other people and hope or expect that we will recognize the allusions. Ginsberg, we saw, alludes to a poem by Browning. When T.S. Eliot, in 'The Fire Sermon' section of *The Waste Land* (1922), writes:

> Sweet Thames, run softly till I end my song,
> Sweet Thames, run softly, for I speak not loud or long,
> But at my back in a cold blast I hear
> The rattle of the bones, and chuckle spread from ear to ear,

he wants us to recognize the voices of Edmund Spenser and Andrew Marvell. As for Auden's 'The Shield of Achilles', here is a masterpiece that somberly gives the lie throughout to another text, namely Homer's joyous account of the forging of the shield in the *Iliad*.

But, besides alluding to other texts, poets may allude to events, customs, objects—any number of non-text realities which may be beyond our immediate field of knowledge. How many American readers would know, without an editor's footnote, that the ominous

HURRY UP PLEASE ITS TIME

answer questions this particular work fails to resolve. Professor Ronald Bush, a prominent student of Pound, advised me that 'Gard' is 'God' and not, as I first surmised, short for 'on your guard'! San Giorgio could hardly refer to a church in the context of the lines I have quoted. The possibility that 'the Romagnolo' is Cesare Borgia is suggested by 'the classical Caesarian cut'. The latter line, by the way, demands from our imaginations a dash before and after. As for the apparent disconnection between the two parts of the quoted section (lines 1-9, then line 10 to the end), this is a theme taken up below in another pointer.

6.   Used for divination. Plath probably took the allusion from T.S. Eliot's *The Waste Land*, itself a bazaar of allusions to texts of all kinds.

which resounds repeatedly in the previous section of *The Waste Land* echoes the English bartender's call for closing time?

If you despair of elucidating all the allusions of a text, console yourself with the thought that we do not completely elucidate much of anything in this vale of tears, yet manage to live and enjoy life in that penumbra. Remember: we do not need to exhaust a poem in order to take satisfactory possession of it.

(7) It often happens that, before we relish a poem, we need to perform the humble task of *unravelling its grammatical structure*. Where is the subject, where is its verb, what are the person, tense and mood of the verb or verbs, to what are the subordinate clauses subordinated, are there appositions, what modifies what, what noun is the antecedent of a given pronoun, what is the sensible word order, what part of speech are certain words that could be noun or verb or adverb or preposition, what hidden words must be supplied in order to establish the syntax?[7] And so forth. As before, you are advised to devise a hypothesis, to test it honestly on the text, and switch to a new one in case the passage in question resists you.

Pope's opening lines for Homer's *Iliad* provide a good terrain for trying out our skills. Let us read them again.

> Achilles' wrath, to Greece the direful spring
> Of woes unnumber'd, heavenly goddess, sing!
> That wrath which hurl'd to Pluto's gloomy reign
> The souls of mighty chiefs untimely slain;
> Whose limbs unburied on the naked shore,
> Devouring dogs and hungry vultures tore,
> Since great Achilles and Atrides strove:
> Such was the sovereign doom, and such the will of Jove!

To begin with, we recognize the 'heavenly goddess' as an indirect allusion (technically: an epithet) that must be inquired into, if necessary, like any dictionary word. But even if we fail to discover that she is one of the Muses, the drift is clear enough, and, whoever she may be, we need to recognize in her the subject of Pope's sentence; otherwise we are lost from the start. As soon as this is done, we might, in our imaginations, reset the word order

---

7. I will keep using the simple 'hidden' instead of 'understood' because of the obviously inconvenient major meaning of the latter. The topic of hidden words will return several times in our discussions.

of the two-line sentence so as to start with the subject—the heavenly goddess—continue with the verb and its object, and then 'mop up' whatever remains. Well now, the Muse is told to sing—for we have also (I hope) recognized 'sing' as an imperative. What is she told to sing? The wrath of Achilles. This leaves, in line 1, a subordinate clause starting out with 'to'. Now, however, we are paralyzed unless we recognize the ghost of two hidden words, namely 'which was'. This yields 'Achilles' wrath, which was to Greece the direful spring of woes unnumbered.' Or, if we feel the need to register this momentarily in prose word order in our imagination, 'Achilles' wrath, which was the spring of unnumbered woes to Greece.'

Two lines are now elucidated thanks to syntactical analysis. But what about the other six? When you read 'That wrath which hurled' (on line 3) you might be confident that another sentence has begun, similar in construction to: '(i) That sign (ii) which pointed East (iii) reassured me (iv) that I was travelling in the right direction.' Here (i) is the subject; (ii) is a subordinate clause with its subordinate verb; (iii) has the main verb + direct object, both attached to the subject; followed at (iv) by another subordinate clause with its subordinate verb. But where is Pope's main verb? What did that wrath do? It is a wrath *which hurled* mighty chiefs to Hell ('Pluto's gloomy reign'—another indirect allusion or circumlocution), but that is only a subordinate clause with its subordinate verb. Again, where is Pope's main verb? What did that wrath, which hurled, do in addition? Forced to conclude at last that no main verb is anywhere in sight, you must rethink your grammatical hypothesis, and you will turn and turn in vain until you realize that the entire six lines beginning with 'That wrath which hurled' stand in *apposition* to the first two words of the epic: 'Achilles' wrath'.[8] In shortened prose: 'Sing, Muse, Achilles' wrath, which was the source of numberless woes for Greece—I mean, sing that wrath which hurled...' etc. A hidden verb is thus restored, and the sentence makes sense. As for 'Since' in the penultimate line, it works whether we take it in its time-meaning

---

8.   Instead of the dictionary definition of apposition, here is a double example: 'My banker, one of the most astute men in the business, gave me, his best friend, the good advice to sell.'

('I have been waiting for you since six o'clock') or its consequence-meaning ('since you have disobeyed me, you will be punished'). Finally, the colon tells us that 'Such' refers backward to the preceding sentence, and is not the start of another, forthcoming, thought.

A more problematic set of difficulties regarding word order, antecedents and parts of speech occurs in the third stanza of Keats's 'Ode on a Grecian Urn' (1820). Keats is looking at a world of soulful activity painted on the Greek vase he has imagined.[9]

> Ah, happy, happy boughs! that cannot shed
>   Your leaves, nor ever bid the Spring adieu;
> And happy melodist, unwearièd,
>   Forever piping songs forever new;
> More happy love! more happy, happy love!
>   Forever warm and still to be enjoyed,
>   Forever panting, and forever young;
> All breathing human passion far above,
>   That leaves a heart high-sorrowful and cloyed,
>   A burning forehead, and a parching tongue.

Line 8 (not the best one Keats ever wrote!) usually bewilders inexperienced readers. The sentence begins innocently enough. The antecedent of 'All' seems to be, collectively, the boughs, the piper and the lovers just evoked. Furthermore, since we are used to hiding the various forms of 'to be', we silently supply 'are' and read that these boughs, this piper, the lovers *are* all of them breathing human passion. 'Breathing passion' is a little strained for feeling (or expressing) passion. Nevertheless, we follow the hypothesis that the boughs, piper and lovers are feeling and expressing passion. Unfortunately, we run at once into the wall of 'far above'. The lovers are breathing far above whom or what? And where is the antecedent of 'That' at the beginning of line 9? We thought that the passion of boughs, melodist and lovers was a fine thing. But if that passion leaves them, or us, in the pitiful condition described in the last two lines, a flat contradiction is thrown at us. The moment we reach a contradiction—a fruitless one—we must turn suspicious eyes on our hypothesis. Line 8 must be re-read, until we realize that a strained word order has been

---

9.   The Greek potters never made a vase or 'urn' of the sort Keats so movingly invented.

imposed on Keats by the necessity of having to rhyme with that most intractable of English words, 'love'. The correct word order, we now realize, is 'All [these] are breathing far above human passion.' This reading erases the contradiction. The passions rendered by Art do not cloy, do not parch; human passions do.

Although the poets who dwell in the Elysium of the established canon tease us on occasion with minor or not-so-minor grammatical difficulties, the as yet uncanonized poets of our own generations often make deep grammatical cracks that leave their meanings open to yawning doubt. The act of poetically energizing meaning was never entirely kind to high school correctness; but nowadays it has a way, very often, of devastating the decent precepts our teachers tried so hard to inculcate into our young brains. We could profitably summon Robert Creeley's 'A Reason' once more in this connection:

> Each gesture
> is a common one, a
> black dog, crying, a
> man, crying.
>
> All alike, people
> or things grow
> fixed with what
> happens to them.
>
> I throw a stone.
> It hits the wall,
> it hits a dog,
> it hits a child—
>
> my sentimental
> names for years
> and years ago, from
> something I've not become.
>
> If I look
> in the mirror,
> the wall, I
> do the same thing.
>
> Let me hit you.
> Will it hurt.
> Your face is hurt
> all the same.

Examine, for instance, the fourth stanza. It acts like an apposition; but an apposition to what? Stones, walls, dogs, children do not sound to us like sentimental names for years. Some other grammatical hypothesis must be launched at this stanza—or so it seems. For that matter, the first stanza offers something of the same difficulty. Its second half seems to be in apposition to the first, and yet it resists our effort to make it play that role. Returning to the fourth stanza, we detect in the word 'from' one of those troublesome connective words mentioned earlier. To begin with, we need to discern the precise meaning of this particular 'from' ('from morning to night' refers to a movement in time, in 'I steal from you' the victim of an action is defined, and 'I come from England' refers to a movement in space). And then we must make the syntactical decision of attaching the 'from' phrase either to 'names' or 'years'—in addition to wondering whether either makes sense!

I will be speaking of hidden or implied words at length in our next chapter; but we can anticipate the discussion to come by querying Creeley's fifth stanza: do we want silently to supply an 'or' after 'mirror'? Is the poet saying, 'Whether I look in the mirror or at the wall, I am equally vicious'? One of my students suggested 'on' ('mirror on the wall')—but what of the comma after 'mirror'? Might 'and' be a better solution? And is the poem worth the trouble of looking for a solution?[10]

You will recall that John Ashbery's 'A White Paper' consists of a sentence fragment—a clause beginning with 'And if' and going grammatically nowhere thereafter:

> And if he thought that
> All was foreign—
> As, gas and petrol, en-
> gine full of seeds, barking to hear the night
> The political contaminations

---

10. In this as in the next poem to be considered, we encounter a situation discussed in Chapter 6, and illustrated there by Tennyson's lyric from *In Memoriam*—to wit, that the difficulty concerns first-ring language ('I throw a stone' is as elementary as 'bird flies'): language directly rooted in the core, but failing to link to the other clusters in the text; and that some of these clusters need to be translated into more abstract language (outer-ring words) before joining their threads to our myriad web of meanings.

> Of what he spoke,
> Spotted azaleas brought to meet him
> Sitting next day
> The judge, emotions,
> The crushed paper heaps.

But the poem presents other grammatical problems for us (they do not, presumably, exist in the poet's mind). We can learn—anticipating again—that we may need to supply hidden punctuation marks as well as hidden words, inasmuch as the 'related signs' of our definition can be essential carriers of information.[11] Should we not try to imagine a bit of punctuation after 'night' in line 4 and after 'day' in line 8? But we also learn that not every one of our commendable moves meets with success. For after placing, say, an imaginary comma after 'night', the question still remains whether 'barking to hear the night' is a proper phrase. What is the antecedent of this present participle? Or is 'barking' a gerund? In the first case, the engine might be barking (remember that Creeley's dog was crying); in the second, there is *a* barking going on. Alas, in neither case does a true meaning peek out. What, after all, is a barking in order to hear the night? (Mind here again the problem of our multi-purpose English prepositions: 'to' is one of our worst offenders.) Are we looking at a cluster of unattachable free-floating beads—a word sequence deliberately pumped empty of meaning? Has Ashbery written a purely aleatory poem?

Perhaps; and yet he offers a series of fairly intelligible items that make up the world that is alien to the 'hero' of the poem, including the political consequences of what the man said in that alien country. Might the White Paper of the title be the official report he is writing about this foreign country? As you can see, we are venturing hypotheses about individual passages and then about the subject or theme as a whole.

With at any rate a drift of a subject-matter in mind, we can try to work on the grammar of the final two lines. Here are three perfectly clear individual items—beads of the first ring immediately in touch with our sensory experiences. But nothing can be made of them until we determine their grammatical roles. Is 'the judge'

---

11. Many twentieth-century poets have conducted a veritable massacre of punctuations! We saw one little example in our Pound selection above.

in apposition to 'him'? Or are emotions the judge of something? Or else, perhaps all three items—judge, emotions, heaps of paper—are additional alien things, parallel members of the series that began with 'gas and petrol'. Perhaps our hero has been arrested; flowers have been brought to him; a judge hears his case; emotions flare; the paper-work lies in heaps... Who knows? And why the incomplete sentence of the poem? Because the affair is as yet unconcluded? If so, we can say that the hanging structure implies a proposition or reinforces an implied one. The point, at any rate, is that without nagging at the syntax we are hard put to formulate *any* decent hypothesis.

Chapter 10

More Practical Pointers for Reading Poetry

(1) The strategy of hiding elements of the text deserves a pointer of its own. Poets often remorselessly cut out not only punctuation marks but also words, phrases and clauses. They do this, we hope, not in order to baffle their poor readers, but in order to 'cut out the fat', or 'unload excess baggage'. I use these two routine expressions to show that the desirability of economy is recognized everywhere. Economy is not always and necessarily attractive—quite a few fine poems go in for abundance and a 'spreading themselves out' which, as Walt Whitman knew, has attractions of its own—yet very often poets will suppress what they consider uninteresting or retarding words and related signs. As a result, poems can appear highly compressed, and our humble task, if we have trouble understanding them, is to decompress them by *supplying the missing elements* in our minds just long enough to take possession, before we dismiss these additions in order to revert to the thrilling original.

The hidden 'which was' in Pope's *Iliad* can be enlisted to represent a myriad suppressions of this simple kind throughout the history of English and American poetry. Or else we can return to Browning's 'Fra Lippo Lippi', which we looked at in Chapter 3:

> 'How looks my painting, now the scaffold's down?'
> I ask a brother. 'Hugely,' he returns—
> 'Already not one phiz of your three slaves
> Who turn the Deacon off his toasted side,
> But's scratched and prodded to our heart's content,

> The pious people have so eased their own
> With coming to say prayers there in a rage;

The pious people have so eased their own what? You will quickly answer the question, I think, now that I have asked it; so let this example stand for the many easy and normal suppressions that our language allows.

A somewhat more 'advanced' couple of cases can be found in Andrew Marvell's 'The Garden' (c. 1650), from which I quote a few lines:

> Fair Quiet, have I found thee here,
> And Innocence, thy sister dear?
> Mistaken long, I sought you then
> In busy companies of men.
> Your sacred plants, if here below,
> Only among the plants will grow;
> Society is all but rude
> To this delicious solitude.

To decompress the fifth line and make it 'good English', we need to pump a few words into it, and spoil it poetically for an instant in order to grasp it. 'If here below' becomes 'if [they exist] here below [at all]' before we quickly revert to the original. As for the last couplet, a serious misunderstanding will be avoided if we mentally insert 'compared' after 'all but rude'.[1]

We have already surmised that our Creeley and Ashbery poems require a great deal of mental filling in before they can yield more than a drift of meaning. In particular, incomplete sentences (much practiced in our times) call for this act of our imagination. Observe, in the following poem by E.E. Cummings, how the poet has wittily suppressed tired words and phrases; but at the same time note how that very act of suppression yields rich implied thematic propositions about 'average people', clichés, war, patriotism, and the family. *Not* saying something can be an eloquent way of saying a great deal.

> my sweet old etcetera
> aunt lucy during the recent

---

1. 'Rude' is another false friend. Its meaning of 'impolite' did not exist in Marvell's time; hence we must stick to 'rough' or 'harsh' and not flirt with ambiguity.

war could and what
is more did tell you just
what everybody was fighting

for,
my sister

isabel created hundreds
(and
hundreds) of socks not to
mention shirts fleaproof earwarmers

etcetera wristers etcetera, my
mother hoped that
i would die etcetera
bravely of course my father used
to become hoarse talking about how it was
a privilege and if only he
could meanwhile my

self et cetera lay quietly
in the deep mud et

cetera
(dreaming,
et
    cetera, of
Your smile
eyes knees and of your Etcetera)[2]

Once more we can dutifully punctuate the text in our imagina-
tion; but chiefly, of course, we find ourselves completing sen-
tences as discreetly as possible before reverting to the original.

(2) Suppressions can go still farther. Poets sometimes pulverize
the bridges between propositions, or blocks of propositions. Let
us begin by looking again at a normally progressing poem, namely
Yeats's 'The Mother of God'.

---

2.   Published in 1926. In *Complete Poems* (ed. George J. Firmage; New
York: Liveright Publishing Corporation, 1991). Like Stevens's 'The Surprises
of the Superhuman', this is a commentary on World War I. I will be mention-
ing the poem again under the topics of sarcasm and repetition. In the mean-
time, note that the fervently humorous final 'Etcetera' carries the sort of
implied proposition we call an innuendo.

The three-fold terror of love; a fallen flare
Through the hollow of an ear;
Wings beating about the room;
The terror of all terrors that I bore
The Heavens in my womb.

Had I not found content among the shows
Every common woman knows,
Chimney corner, garden walk,
Or rocky cistern where we tread the clothes
And gather all the talk?

What is this flesh I purchased with my pains,
This fallen star my milk sustains,
This love that makes my heart's blood stop
Or strikes a sudden chill into my bone
And bids my hair stand up?

In the first stanza Mary is terrified by the angel of God who announces that she is bearing 'the Heavens in her womb'. She goes on in the second stanza to tell us by means of a rhetorical question (i.e. a question that only pretends to be one, and is actually a statement) that before this terrifying event she was content with ordinary village life. All the propositions so far are first-ring clusters of beads. The connective bead between the two stanzas consists in the notion 'before'. This merits two observations. The first is that 'before' is also a first-ring bead. It threads directly into our pre-verbal life and is of course available even to an insect, let alone our faithful dog. The second is that Yeats has not bothered to use the word 'before', since the time-before-a-time is efficiently conveyed by the past-perfect tense. As a result, when Mary returns to the present tense in the third stanza, we know that we are reentering the scene of the Annunciation. Here another unobtrusive word plays the part of connective tissue: 'this'. It reconnects us to the first stanza and tells us that the 'flesh' Mary speaks of is the Heavens she carries in her womb. As a result, we can proceed to Mary's frightened question about who and what the child might be.

Thus we see that a smooth narrative flow is not necessarily a steady flow into the future. As early as in the *Iliad* and the *Odyssey* we find the poet or poets already running their narratives back and forth in time, and yet they ensure a smooth flow by means of sufficient bridging material.

Instead, many modern artists have burnt their bridges. Giving up smoothness of flow, they require of us that we leap across a vacuum from one image or proposition to another (see Fig. 7 for an example in the visual arts). Or rather, having leaped, we are expected—for our pleasure, of course—to work at filling in the vacuum by applying our own intelligence and imagination (and perhaps some off-stage illumination); or, to use our other metaphor, to install the bridges ourselves. Here is a tragic but enigmatic poem by Adrienne Rich (b. 1929) in which a number of propositions, some difficult in themselves, are severed from one another. Can we fill the gaps without off-stage help? Do we catch at any rate a drift?

A VALEDICTION FORBIDDING MOURNING

My swirling wants. Your frozen lips.
The grammar turned and attacked me.
Themes, written under duress.
Emptiness of the notations.

They gave me a drug that slowed the healing of wounds.

I want you to see this before I leave:
the experience of repetition as death
the failure of criticism to locate the pain
the poster in the bus that said:
my bleeding is under control.

A red plant in a cemetery of plastic wreaths.

A last attempt: the language is a dialect called metaphor.
These images go unglossed: hair, glacier, flashlight.
When I think of a landscape I am thinking of a time.
When I talk of taking a trip I mean forever.
I could say: those mountains have a meaning
but further than that I could not say.

To do something very common, in my own way.[3]

Here we get both local suppression—the sentence fragments of the first stanza and the last line—and, in addition, disturbingly unbridged gaps between blocks of text.

---

3.   From *The Will to Change* (New York: W.W. Norton, 1971). The title copies that of a famous poem by John Donne—another instance of allusion. A valediction is a farewell. See the Appendix to this chapter for more discussion.

Fig. 7. Julio Alvarez, 'El Grito' (The Shout)), black and white drawing, 1978. A nude figure, presumably shouting, echoed by two denuded trees, or else echoing them. Three other nude persons. One holds up another. Everybody and everything sunk more or less deeply into the soil. By what ideas (propositions) do these images connect and cohere?

To make the effort of filling the gaps, we must presuppose that the poem before us is not a fringe one that refuses connections to begin with. Most readers, I believe, will feel that somehow the gaps in Rich's poem can be bridged, even though, as with Sylvia

Plath's poem, we may want some off-stage lights to be beamed at it. Can we put our trust in that assumption with regard to a poem like 'A Reason'? If we do, we shall need to build a bridge, for instance, between its fifth and last stanzas. Try 'For example':

> If I look
> in the mirror,
> the wall, I
> do the same thing.
>
> [For example:]
>
> Let me hit you.
> Will it hurt.
> Your face is hurt
> all the same.

Will this work? Does it help? You may be skeptical...

The classic poem of suppressions in our language remains T.S. Eliot's *The Waste Land*, where, abetted by Ezra Pound, the poet made a collage of powerful scenes from which he had carefully scissored the bridging elements. In doing so, he obtained, among other things, an implied proposition—a proposition created not only by the scenes as such, but also by the very act of fragmenting them. Social fragmentation as theme of the text was also implied by the formal act of fragmenting that text. Form expressed content.[4]

Another glance at the opening lines of Pound's Canto XXVIII will yield a final illustration.

> And God the Father Eternal (Boja d'un Dio!)
> Having made all things he cd
> think of, felt yet
> That something was lacking, and thought
> Still more, and reflected that
> The Romagnolo was lacking, and
> Stamped with his foot in the mud and
> Up comes the Romagnolo:

---

4.   As did, you will remember, Susan Howe's poem quoted in Chapter 5, and the very fact of brevity at the end of George Herbert's 'The Collar', discussed in Chapter 6. The gaps in Adrienne Rich's poem also suggest, in the context of the actual words of the poem, a mind in disarray.

'Gard, yeh bloudy 'angman! It's me!
Aso iqua me. All Esimo Dottor Aldo Wallushnig
Who with the force of his intellect
With art and assiduous care
 Has snatched from death by a most perilous operation
The classical Caesarian cut
Marotti, Virginia, in Senni of San Giorgio
At the same time saving her son.
May there move to his laud the applause of all men
And the gratitude of the family.
        S. Giorgio, 23d May. A.D. 1925.

Pound deletes the connection between the Romagnolo and the Dr Wallushnig scenes. It is up to us, if we think it worth our while, to reconstruct it in our minds. I might add that the unquoted remainder of the Canto presents several more fragments of Pound's assemblage of verbal scenes.

Now, the truth is that neither the sane nor the insane ever think in fragments or delete transitional passages in their own thoughts, unless they are in a condition of delirium. Why then, you may protest, do poets suppress these texts for us readers? Are we enemies from whom important information must be withheld? The answer has to be that the not-saying in a poem, minor or major, plays its part in the artist's overall gamble: will he succeed or will he fail? To succeed, the not-saying must be pregnant with energized meaning; or it must provide energy to some of the uttered meanings; or it must prevent energy from being lost through uttered text. If it does none of these things, the poem suffers.

(3) *Look for leitmotifs*: words, phrases, allusions that are repeated, or synonymized, or modified, or amplified, or corrected, or contrasted, or countermanded, as you proceed through the poem. The recurrence of *hit* and *dog* in 'A Reason' can serve as a beginning instance. The repetition of 'etcetera' by Cummings is another. Here, however, is an ampler illustration from the work of G.M. Hopkins. Pay attention to the words I have italicized and bold-faced.

THE LANTERN OUT OF DOORS

Sometimes a *lantern* moves along the **night**,
   That interests our *eyes*. And who goes there?
   I think; where from and bound, I wonder, where,
With, all down **darkness** wide, his wading *light* ?

Men go by me whom either beauty *bright*
    In mould or mind or what not else makes rare:
    They rain against our **much-thick** and **marsh** air
Rich *beams*, till **death** or **distance** buys them quite.

Death or **distance** soon consumes them: wind
    What most I may *eye* after, be in at the end
I cannot, and out of *sight* is out of mind.

Christ minds; Christ's interest, what to avow or amend
    There, *eyes* them, heart wants, care haunts, foot follows kind,
Their ransom, their rescue, ánd first, fast, last friend.[5]

These repetitions, modifications, contrasts and so on provide important markers for us that trace out pathways of meaning. When we are faced with a difficult poem, one of our early moves should be to look for these signposts.

(4) 'Theoretical physics,' writes a scientist, 'is a science of approximations. What counts is the ability to see what is "big" and what is "small"—which effects are important and which can be neglected.' True words that apply to art in general, literature in particular and poetry most especially. The repetitions we have just observed, the leitmotifs as they would be called in music, are clearly 'crowns' of meaning—important moments in the text—by virtue of the very fact that the poet insists on them. But in any text—whether or not it displays these signposts—in any poem that presents some initial difficulty, you could *try to distinguish between words, phrases or clauses that seem to be crowned with essential meanings, and others that merely support and minister to the essentials.* Let us re-read W.H. Auden's 'A Misunderstanding' at this point.

A MISUNDERSTANDING

Just as his dream foretold, he met them all:
The smiling grimy boy at the garage
Ran out before he blew his horn; the tall
Professor in the mountains with his large
Tweed pockets full of plants addressed him hours
Before he would have dared; the deaf girl too
Seemed to expect him at the green chateau;
The meal was laid, the guest room full of flowers.

5.   I have omitted all but one of the prosodic accents put in by the poet. For 'wind', in line 9, the reader had best choose one of the meanings (and pronunciations!) the dictionary suggests, and again avoid ambiguity.

More, the talk always took the wished-for turn,
Dwelt on the need for stroking and advice;
Yet, at each meeting, he was forced to learn,
The same misunderstanding would arise.
Which was in need of help? Were they or he
The physician, bridegroom, and incendiary?

Is 'before he blew his horn' in line 3 majesty or retinue? If retinue, shall we crown 'the need for stroking and advice'? Clearly the answer is yes. Even in a short poem, by the way, you are apt to find an alternation between major and minor players in the textual drama, as we might also call these two elements.

(5) Still re-reading Auden's poem, we are faced with its basic enigma, namely the identity of the 'he' visiting the chateau as, possibly, a provocative (incendiary) healer who is himself in need of healing (?). Might he be a psychotherapist? Does that hypothesis at any rate fit every element of the text? Or do we need to run off-stage again and switch on a biographical light? And who is the 'he' in line 6 of Rich's 'A Valediction Forbidding Mourning'? The truth is that *modern poets love to play with personal pronouns to which they refuse to attach specific referents.* They prefer to have us readers supply a name or at any rate a type. As usual, this is a challenge we will happily accept if we like the poem to begin with.

'He' could even be the equivalent of the poetic or real 'I':

MEETING THE MOUNTAINS

He crawls to the edge of the foaming creek
He backs up the slab ledge
He puts a finger in the water
He turns to a trapped pool
Puts both hands in the water
Puts one foot in the pool
Drops pebbles in the pool
He slaps the water surface with both hands
He cries out, rises up and stands
Facing toward the torrent and the mountain
Raises up both hands and shouts three times![6]

6. Gary Snyder (b. 1930) in *Regarding Wave* (New York: New Directions, 1970). 'Shouts three times' is a cluster of first-ring beads that make important sense only via a more abstract idea (e.g. 'he is exalted' or 'he manifests his joyful unity with nature') that 'collects' numerous first-ring statements *and* non-verbal experiences.

Most readers will suppose that the poet is really talking about an experience of his own. However, as anyone would guess, the most frequent character to appear in poetry is a bare-faced *I* and *me* towing their *my* and *mine*. The elementary advice to be given here is not to worry whether this 'I' truly represents the author or whether it is a mask he has decided to wear. When we read a poem like Donne's 'The Apparition' and numberless others written in the first person, the problem of what they mean (if there is a problem at all) has nothing to do with the question whether the 'I' is truly, truly the author pouring his heart out, or 'a speaker'.

If we feel that biographical information might elucidate certain passages, we should never be stopped merely because the 'I' is perfectly obviously *not* the author; not even when, as in 'The Mother of God', the poem is a first-person narrative fiction remote in time and place from its author. Moreover, neither there nor in 'The Hanging Man' do we rule out biographical information on the ground that the speaker is of one sex and the poet another. I who am a male adult can impress some urge, fear or idea of mine on any character I choose to create: the mother of God, any woman, a child, a ghost, an ancient hero, a dog, a tree, and, as we shall see, a snail. So then, if you think that my 'I poem' in which the I is clearly not I might be explicated through a reference to some letters I sent my mother 25 years ago, by all means refer to it—if you can.

(6) But beware! I have encouraged you so far to look for off-stage illumination when the text apparently fails to speak for itself. Now, however, you must be cautioned that tact and prudence are called for when you go foraging into the poet's other works, his life and letters, his sources, the historical moment in which he happened to live, etc. For example, we may be helped by finding out that Wallace Stevens had indeed been reading Nietzsche at the time he composed his poem, and that the poem originally appeared during World War I. But could not Stevens have made use of his reading, and of the concepts and words he got from his reading, for his own quite different purposes? We must always allow for a 'mental space' between, on one side, the facts of and pressures on a poet's personal life and readings, or the socio-economic conditions (or any other 'large' conditions) in which he lived, and, on the other side, the words he decided to

place on paper. If a poet writes mysteriously about black things, it may be of help to ascertain that he was just then concerned with death, or ignorance, or the different races of mankind, or interstellar space. But even if we know him to have been obsessed with one or the other of these matters, there is no airtight guarantee that the obsession influenced that particular passage. For all we know, the poet may have taken a holiday from his obsession that one time. 'Handle with care,' then, is our parting precept for offstage data—and our final practical pointer.

APPENDIX

'A Valediction Forbidding Mourning' illustrates a number of points made so far in this book.

(1) Mentally supplying bridges between the fragments of a text. In line 1, for instance, we might plausibly (not certainly!) insert 'to unfreeze' between the two incomplete sentences. Between lines 4 and 5 we might imagine a transition toward a (mental?) hospital, where the treatment only made matters worse. (Of course the drug and the wounds might be metaphors for a purely social or psychological situation.) Before line 9 (note the absence of punctuation marks) we could insert an 'I remember'—namely, the sight of some poster promising a cure. And in front of the isolated line 11, where the poet seems to claim a superior humanity for herself over the rest of mankind, we might imagine a phrase like 'When I die I want,' unless we prefer 'I am like.'

(2) Deciding parts of speech. In line 1, is 'wants' a verb in the third person singular, with 'swirling' as its subject, or a plural noun, with 'swirling' as its qualifying adjective? Or either, or both?

(3) Decompressing compressed passages, for example, guessing something like 'when we enjoyed it together' or a contrary 'when I didn't know you' after line 14, or, with a higher degree of probability, restoring a suppressed 'I want' at the start of the last line.

(4) Coping with first-ring sets of beads that fail to thread into our core, like 'I rode my bicycle into the pudding.' Thus line 2 could become 'language defeated me', an intelligible equivalent that seems to be confirmed by line 12, perhaps to be read as 'I can't make a direct, clear statement.' Or glossing line 7 perhaps as 'The experience of repeating over and over again my futile attempt to communicate is like a death.'

(5) Looking for leitmotifs. Here, obviously, repeated references to speaking, communicating, expressing oneself.

(6) Distinguishing between essential and subordinate elements. Are 'hair, glacier, flashlight' absolutely essential to the poem, or might Rich have

chosen other 'unglossed' (unexplained) images, just as Auden, in 'A Misunderstanding', might have selected a housemaid instead of a grimy boy.

(7) Catching a drift, even if the poem can't be pinned down with high precision. From what has been said so far, I think the drift is clear enough—a radical and desperate failure to reach others or one other with words, perhaps a mental breakdown, perhaps a divorce, perhaps even a contemplated suicide.

(8) Formulating hypotheses both for individual passages and for the poem as a whole. This is what we have been doing in this appendix. Should some other hypotheses be tried?

(9) Finding that form often expresses content. Compare with Susan Howe's 'five princes' in Chapter 5. In Rich's poem, grammatical fragmentation and disconnectedness reproduce, in themselves and as such (i.e. aside from what the propositions convey), the mental disarray the poem expresses in its words.

(10) Seeking off-stage illumination. Is the enigmatic and fragmentary character of the poem, and the drift of meaning it radiates, satisfying enough? Or would a fuller 'taking possession' of its propositions yield an even stronger pleasure? If so, we will want to read more poetry and prose by the poet, look for cues in whatever we can find out about her life, and read the commentaries of those who have written about her. Any or all of these explorations outside the text of the poem may explicate some of its mysteries—that poster in the bus, for instance—and perhaps increase our satisfaction as a result. We will not go to the trouble, of course, if we dislike the poem as it stands.

Chapter 11

Acceptable and Unacceptable Propositions

I ask you to return for a moment to our definition of Art, as boxed in Chapter 1 and then again in Chapter 5; and to pick out—for the second time, as it happens—one of those 'minor' words that sometimes make their way into sentences, unnoticed even by the writers themselves. The work of art, our definition tells us, produces pleasure *largely* through the energizing of appropriate materials. Chances are that this 'largely' escaped your attention. Even now, as I detach it for observation, it looks like the kind of word one throws in just to be prudent—to forestall querulous readers who might be lying in wait with objections. The fact, however, is that 'largely' plays an essential role in this guidebook. It is emphatically not a throw-away word.

What 'largely' implies is that something else produces pleasure (if pleasure is produced at all) besides the poet's talent in energizing his propositions. That something is simply the power of the bare, pre-energized propositions as such. All the notions the poet will work with and work upon exist *beforehand* radiating already, for this or that portion of the public, a certain degree of built-in energy—that is to say, a presumed power to arouse feelings and therefore, potentially, to thrill. Whether we paraphrase in our own prosaic words an approximation of a stated proposition in the poem, or formulate in our own prosaic words an implied one that we have deduced from the poet's words—either way, the prose propositions possess a certain energy *to begin with*. Thus, although our pleasure in the poem is due 'largely' to the energizing of propositions, it owes something as well to their intrinsic raw,[1] pre-poetic power. In Chapter 13 we will see that energizing raw propositions *ipso facto* alters them to a degree, and vitally so. But for the time being we can allow ourselves to ignore this phenomenon.

Analogies readily come to mind. For instance, a wonderful meal is the result not only of the magic the chef has performed upon his ingredients; the ingredients themselves come beforehand pregnant with their intrinsic quality. Or: the beauty of a building depends not only on how the architect has disposed his building materials; the building materials themselves display a certain quality to begin with. Or: a body given an impulse of energy will move at a higher velocity if it was already in motion in the same direction.

In literature, colorless pre-poetic raw statements like 'my love is beautiful', 'let us enjoy ourselves while we are young', 'duty not enjoyment is the aim of life', 'here was a man we thought happy and yet he committed suicide', 'the voice of a singing girl deeply moved me', 'I tell the tale of Sir Lancelot who loved Queen Guinevere yet remained loyal to King Arthur', 'may God protect my country', 'patriotism is a disgrace to mankind', 'a brilliant person ought to beget children', 'let poetry evoke moods and not philosophize', 'war is exciting', 'war is hell', and a million others, exercise a power over most of us most of the time, distinctly greater than a statement like 'bookshelves should be at least eight inches deep'. Even blandly stated, they are more energetic than the mass of daily propositions that make up the routine of ordinary life. And more energetic whether we agree with them or not; whether they seem true or false to us; whether we have or have not experienced what they report; and whether or not they make us wiser or better. No wonder therefore that poems usually form themselves out of these more significant and therefore potentially more satisfying raw propositions. All other things being equal, the better of two poems is the one whose raw propositions—stated or implied—excite us more than those of its rival. Its raw material is, so to speak, in motion to begin with, hence will receive more benefit from an input of new energy.

Of course, other things are seldom if ever equal. To pursue another one of our analogies, you might spoil a house even

---

1.   'Raw' means 'pre-refined', 'pre-treated' throughout this discussion, as in 'raw material'; not 'crude', as in 'raw humor'.

though you were using the very best materials, while your fellow-builder might produce a superior dwelling even though his materials were relatively poor. For here we come upon another one of our facts of the aesthetic life: however thrilling a raw, pre-poetic proposition is in itself, it cannot ever, ever account in itself for the success of a poem. That is why our definition insists that success must be *largely* due to the operations the poet performs upon the raw propositions. Imagine the most electrifying of all possible ideas: 'We shall be happily reunited with our loved ones after death.' What idea could be more moving and powerful *to begin with*, before literature has taken hold of it? And yet, even this—or any stirring proposition you care to formulate—is but a resource for the poet. All the perspiration is still to come. If every great theme guaranteed good poetry, the world would be flooded with masterpieces, all written by theologians, philosophers and physicists.[2] No: the poet is an *artist* (let us never forget it); his grand enterprise is not to invent propositions but to energize them, no matter what amount of energy they possessed before he began to work on them. All the same, he makes a better start with exciting propositions than with something on the order of 'We need another spoon on the table.'

Keep in mind that we are talking about propositions at every level: those that are stated in the poem; those that the stated ones imply for us; and those intimated by any devices of form that the poet applies to his text. Also that we are talking both about the individual propositions (intelligible semantic units) and the overarching ones (subjects and themes). And also that the propositions can be stories, ideas, descriptions, characterizations, moods—whatever.

If you are wondering whether the poet literally operates by taking hold of some raw proposition and then rolling up his mental sleeves in order to make it beautiful, powerful, magical or

2.   This is equally, and most vividly, true in the visual arts. Choosing a great theme is easy; painting it well is hard. This is charmingly suggested in one of our best comic strips, 'Calvin and Hobbes' by Bill Watterson, where Calvin's imaginary tiger-friend helps him draw a tiger for school, informing Calvin as he does so, 'The good thing about drawing a tiger is that it automatically makes your picture fine art.' The reader of this most sophisticated strip is to understand that the amiable tiger is dead wrong.

funny—as a diamond cutter picks up the unlovely rough stone, places it in a vise and then applies it to the rotating disk in order to create the facets that turn it into a precious jewel—the answer to your query is that poets work in all sorts of ways; indeed, that any given poet may work in different ways at different times. Sometimes he does act like the diamond cutter, beginning with raw propositions and then trying his best to 'bring them to life'. Sometimes a perfected energized proposition strikes him all formed. More often this perfected proposition turns out to be less perfect than he had believed at first, and then he proceeds to perfect it (he hopes) by the sweat of his brow. Sometimes he has not even a raw proposition in mind when he begins: a word, a phrase, a rhythm may excite his imagination, and notions will come later.

Our business, however, is not with the secrets of the poet's shop, but with the product that comes out of it. We leave him alone hammering away at his words in his own private way and proceed to the topic announced by the heading of this chapter. Let us start with our architectural image again. Although a beautiful house can unquestionably be built out of less-than-optimal materials, somewhere a line must be drawn; there is a limit to this hopeful principle. A superb mansion cannot be built of twigs. Similarly, a superb poem cannot be built out of what I choose to call 'unacceptable' propositions. You have certainly understood by now that I am not about to sneak a dictator into our discussion—some awe-inspiring personage who will decide for us what is and what is not acceptable. As before, each one of us judges; but as before, I am operating upon the axiom that we all fall into more or less large and more or less durable groups. In any event, the underlying principle remains: raw propositions weaken or kill the poem for any reader who finds them unacceptable; and this, no matter how the poet has gone about trying to energize them.[3]

I am using a vague term like 'unacceptable' in order to cover the largest possible territory. But now we need to ask what in fact is unacceptable to people. Broadly speaking, people *cannot* enjoy poems (or any other literary works) whose raw propositions they regard as one or more of the following:

---

3. This includes the alterations that, as I have mentioned before, the act of energizing inevitably produces and will be discussed in Chapter 13.

> stupid
> evil (vicious, disgusting, odious, vile)
> dull (boring)
> emotionally unbearable

Stupid, vile, dull or unbearable propositions, like the twigs with which you might vainly try to build a mansion, constitute resources that cannot be energized so as to satisfy any reader who regards them as such.

No one enjoys a stupid poem. Summon to your mind a person you bluntly rate as a simpleton. Be assured that this simpleton is perfectly contemptuous of any poem *he* considers fundamentally dumb. And now imagine a person whom you consider extremely evil. That person too, just like you and me (who are of course very good), dislikes poems *he* considers evil. And dullards dislike poems they find dull just as the most fascinating people in the world do.

I will speak separately in the next chapter of the area occupied by unbearable art—poems or other works of art that terribly upset us without being stupid or odious.

An immediate corollary of these several axioms is that, inasmuch as there are gradations in our judgments of what is dull, stupid or morally offensive, so there are degrees to which poems are injured for us through failures in these areas. For instance, a feeling that the theme of a poem is morally deficient will injure the poem less in my mind than a reaction of utter hatred for its propositions.

Looking at things from the positive side, we can affirm that all readers demand that the raw, pre-energized propositions of a poem be acceptably intelligent, moral and interesting. 'Acceptably' is not only a very broad adverb; it is also a modest one. Why do I not say 'highly' or 'extremely' intelligent, moral and interesting? How is it that a merely 'acceptable' proposition suffices for the creation of a successful poem? I have already given the reason: so very much depends on the energizing skill of the artist that, like a great chef handed average ingredients yet concocting an unforgettable meal, the good poet can be trusted with modest propositional resources. Granted that, all other things being equal (again!) the grander propositions will yield the grander poem. But the proof is in the pudding; and the truth for literature is that many poems on relatively small subjects are venerated classics, thanks to what their creators accomplished with the pre-poetic propositions they manipulated. I could go back to ancient Greece and Rome for any number of examples; in Chapter 3 I quoted a very modest lyric by Shakespeare; but here is another illustration:

UPON JULIA'S VOICE

So smooth, so sweet, so silv'ry is thy voice,
As, could they hear, the Damn'd would make no noise,
But listen to thee (walking in thy chamber)
Melting melodious words to Lutes of Amber.[4]

If the pre-poetic subject—namely 'a compliment to a girl's beautiful voice'—is acceptably interesting and intelligent for you, and if it does not shock your morals, the poet has at any rate materials of sufficient quality to make a fine poem for you. And this on the basis of something distinctly less grandiose than the fate of the cosmos. Now examine one of the individual propositions in the poem. I paraphrase it by saying that Herrick imagines the very damned stopping their din in order to listen to the lady. For me, at any rate, this is a modestly witty little thought, and for me it is already 'something': an invention, an act of the poetic imagination, even when presented in my colorless prose words.[5] And again, nothing earth-shaking has transpired. Good poems do not require earth-shaking thought or moral fervor. In a word: our 'acceptable' will do.

All this time I have been sedulously avoiding the word 'true' in favor of 'interesting' and 'intelligent'. Not, however, because the notion of 'truth' offers insuperable philosophical difficulties in the present context. As far as this book is concerned, 'true' means nothing more arduous than 'seems true to the reader'—and we know that all of us have strong opinions regarding what is true and what is false without bothering to check into the absolute nature of Truth. The real point is that in works of art we tend to

4.   Robert Herrick, in *Hesperides* (1648). 'Chamber' should be pronounced to rhyme with 'amber'.
5.   Herrick's poem is of course highly energized by its verbal music; its first line alone is a tiny masterwork in this respect. See Chapters 14 and 15 for an extensive treament of this subject.

accept propositions (stated or implied) that appear untrue to us, provided they seem reasonably intelligent, interesting and morally acceptable.

Our friend 'The Red Wheelbarrow' can be cited again in this connection. Williams, you will recall, is telling us that certain humble things in life have great importance. Suppose you feel that this is deeply true; and then suppose I offer a pseudo-Williams poem by turning the 'so much' of his first line on its head:

> nothing depends
> upon
>
> a red wheel
> barrow
>
> glazed with rain
> water
>
> beside the white
> chickens.

Is the poem poisoned for you because it now makes a claim that, according to our premise, you regard as untrue? I doubt it. For the fake version is as intelligent as the original. It suggests that we value things in a perfectly disinterested way, we love them when they are perfectly inconsequential. Be that as it may, the point I am making is that most of us can, and in fact do, enjoy works of art with whose propositions we disagree. The artist claims that so and so is true. We feel that the opposite is true. And yet we like what we are reading; we admire the poem. Clearly, it is enough for us that the propositions be acceptably intelligent, moral and interesting.

Here is the finale to the first Epistle of Alexander Pope's *Essay on Man*, published in 1733:

> All Nature is but art, unknown to thee;
> All chance, direction, which thou canst not see;
> All discord, harmony not understood;
> All partial evil, universal good:
> And, spite of pride, in erring reason's spite,
> One truth is clear, WHATEVER IS, IS RIGHT.

Against this, set 'A Dirge' by Percy Bysshe Shelley, published posthumously in 1824:

Rough wind, that moanest loud
  Grief too sad for song;
Wild wind, when sullen cloud
  Knells all the night long;

Sad storm, whose tears are vain,
  Bare woods, whose branches strain,
Deep caves and dreary main,—
  Wail, for the world's wrong![6]

If, like most readers, you admit both poems to your private canon (both are already securely lodged in the established one), it is obvious that truth has not been your criterion, for if one poem is right about the world, the other must be wrong. 'Sufficient intelligence' has been the test applied. We may have our doubts about the validity of both sweeping statements; we may agree with one and not the other; we may lean in one direction or the other; we may feel that 'it's all a question of what mood you happen to be in'—any of these responses is compatible with a love of both poems. But should your verdict be that one of the two is stupid, evil or dull, this would present a fatal or near-fatal obstacle to your aesthetic pleasure.

However, I do not mean to suggest that the true/false category of judgment is flatly inapplicable to Art in general and poetry in particular. Invoking once again our old friend 'all other things being equal', we can assert that if they are, we invariably prefer poems whose propositions we deem true to poems whose propositions seem in error, for the combination 'intelligent-and-true' is unquestionably more satisfying than 'intelligent' alone. But the fact remains that, whereas a basic intelligence is an absolute requisite for us before we can admire a poem, truth is not.

Similarly, even though, as we have seen, a poem need not be instructive in order to please (whether you take this term in the narrow sense of giving out new information, or in the generous

6.   The comma in the last line is the best possible reminder that the basic resource of poetry consists not only of words but also of 'related signs'. Consider how Shelley's meaning would be subverted and redirected if the comma were left out. Furthermore, that little 'for' would be a key agent in redirecting the poet's theme, since it would leap from one of its meanings to a very different one. Remember, in this connection, Chapter 9 (5) concerning 'articulators'.

sense of somehow making you a wiser person, with deeper and richer insights into Life), it cannot be gainsaid that 'intelligent-and-instructive' produces more enjoyment than 'intelligent' alone. We amply covered this topic in our chapter on the mediated and unmediated pleasures of art, where we saw that additions to our stock of wisdom (like increases in our bank accounts) are desirable without, however, being conditions for the success of any work of art.

So much for truth and instruction. Returning now to the basic dimension of intelligence versus stupidity, I suggest we examine a couple of illustrative poems. With our several constituencies in mind, I shall assume that I am now addressing students and other persons at a fairly high level of sophistication along the continuum who will not be offended if I retrieve Eddie Guest's deplorably useful poem and display it as a work ruined (for 'us') by, among other things, a radical failure of intelligence.

DEPARTED FRIENDS

> The dead friends live and always will;
> Their presence hovers round us still.
> It seems to me they come to share
> Each joy or sorrow that we bear.
> Among the living I can feel
> The sweet departed spirits steal,
> And whether it be weal or woe,
> I walk with those I used to know.
> I can recall them to my side
> Whenever I am struggle-tied;
> I've but to wish for them, and they
> Come trooping gayly down the way,
> And I can tell to them my grief
> And from their presence find relief.
> In sacred memories below
> Still live the friends of long ago.

Now, there are reasons other than lack of intelligence why this is a very poor poem for a certain class of readers. Here are four of them: the babyish sing-song rhythm and rhymes that run counter to the gravity of the theme; the syntactic clumsiness of line 13 ('And I can tell to them my grief') caused by the versifier's wish to keep the sing-song going; commonplaces of the 'sacred memories' variety[7]; and the repetition of one and the same idea so that the poem walks without advancing. But what is chiefly relevant at present is the jaunty ease with which the writer is comforted. It seems that for him death is a downright jolly experience. Is he in a bad mood? He summons his dead friends; they come running; all is well again. They even come running, or rather trooping, *gaily*. There is not a speck of black in Guest's rose-colored glasses. Indeed, so childish is the poem's idea of death that the only compliment the poet deserves is that his infantile sing-song music is, after all, congruous with his childish concept.

Another weakness is that no propositions radiate from those that are stated over and over again. Guest's 'basic English' hints at nothing beyond itself. This is poverty of intellect and poverty of invention (imagination). Metaphorically, we speak of such a work as *flat*.

For most readers, even if they do not believe in an afterlife, an optimistic view of our departed friends can be acceptably intelligent. But intelligent readers cannot accept so light-hearted, so bouncing a disregard of the pain and sorrow that normally flow from the death of our friends. This sort of simplification (usually called 'sentimentality') strikes them as so silly that it cannot be energized into a valuable serious poem.

As a powerful contrast, we read John Milton's sonnet on his wife, written in 1658, when Catherine Woodcock died in her twenty-ninth year.

> Methought I saw my late espoused Saint
>   Brought to me like Alcestis from the grave,
>   Whom Jove's great Son to her glad Husband gave,
>   Rescued from death though pale and faint.
> Mine as whom washt from spot of child-bed taint,
>   Purification in the old Law did save,
>   And such as yet once more I trust to have
>   Full sight of her in Heaven without restraint,
> Came vested all in white, pure as her mind:

---

7. The trouble with commonplaces is not that they are stupid or untrue-to-life, but rather a combination of two defects: *what* they say has been said too often before, and *how* they say it has been heard too often before. This double defect drains them of energy. Of course, what is a commonplace for you may not be one for me; but as usual, there is a very large group-consent in these matters.

> Her face was veil'd, yet to my fancied sight,
>   Love, sweetness, goodness, in her person shin'd
> So clear, as in no face with more delight.
>   But O, as to embrace me she inclin'd,
>   I wak'd, she fled, and day brought back my night.[8]

Perhaps the first contrasting element we notice is the density and complexity of the music and the syntax, which are as congruous with the complexity of the thought (the propositions) as the namby-pamby music and syntax was with the childish matter in Guest's verses.

Also noteworthy are the allusive propositions that draw into the poem three worlds: the pagan, the Hebrew and the Christian; here is no poverty of invention!

But the essential intelligence is that, unlike our poetaster, Milton knows that death is a hard foe to conquer, even for the faithful Christian; and this, as we have seen, is an intelligence we cannot dispense with. His Alcestis does not come 'trooping gayly' out of Hades in order to go out for a post-mortem hamburger with her hubby Admetus. Emerging from death after her dark sacrifice, she is understandably 'pale and faint'. As for the dead wife, whose face is veiled, the poet *trusts* he will see her in Heaven; yet as he holds out his arms to her, she vanishes, and the poem, despite that trust, ends sadly upon the word 'night'. This gives us the density or complexity—the intellectual stature—such a subject requires. We feel it even in the paraphrase—in the raw approximate propositions before they have been refined into poetry.

Just as we can state axiomatically that a stupid poem is a bad poem, so we posit the axiom that an odious poem is a bad poem. Again I add: 'as judged by any given reader'. If we hate what the poem admires or advocates, or love what the poem hates, the poem sickens or dies for us. Remember that I have allowed for degrees in this process; but the point is most sharply made by considering the extreme positions. Since my readers are unknown

8. Alcestis, the heroine of a play by Euripides, offers herself to Death in lieu of her husband, but is rescued by Heracles, son of Jove (Zeus). In lines 5-6 Milton says that he sees his wife like a Hebrew woman ritually purified after childbirth (Katherine Woodcock had borne him a child in the year before her death.) These two lines will yield their meaning more easily if you read them 'Mine, as *one* whom', etc. A good example, by the way, of compression.

to me, I cannot easily give 'universal' instances. But you can see that a member of the Ku Klux Klan will probably be repelled by a poem exalting the black race, and that a Jew will draw away in horror from a poem singing the praises of Nazi gas chambers. Some persons are violently disgusted by the explosion of genital display in all the representational arts of our time, including the art of poetry, and therefore cannot abide the works in which this occurs. It is true that educated people today are on the whole more tolerant than their educated ancestors were. We are not obsessed, like our forefathers, with a thousand-and-one damnable heresies, sins and taboos. All the same, we too, no matter how sophisticated we are, nurture our moral loves and hatreds, especially in the social-economic-political arenas of the moral world. A perfectly amoral, indifferent person would exhibit a total tolerance for any moral-political point of view whatsoever in a work of art. But I doubt that such a person exists. These years, for instance, many intellectuals who disdain 'conventional morality' are disgusted by works of art in which they detect an oppressive attitude toward women or victims of colonial domination. I doubt that many of our elite readers could bring themselves to admire poems that advocate forcing children to work in the mines, obtaining confessions in our jails by torture or even sending women back to housework, minding babies and darning their husbands' socks. They also tend to dislike patriotic works of art. In practice, to be sure, the moral revulsion that kills aesthetic delight is a rare occurrence, because poets normally reach and interact with the very group whose ethics they share. But the axiom stands nonetheless. The less moral a poem is (from our point of view), the less we will like it—all other things (as usual) being equal. The more moral a poem is (from our point of view), the better we will like it. And at the boundary, both phenomena come to their logical conclusions. On the one side, as mentioned already, profound moral revulsion will poison aesthetic pleasure. But on the other side it may happen that a moral stand in a poem makes us so deliriously happy that, overlooking all manner of defects in the artistry, we are aesthetically carried away.[9]

9. Here is a not untypical call for scripts by a theater company in New York City: 'The group is dedicated to produce new plays which promote the understanding of cultural diversity and will strive to serve as an educational

An interesting side-issue is that our moral revulsion can also poison a work of art not because of the work as such, but because we hate the person (or group) that produced or even just admired it. For example, fifty years after the Holocaust, the Israeli Philharmonic Orchestra still refused to play the music of Richard Wagner, who disliked Jews and whose music Adolf Hitler admired; while the Nazis, in their few but lethal years of power, prohibited as best they could music composed or literature written by Jews.

At the other pole, a burst of sympathy or love for a person may cause us to be charmed or moved by almost anything whatsoever this person has produced. It is then no longer a case of sympathizing with a proposition *in* the poem, but approving of the person who wrote it. Take the following little poem:

> 'Twas midnight and he sat alone,
> The husband of the dead.
> That day the dark dust had been thrown
> Upon her buried head.
> Her orphan children round me sleep,
> But in their sleep do moan.
> Now bitter tears are falling fast.
> I feel that I'm alone.

As poetry, this is not much better than 'Departed Friends.' And yet, when we discover that these lines were scribbled in 1853 by a broken-hearted pioneer (John Tucker Scoot by name) on the harsh Oregon Trail, a burst of sympathy may well make us like the poem with a liking we withhold from a professional poetaster like Eddie Guest.[10]

Turning very briefly to our next category: Many raw, pre-energized propositions—many basic subjects or themes—are neither stupid nor vicious in our opinion but merely uninteresting. They

process.' This does not imply that the producers dislike, say, fluffy farces; but it does imply that they will, inevitably, experience a greater satisfaction (other things being equal) when they see a work of art that conforms to their moral passions. Hundreds of similar citations could be garnered, whether at the rather naive level of the one I have chosen, or from the writings of the most sophisticated critics.

10. The poem is printed by Stephen Dow Beckham in his *Many Faces: An Anthology of Oregon Autobiography* (Corvallis: Oregon State University Press, 1993).

bore us. Nothing, we feel, that the poet can do with them will arouse much or any enthusiasm in us. Examples? This is even harder than before—if, that is, we try to rise above the level of ideas regarding the depth of bookshelves. Topics that leave some of us cold are apt to fascinate others. One of my readers might be fundamentally uninterested in minute descriptions of nature; another in theological speculations; another in tales about King Arthur. Boring his audience is probably the sort of failure an artist dreads the most; and when we examine the history of any of the arts, we often see that once exciting types of painting, music and literature ended in the dustbin of history because later generations found them merely tedious.

This leaves us with the fourth class of unacceptable propositions to be considered—those that are neither morally revolting nor stupid, and quite the contrary of dull, namely emotionally devastating. I propose that we take up this subject in the next chapter, at the end of our discussion of emotions in general.

Chapter 12

Emotions

I

'Satisfaction' is the only feeling mentioned in our definition: of Art in general, of literature, and of poetry in particular. I remind you that there is nothing sacrosanct about this word. I like its simplicity; but you will find other and grander ways elsewhere of naming the ultimate emotion that vibrates in us when we rejoice in a work of art. Another reminder: the intensity of this satisfaction varies, and we welcome the little pleasures Art affords as well as the highest raptures.

A third reminder: although raw, pre-poetic propositions can move us in themselves, in the work of art they are invariably *charged* ('energized' is the word used in our definition) in a variety of ways. For instance, they are given a *form* that they otherwise do not possess. Form is a way of *ordering* the materials and resources of a work of art. And human beings generally welcome and admire the ordering of phenomena—indeed, from some very deep biological causes. The satisfaction we take in a well-crafted form is thus one of the emotions connected with works of art.

The raw propositions in their intellectual and moral power, the form, the music, the special words through which the raw propositions are refined, and an endless variety of rhetorical maneuvers that further empower the text—all these fuse (when successful!) so as to endow the intelligence of a text with a certain emotional quality and a certain intensity *in* that quality. A poem feels melancholy, or cutting, or serene, or bleak and dreary, or terrifying, or sprightly, and so on. Cummings's 'My sweet old etcetera' is obviously sarcastic in 'tone'. Herrick's 'Upon Julia's Clothes' can be called delicately charming. Artists have even discovered that appearing to *suppress* the emotionality of a text (matter-of-factness, understatement, 'tough talk') might deliver more emotion to the reader than turning the full orchestra loose. Remember Robert Creeley's

> Let me hit you.
> Will it hurt.

— with its suppression of a 'warm' question mark in favor of a 'cool' period. Not so incidentally, power-through-understatement ('less is more') is largely practiced nowadays in the other arts as well. Early in the twentieth century the lush orchestrations of Gustav Mahler and Richard Strauss gave way to the dry tones of Alban Berg and Anton Webern, while in the visual arts the luxuriance of Delacroix and the Symbolists yielded to the coolness of Braque, Mondrian, Klee and many others. But Sahara-dry or Amazon-copious, the successful work of art is like a vibrating object that produces a vibration in response. The consciousness of these inner vibrations is the happiness that successful Art begets in us.

Thus, our definition of Art makes no attempt to specify emotional quality or intensity. A successful work of art can have evoked any one or several of a great number of moods (another useful name for feelings and emotions) at almost any degree of intensity—and even alternations of moods that feel like contradictory emotions within us. Indeed, feelings are impossible to enumerate; not, perhaps, because there are so many of them, but because they come in so many shades and are often too subtle, too private for labeling. Our vocabulary for the inner life is largely a groping in the dark—the dark of each unique inner life. It is ever so much easier to name what we see than what we feel—blushing, goose-pimples and swooning, for instance. Compare such public manifestations of emotions with attempted inner-world descriptions like 'I detect in this poem a beginning of joy still tinged with rueful melancholy.' No wonder that beginners had rather give an account of 'what the poem says' than formulate precisely what they feel.

One thing is sure: we human beings are restless creatures that want to be stirred. We go chasing almost untiringly after pleasurable excitement. The Chinese philosopher meditating in perfect silence on a bluff overlooking a lake seeks the joy of deep emotion in that silence as truly as the American teenager looking for it in the bawling and banging of a rock concert. I mentioned our movie house experience in the first chapter of this book, where I spoke of our progress from near-indifference as we settle into our seat to the growing excitement that takes hold of us when the motion picture begins to 'grab' us. Of course, we have entered the theater *in order* to be stirred. The very names of some of our motion picture theaters bespeak excitement: Rialto, Alhambra, Lido—as if to say that Main Street is a bore. Normal humdrum life does not electrify us sufficiently to satisfy our needs.

When a work of art has thoroughly satisfied us, another emotion is born; and this one is easily named: admiration. We readily speak of 'an admirable lyric by Tennyson' or, more briefly and pointedly in the world of the visual arts, 'an admirable Monet'. Beethoven expressed this emotion for all of us when he spoke of Handel to a friend: 'I would uncover my head, and kneel down at his tomb!' We are told of certain twin stars in the heavens—two bodies shackled by the force of gravity into an eternal dance around one another. So it goes with the admiration that dances round our delight: admiration for the work the artist has created, admiration for the artist who created it, or else, if the artist is unknown, admiration for the unknown but living individual force that made the thing we love.

No wonder, therefore, that if we discover lack of originality or downright plagiarism in a work of art we loved, the ensuing collapse of admiration—'so this was not *his* idea after all!'—brings about an immediate deflation of our aesthetic pleasure. That is how we punish 'mere imitators.'

II

Do we know for sure that the poet intended us to feel the particular emotions we experience as we read his work? Seldom. Seldom do we have indubitable proof of his intentions. If and when we are convinced that we do know what he intended us to feel, we remain as free as before to feel whatever the text made us feel.

Do we know for sure what *he* felt as he was composing? Rarely if ever.

Is it possible that he felt nothing like the mood his text produces in us? Yes, quite possible. We cannot even exclude the possibility that a passionate work of art was produced in a mood of cynical calculation.

Do all the people who like a poem experience the same feelings? Most improbably.

Are we therefore (once again!) threatened with chaos? Certainly not. What is true of meaning is also true of feeling. We differ in detail within a broad sameness. We laugh pretty much in the same places. We cry pretty much in the same places. No one— no one, at any rate, in our culture[1]—registers the following lines by Donne as placid:

> At the round earth's imagined corners, blow
> Your trumpets, angels! and arise, arise,
> From death, you numberless infinities
> Of souls, and to your scatter'd bodies go.[2]

No one apprehends Shelley's 'Dirge' as angry or merry:

> Rough wind, that moanest loud
>   Grief too sad for song;
> Wild wind, when sullen cloud
>   Knells all the night long;
> Sad storm, whose tears are vain,
>   Bare woods, whose branches strain,
> Deep caves and dreary main,—
>   Wail, for the world's wrong!

III

Few natural phenomena are as frightening as the blow to our houses and streets struck by a violent earthquake. Suppose someone writes a poem that powerfully expresses this frightfulness. An

---

1. This is a qualification worth keeping in mind. The feelings as well as the meanings of numerous works of art depend on a sort of cultural collusion between work and audience. Works of art do not register outside the cultural circle as they do inside. Take 'my sweet old etcetera'. A person belonging to a truly distant culture (distant in time or place or both) might very well not catch the poet's sarcasm at all.

2. John Donne, opening lines of No. 7 of his *Holy Sonnets*. The second and third lines rhyme.

obvious point, but one that needs to be made, is that fright for fright, the feeling of terror during the real earthquake is not the same as the feeling of terror produced by that representation, however successful and 'true to life', as long as the representation is felt as art, that is to say, as a man-made form. Should we ever witness the Resurrection of the dead, it will feel quite unlike the emotion Donne's lines produce, no matter how intense they seem to us. But this is true also of happy events, like walking among the daffodils. I am not saying, however, that real-life emotion is always and necessarily stronger than the feelings aroused by works of art. It is just possible, for instance, that Wordsworth instills in some readers a stronger pleasure in his poem than what they would feel while actually walking among the daffodils, even if they were lucky enough not to be stung by a swarm of mosquitoes. In short, even where poets try to reproduce, in their text, the authentic feel and mood of an event, the text, being just that, a text, inevitably delivers something else, however close to the real-life feelings.

But beyond this, the poet can drop the resemblance altogether. He may incite within us emotions-from-the-text startlingly different from the expected emotions-from-the-real-thing. This was beautifully said by the fifteenth-century Spanish poet Juan de Mena: 'The last hours of Priam were no more lamentable than Homer wished them to be.'[3] But the very sharpest break between art and life occurs at the moment the artist introduces the emotion of the *comic.* This is a very large subject, which, as far as literature is concerned, has received far more attention with respect to the novel and drama than in connection with poetry. And yet an enormous amount of good poetry strikes the comic note too. Or rather: the comic notes, in the plural, for humor can sweep across the gamut from the lightest to the grimmest. What is so remarkable about humor for our present purpose is that incidents treated by artists so as to make us smile, grin or laugh would seldom amuse us if we truly lived them.[4] We saw a feather-light instance in Armour's ditty on self-admiration. There is nothing

3. Except, to be sure, that it was Virgil, not Homer, who described the final carnage at Troy and the killing of Priam, its king, by the son of Achilles.

4. Nor, by the way, do they often amuse the fictive personages themselves within the comic work.

feather-light about the rampaging ego when we truly own one, or endure it from others.

The craving for fun is universal, and although cats, dogs and monkeys do not laugh or smile (why not? one wonders), they surely experience the emotion of amusement as we do, and some-times even more so—what can compare to the fun kittens at play are having? For human beings, however, humor light or grim is a peculiar way of energizing serious, troubling and even horrifying raw propositions. Its effect in works of art seems to be to 'demote' such propositions so as to make them acceptable and emotionally accessible to us. It enables the artist to bring into his works terri-tories of experience that no chimpanzee would dream of explor-ing as sources of fun—for example, hunger, sex, competitions and struggles, war, deformities, disease and death.

Take shipwreck and cannibalism. One supposes that they hardly register as amusing when they really happen. And yet Byron makes us laugh when he has Don Juan's old tutor Pedrillo devoured by his shipmates on a raft:

> And if Pedrillo's fate should shocking be,
> Remember Ugolino condescends
> To eat the head of his arch-enemy
> The moment after he politely ends
> His tale: if foes be food in hell, at sea
> 'Tis surely fair to dine upon our friends,
> When shipwreck's short allowance grows too scanty,
> Without being much more horrible than Dante.[5]

Nor do we usually treat the real-life suicide of a friend or the spectacle of indifference and the failure of human relations with the macabre humor carefully crafted by Frank O'Hara in 'Poem':

> The eager note on my door said 'Call me,
> call when you get in!' so I quickly threw
> a few tangerines into my overnight bag,
> straightened my eyelids and shoulders, and

---

5.   *Don Juan Canto* II, Stanza 83. Published in 1819. As Dante tells the tale in the 32nd and 33rd Cantos of his *Inferno* (written in the first decade of the fourteenth century), Count Ugolino, himself a traitor, was betrayed in turn by Archbishop Ruggieri. Both are buried up their necks in ice, but Ugolino has the privilege of gnawing at Ruggieri's 'brain above the nape' for all eternity.

headed straight for the door. It was autumn
by the time I got around the corner, oh all
unwilling to be either pertinent or bemused, but
the leaves were brighter than grass on the sidewalk!

Funny, I thought, that the lights are on this late
and the hall door open; still up at this hour, a
champion jai-alai player like himself? Oh fie!
for shame! What a host, so zealous! And he was

here in the hall, flat on a sheet of blood that
ran down the stairs. I did appreciate it. There are few
hosts who so thoroughly prepare to greet a guest
only casually invited, and that several months ago.[6]

Propositions concerning the extinction of mankind, whether by means of hydrogen bombs, because of world pollution, through a collision with a comet, or by some other cause, are usually treated with the greatest seriousness. In the following lyric, however, the cheerful nursery rhyme humor directs us to an implied proposition that belittles the importance of humanity:

> I am a little snail
> On the green grass I sail
> Sometimes I live sometimes I die
> And in between I hear great mankind cry
> We mankind must survive
> How ghastly to deprive
> The cosmos of mankind
> Although the reason I don't find
> Being a simple snail
> On the green grass I sail.[7]

However, humor is not the only means of creating a disparity between our normal perception of a situation and the emotion infused into it by a work of art. When Thomas Gray wrote his 'Ode on a Distant Prospect of Eton College' in 1742, he did so in a solemn mood:

6. Frank O'Hara (1926–66), *A City Winter, and Other Poems* (1952). From *Collected Poems* (ed. Donald Allen; New York: Alfred A. Knopf, 1971). The powerful theme of indifference (which can be formulated in many ways) is implied not only by the action (or inaction) described in the poem, but also by the tone of understated everyday casualness O'Hara has imparted to it.

7. From *Collected Lyrics and Epigrams* by Oscar Mandel (Los Angeles:

Say, Father Thames, for thou hast seen
　　Full many a sprightly race
Disporting on thy margent green
　　The paths of pleasure trace,
Who foremost now delight to cleave
With pliant arm thy glassy wave?
　　The captive linnet which enthrall?
What idle progeny succeed
To chase the rolling circle's speed,
　　Or urge the flying ball?[8]

The elevation, the sense of nobility imparted to this scene hardly matches the mood in which most of us register schoolboys taking a swim, catching birds and playing with hoops and balls. The sweaty lads are called a sprightly race; the gang disports itself instead of running about; the river-bank is a green margent (a promotion bestowed on the simple 'margin'); plain swimming becomes the cleaving of a glassy wave with pliant arm; the sons of the wealthy are an idle progeny (words redolent of Latin were thought nobler than those of Germanic origin);[9] and they do not kick the ball (God forbid!), they urge it. The strategic aim of this diction was obviously to place Eton on a par with the inspiring fictions of Antiquity. For us, it demonstrates that the discrepancies which are our subject just now need not be based on humor.

To sum up: The the raw propositions of a poem and the real-life situations behind them do not lock into a predetermined emotional treatment.[10] This basic law of aesthetics can be stated in grammatical terms: no noun is locked into a predetermined

Spectrum Productions Books, 1981).

8.　Gray wrote this hundred-line poem when he was a mere 26 years old, and allowing his 'weary soul' (line 18) to philosophize over a new generation of schoolboys at Eton, the prestigious school he had entered in 1727 at the age of 11. If you are momentarily baffled by the syntax, try 'a sprightly race *that was* disporting' and then move 'trace' to the start of its own line.

9.　Normally, 'idle progeny' would be read as an insult to the upper classes; but Gray's poem discourages this reading (remember, in Chapter 9, section [5], what was said about controlling proliferations of possible meanings), for it would introduce an inexplicably isolated undercutting of the text as a whole.

10. This is of course equally true if the inspiration for a poem is another poem, some other work of art, any text whatsoever or a purely imaginary character or situation.

adjective or adverb. Or in the terms of Juan de Mena: it is the poet who decides how lamentable Priam's end will be—in a work of art.

IV

A visitor from Mars would probably take it for granted that mankind rushes toward pleasurable emotions and away from the painful ones. What could be more natural? But while the Martian would be right with regard to animals, the facts about *homo sapiens* are more complicated. Let us begin with real-life situations. Some dreamed-of future thrills are so powerfully attractive to our antic-ipating imaginations that we consent to suffer all manner of dis-comfort, fear, horror and even torture for the chance of enjoying them. Saints will endure martyrdom for the sake of salvation. Explorers to the North Pole will suffer aches and privations of the worst sort in order to be triumphantly cold at the top of the world. Colonels will risk their lives in order to become the military dictators of their wretched countries. Businessmen will work end-less hours in order to bank more millions than their rivals. Many women and not a few men will opt for painful operations in order to remain beautiful longer than naive Nature decrees. Poets will starve in order to write beautiful poems instead of making a decent living in an office. And readers will perspire over baffling poems in order the better to enjoy them. Why go on? *Everyone* will accept pain now in order to obtain some satisfaction later.

Besides the suffer-now-and-enjoy-later complex there is also the here-and-now *mixture* of light and dark emotions that we often tolerate and sometimes seek out. We love excitement so much that we often flirt with fear, disgust, pity, embarrassment and the like; we test ourselves at the limits of endurance. Dante has expressed this eloquently in his *Inferno* :

> I turned like one who cannot wait to see
> the thing he dreads, and who, in sudden fright,
> runs while he looks, his curiosity
> competing with his terror.[11]

11. Canto 21, lines 25-28, in John Ciardi's translation of the *Inferno* (New York: The New American Library [Mentor Books], 1954).

In prosaic terms: we try to play what the economists call a posi-tive-sum game; that is to say, we accept and absorb a variety of emotions, some in the negative and some in the positive sector, and pronounce the experience a success when the sum is positive, when the final sense is that of satisfaction. A trivial but convenient illustration is the excitement of riding a 'terrifying' roller-coaster. This strange amusement colorfully represents all our real-life adventures in high-risk emotions. And all the more so because it also enables us to assess our varying limits. You can hear the patrons screaming as their vehicle careers down a violent slope. You reasonably suppose that, having boarded the ride of their own free will, they are all hugely enjoying themselves at the bor-derline of terror. And for many of them the game is in fact posi-tive-sum, as is suggested if not proved by their presently boarding the ride again. Some, however, may emerge at the exit silently (or not so silently!) promising themselves 'Never again...' For them, the sum has been negative; the terror or nausea has overwhelmed the thrill.

Whatever our personal limits may be for the toleration or acceptance of the unpleasant emotions, it must be confessed that we are considerably less sensitive to the calamities that befall strangers than to those we experience ourselves.[12] As a result, when the mix of dark and light emotions concerns strangers, the chances for a positive-sum improve. This calculus does not do mankind great honor, but alas, except for a few superior per-sons—our genuine saints—such is the reality. A fire, an accident, a murder in our neighborhood are apt to arouse our curiosity and a sort of 'morbid interest' that is, alas and twice alas, more plea-surable than painful. The Roman philosopher Lucretius (c. 99–55 BC) expressed this in a famous passage: 'It is sweet, when on the great sea the winds trouble its waters, to behold from land anoth-er's deep distress.' The reason, Lucretius added, is not that we delight in the afflictions of others, but that 'it is sweet to see from what evils you are yourself exempt'.[13] I think that Lucretius was

12. For the sake of brevity, I leave out the intermediate class of persons more or less close to us—that is to say, neither ourselves on the one hand, nor strangers on the other.

13. This is from the opening of Book Two of his *Of the Nature of Things* (*De Rerum Natura*), trans. H.A.J. Munro, in *The Stoic and Epicurean Philosophers* (ed.

partly right and partly wrong: it is normally true that our fascination is not sadistic, but I do not believe that our pleasure is due simply to a smug sense of our own safety. It is due, rather, to our craving for and pleasure in excitement, provided the sum remains on the other side of pain, a sum arrived at more easily when we ourselves are safe. Note our typical limit once again. We may be drawn to the scene of a murder, experience a 'morbid' thrill as we approach the body, but perhaps this thrill will darken into horror when we see the gore and the mangled flesh, and be suddenly replaced by an overwhelming pity and an urgent desire to run home.

An interesting series of steps can be outlined. When pain and pleasure mix (or, what is probably a truer description in physiological terms, when they alternate so rapidly within us as to constitute subjectively a single experience), pain is most likely to overwhelm when we ourselves endure it, less likely when we see others enduring it, still less likely when we imagine it or else read, see or hear what we consider to be factual reports of it (e.g. an airplane crash on television), and—proceeding to our proper theme—least likely when we watch others enduring it in what we take to be more or less fictive representations—and notably in works of art. Few of us would pay money in order to be allowed to witness, through a window, the savage strangling of an innocent girl. But we cheerfully buy our tickets to watch Othello strangling Desdemona on stage.

We are now approaching the subject of unbearable propositions in the arts that was listed but not discussed in the previous chapter. At each of the several steps just mentioned, the threshold of 'unbearable' normally rises. In a real-life situation that we ourselves experience, the threshold is relatively low: our pleasurable excitement is most swiftly overtaken and overcome by intolerable pain. Our sense of pleasure resists a little better when the pain concerns strangers. Still better when we merely read about it in the newspaper. And best in the perceived fiction of works of art. In works of art, we can remain pleasurably excited even when some extremely upleasant emotions—fear, horror, disgust, indignation, shame, pity, gloom, and so on—are being stirred in us.

W.J. Oates; New York: Random House, 1940).

That is why we voluntarily seek out or at any rate happily accept grim, tragic, pathetic or shocking art. Through the artificiality of art, because, that is, art is an artifact, a manufactured form, our love of excitement can satisfy itself without spilling over into unbearable pain in the presence of an enormous range of situations we find too unpleasant to face in the flesh—even in the flesh of strangers. Consider such emotions as anxiety about our careers, the pain and terror of cancer, the fear of aging, the fright when faced by an armed robber or a rapist, mourning over the loss of a child, the desolation of a financial reverse, a humiliating put-down before strangers, sexual shame, jealousy of a rival, envy of someone's happiness, desperate loneliness, pity for an orphan, and then, in a larger arena, the sorrows brought about by fires, famines, epidemics, wars...All of these, normally so hateful in real life, can become, and frequently have become, the subjects of any number of 'marvelous' motion pictures, paintings, novels, plays and, of course, poems. Even boredom, an extremely unpleasant emotion, can be happily transmuted into wonderful art. Duly 'enarted', the dark emotions can be absorbed and managed long after we would have panicked and fled in real life. Hence the artist can go far indeed with his 'uncompromising' vision of reality before he loses his public.[14]

Take Othello again as he is murdering Desdemona in a blaze of poetry:

> Not dead? not yet quite dead?
> I that am cruel am yet merciful;
> I would not have thee linger in thy pain...

The fictions are obvious: what man about to murder his angelic wife ever spoke in iambic pentameter and indulged himself in an elegantly turned paradox? To be sure, there are readers and spectators for whom this scene, like that other one in *King Lear* where the pathetic old dying king bends over Cordelia's corpse, is truly intolerable; for, as I just remarked in a footnote, it is a paramount fact that our vulnerabilities differ enormously.[15] But for most of

14. Of course he would not lose his entire public at one blow anyway. He would lose the most vulnerable first and the least vulnerable last.

15. I recall, in this connection, a production of Shakespeare's *Titus*

us, the sense of fiction assuages just enough of our pain to allow our admiration for the power, complexity and beauty of this scene to 'win out'. We then experience a strong emotion that we (or rather: many of us) find richer and finally more satisfying than easy merriment. Experiencing 'a roller-coaster' of emotions is an apt if trivial image for this state, as we saw before.[16]

Even so-called realistic art is normally felt as fiction. But poetry is particularly active in the satisfying distortions it operates on reality. Unlike (say) the typical war novel, the poem presents itself ostentatiously as an artifact by delivering its propositions in 'unnatural' quanta, by turning them to some extent into music through cadence and rhyme, by experimenting with words, images and grammar, by appearing as a carefully devised structure (the sonnet, to give a familiar instance), and by resorting to any number of rhetorical strategies (Othello's paradox, for instance)—to which, by the way, we will shortly be turning our attention. Typically, therefore, poetry is a 'safer' art than the novel, the play and the film. It seldom provokes the phenomenon of literally walking out in horror, terror, disgust or embarrassment, which is not unusual in theaters. Poetry is thus singularly successful in integrating the dark emotions into the overall aesthetic experience not only without poisoning the latter but positively by obliging them to contribute to the excitement we all seem to crave.

Be that as it may, for almost every one of us, even in the world of art, removed though it is from real life, there is a border across which we step unwillingly. Across that border are unbearable emotions—even in art. Just as, in real life, not every patron of the roller-coaster ride truly enjoys himself, so the grim, the tragic, the pathetic, the shocking work of art may produce a negative-sum effect on anyone, anytime. There comes a time in the movie

Andronicus in London in which a Red Cross station had been placed in the rear of the theater to give first aid to fainting spectators! *Titus Andronicus* is replete with mangled limbs and other physical horrors. In *Othello* and *King Lear* the painful emotion is principally pity.

16. It goes without saying that the same process occurs in all the arts. In music, a good instance would be the death scenes in Verdi's *La Traviata* and Puccini's *La Bohème*. In the visual arts, we might instance the Goya etching pictured in Chapter 1.

house when the spectator, disturbed by a scene of torture, warfare, misery of any sort, rises from his seat and leaves; a time when a reader shuts the excessively sad novel and refuses to re-open it; a time when the visitor in a gallery turn his eyes away from too embarrassing a picture.[17] It is an old story. Around 500 BC a dramatic poet by the name of Phrynichus so upset the Athenian audience with a play concerning a recent victory of the Persians and massacre of the Greeks that he was fined, and the city decreed that no play on that subject should ever be produced again.

Obviously, the kind of art we call realistic is the most likely to upset us beyond endurance, for, even though it too, by definition, is an artifact—a manufactured form—its careful imitation of what we know as reality places it closer to the previous step I have mentioned, that of the credible newspaper account, for instance. And yet, even a lyric poem can be 'too much to take'. Suppose that you have recently lost a beloved brother on the battlefield. Someone shows you a poignant poem in which you recognize your very own grief. You try to read the poem, but you cannot go on, you return it half-unread, with tears of anguish in your eyes. There is no question here of your feeling that the poem is stupid or evil—let alone vapid—grounds for rejection we discussed in the previous chapter. No; the poem is simply unbearable. At that frontier of feeling, Art fails and retires. If this failure affects only you or me and a few others, the work of art easily survives; but it will not survive if it inflicts an excess of pain for a long time over a broad sweep of the public.

17. True non-representational ('abstract') art seldom or never faces this problem, since, by definition, it does not depict or even suggest real-life situations or objects at all. It is hard to imagine a non-representational painting or sculpture suggesting such grief or horror (for instance) that it could overwhelm us with pain. It might, however, become *physiologically* unbearable if it were to become blinding—just as music can become too loud to be endured.

Chapter 13

The Right Word in the Right Place

The really hard work for the poet does not consist in thinking up interesting things to say or powerful emotions to express (these are available to almost anyone), but in finding precisely the 'right', that is to say the effective words for his pre-poetic impulses. These words must be intellectually and emotionally satisfying; they must cohabit with the surrounding words (the context) without poisoning *their* effect or being poisoned by them; and they must at the same time make the right sound and carry the right rhythmic beat—subjects we will consider separately in our upcoming chapters. So difficult is this task, so hard is it to please an audience beyond one's doting relatives, that of the thousands of poems published every year (not to mention the countless ones written but not printed), no more than a few are destined to survive. Indeed, when we study the poetic history of any given nation, we quickly discover that there are years, and even decades, of poetic productivity from which *nothing* is prized any longer. And by the way, this is true of all the arts. The elite publics of literate countries are incredibly fussy! Making works of art for them is like walking a tightrope: success lies along a very thin line; failure gapes all around.

The need to find precisely the right words or phrases for some overall raw proposition and then place them where they should be placed, is normally more critical for poetry than for literary forms like the novel or the drama. To be sure, in long narrative poems like Chaucer's *Canterbury Tales* or Tennyson's *Idylls of the*

King, this necessity is slightly relaxed, because in such poems the writers, like novelists and playwrights, can draw on the excitements of story and character to stimulate the desired pleasure in their audiences. An occasional linguistic weakness is readily forgiven in an exciting thousand-page novel or ten-thousand-line epic poem. That is why Horace could write, famously, that 'even Homer nods' without meaning any offense. But shorter, non-narrative poetry, having renounced these pleasures, finds itself focusing narrowly—not exclusively, of course—on the potential for excitement in individual words, phrases and 'related signs'. No wonder lyric, confessional and meditative poets agonize over their work and often spend hours, weeks, years polishing and repolishing their words.[1]

The selection of the right or best word or phrase in the right or best place is so delicate a task because—the exaggeration is minute—*there are no synonyms.* All words and all semantic units are unique—even those that resemble each other as closely as the proverbial snowflakes. No two snowflakes are alike; no two words or sets of words are alike.

To a foreigner with a limited knowledge of English, the difference between 'Please close the door' and 'Please shut the door' is nil. As far as a Frenchman is concerned, for instance, both clauses are adequately translated as *fermez la porte, s'il vous plaît.* But for the anglophonic poet the difference is considerable. He knows, and he knows that we anglophonic readers know, that the first word is gentler than the second, the second harder than the first. If he is about to write, 'The nurse tip-toed away and gently...the door behind her,' the likelihood is that he will choose 'closed' rather than 'shut'. By the same token, we slowly close our eyes as we fall asleep, but rapidly shut them when we are scared. Alexander Pope would not have dreamed of opening his vehement 'Epistle to Dr. Arbuthnot' with

> Close, close the door, good John! fatigu'd, I said.
> Tie up the knocker! say I'm sick, I'm dead.

1.   The cartoonist Don Addis has wittily illustrated the problem. He shows us Shakespeare working hard at his desk, quill in hand and a pile of papers before him. In the wastebasket beside the desk we see a crumpled sheet with the words 'Romeo & Debbi' written on it. Not *quite* right, apparently!

Obviously he needed, 'Shut, shut the door,' and that is what he wrote. And Thomas Gray as a matter of course wrote of tyrants that they 'shut the gates of mercy on mankind' in his 'Elegy Written in a Country Churchyard', not that they closed it.

We may as well anticipate our examination of the sounds of poetry by noting incidentally at this point that the distinction in meaning between the two words is surely due to the difference in their music—the long *o* of the one, followed by its mild and drawn-out *zzzz*, versus the short vowel and hard *t* of the other. The moral of this observation is that while we students separate the elements of poetry into distinct chapters, the poems themselves are constituted by totally interpenetrated elements—in this particular instance, the elements of sound and meaning.

We can now spell out, having dispensed a number of hints, the all-important distinction between the 'raw propositions' to which I have given a great deal of attention in these pages, and the precise, the unique propositions made up of the specific words in their specific linguistic context and making their specific music and laid out on the page in their specific way—that, in short, which the poet has actually written and spaced. The raw propositions are the approximations that underly the poet's work, and we can equate them, roughly speaking, with the paraphrases, explanations or summaries we apply to any passage in the poem, or to the poem as a whole. These raw propositions, pre-poetic in the poet's mind or post-poetic in ours, consist of so-called synonyms that take us close enough to the poem's actual text to enable us to leap across the narrow gap into the poem itself, the way we leap from one boat to another after maneuvering ours close to it.

However, an approximation is an approximation, and the real thing is the real thing. The approximations to great poetry are never themselves great literature. For the poet's infusion of energy into the raw propositions that were floating more or less consciously in his mind is an infusion of alterations to these raw propositions, however minute, however subtle. The little crafty 'magic' performed by the music, rhythm, spacing, context; the cunning choice of one word or phrase over its pseudo-synonyms; all these energize meaning by altering meaning. So too a minuscule alteration in a chemical compound can transform the latter from useless or inert to prodigiously serviceable. Of course, the alteration might leave the compound as inert as before, or even turn it into a poison. The same thing is true of the arts. The mediocre artist may work just as hard at refining his pre-poetic propositions as his more gifted rivals; but with him they gain no energy; and they may lose the amount they came with at the start.

The main reason why so few poets become 'immortal' resides in the tremendous difficulty of this tweezer-work of refining and yet again refining the language/music/contextualization, that is to say, enforcing the tiny or not-so-tiny shifts of meaning that move readers from indifference to admiration, or from *some* admiration to more of it. Inspect Donne's lines again:

> At the round earth's imagined corners, blow
> Your trumpets, angels! and arise, arise,
> From death, you numberless infinities
> Of souls, and to your scatter'd bodies go;[2]

and consider why the poet wrote 'round earth' instead of 'curved globe', why 'blow' instead of 'sound', why 'arise, arise' instead of 'get up, get up', why the utterly redundant 'numberless' next to the illogical plural 'infinities'. Sometimes the answer is obvious; at other times we sense yet hardly know why one word or phrase is better than the other; and sometimes we feel that here or there the poet has misjudged, even though the poem as a whole remains a strong one. All this without forgetting the interpenetrations of elements that go toward making a successful poem. There is no such thing, for example, as a right word that makes the wrong sound or rhythm.[3]

The aesthetic difference between 'get up, get up' and its near-synonym 'arise, arise' is gross—although it would be worth analyzing the reasons why a ludicrous alternative *is* ludicrous. 'Numberless infinities', on the other hand, represents a subtler decision over its alternatives. Why would not 'infinity' suffice, or 'numberless' by itself? Donne's idea seems to have been to make the number so outrageously large as to require a wrenching of

2. The music of these lines is essential to their beauty as well, but we are trying not to listen to it just now.

3. 'Right' and 'wrong,' in these contexts, can always be translated in the terms of our definition of Art: 'succesful' and 'unsuccessful', namely with you, with me, with anybody.

language and logic. Perhaps he remembered Augustine's 'Whatever you can understand cannot be God.' He wanted to say something unsayable—like the great mystics of his age—and found a solution of sorts in the act of 'impossibilizing' language. In our terms, he altered the limp 'infinity' into something endowed with great energy.

Back on earth again, we dream up John Donne at his desk composing his first line as follows:

O'er the vast earth's mountains and oceans, blow

etc. Presently he decides that 'mountains and oceans' is a routine phrase, hence boring, though not ridiculous like 'get up, get up'. The proverbial expression 'the four corners of the earth' flashes through his mind as a possible replacement. Although this is also an obviously undesirable commonplace, he toys with the funny notion of the earth having corners. These are of course imaginary, and so, on an impulse, he rids himself of the worn phrase by writing 'imagined corners'. Then, obeying another impulse (where would poets be without impulses?) he exchanges 'vast' for 'round'. This gives him something like the corners of a circle: a bit of wit and paradox. Donne is satisfied. And so are we. But wit in such a solemn context? The poet, it appears, liked the fusion of these opposites; and most of us will feel that 'the round earth's imagined corners' has the energy to compel us to sit up and take notice, if nothing else; whereas 'the vast earth's mountains and oceans' would have slipped by without arousing our attention.

As for a valid system of synonymies, that is to say a paraphrase for the line we are considering, a flaccid 'Angels, blow your trumpets over the whole wide world' will do; it works as an approach to Donne; but it took Donne himself to refine and so alter this raw, pre-poetic proposition that it was transfigured to an 'eternal' life.

II

Our view of John Donne at work is purely imaginary; we have no information about his way of writing poetry. But there are times when we are privileged to watch the actual tweezer-work going on in the poet's shop. In some instances we can follow the evolution of a poem its author has revised through several editions. At other times, we are lucky enough to possess some of his rough drafts, which invite an even more intimate—and sometimes downright embarrassing!—inspection of the artist grappling with those 'materials and resources' mentioned in our definition.

For instance, the Harvard University Library owns the first draft of most of John Keats's *The Eve of St. Agnes*, a work he wrote in 1819. At one point in this narrative of 42 stanzas, the Romeo-like lover, Porphyro, is peeping from a hiding place at his beloved Madeline undressing before going to bed. It is the eve of the feast of the martyred St Agnes, when chaste maidens may, in their dreams, catch a glimpse of their future husbands. Presently Porphyro will manifest himself to Madeline not in a dream but in flesh and blood, whereupon they will escape from the castle and their feuding relatives in order to live happily ever after. But for the moment he is watching her at prayer ('She seem'd a splendid angel, newly drest, / Save wings, for heaven') and then, in stanza 26, disrobing:

> Anon his heart revives: her vespers done,
> Of all its wreathed pearls her hair she frees;
> Unclasps her warmed jewels one by one;
> Loosens her fragrant bodice; by degrees
> Her rich attire creeps rustling to her knees:
> Half-hidden, like a mermaid in sea-weed,
> Pensive awhile she dreams awake, and sees,
> In fancy, fair St. Agnes in her bed,
> But dares not look behind, or all the charm is fled.[4]

This stanza gave Keats a great deal of trouble. We can guess that he was searching for a way of harmonizing the erotic with the tastefully and delicately romantic, and both within the medieval flavor of his romance. Thus, before settling on 'Anon' as the opening word, he had written 'But soon'. Like our 'close' and 'shut', 'anon' and 'soon' (along with 'presently') are what anyone would ordinarily call synonyms. Keats had obviously no problem here with his raw proposition. There was no question, for instance, of choosing between the immediate future or a future two years away or never to come. The problem lay with refinements. The refinement in this instance consisted in giving preference to 'anon' over 'but soon'. Why? Perhaps, or probably, because 'anon' is (and was in 1819) an archaizing word, literary rather

---

4.   I have modernized some spellings.

than colloquial, and therefore more at home in the Gothic romance than the plain, modern 'but soon'.[5] Its connotation was of a near-future envisaged long ago. But Keats may also have felt that 'anon' is a more melodious word than the rather unpleasant sound-sequence 'buttssoon'. For keep in mind once again that although we who analyze a poem can deal with meaning and music in separate chapters, the poet must solve all his problems together.

Would the line, or the stanza, or the whole poem have been murdered if Keats had left 'But soon' unrevised? Most of us, I think, would answer in the negative: at worst it would have suffered a tiny lesion. A few readers might conceivably prefer the dropped alternative. And if so, we would be reminded of the reassuring fact that good poets may make mistakes—in your view or mine. Be that as it may, the choices a poet makes are not necessarily between wonderful and awful, between success and failure. Many choices are between good and better, or better and best.

This is strikingly illustrated by Keats's decision to write (still in the first line) 'vespers' instead of an earlier 'prayers'. 'Prayers' is acceptable; 'vespers' more concretely an evening devotion, also a bit less ordinary, distinctly more Roman Catholic.

Keats's toughest struggle came with the disrobing itself. At first, we find him toying with the notion of having Madeline laying aside her veil before taking the jewels out of her tresses. But he dropped this neutral episode, and the veil disappears from the final version: Madeline simply removes a wreath of pearls from her hair. 'Removes' is my word, however, not Keats's. After trying twice to have Madeline *strip* her hair of the pearls, Keats went over to:

Of all its wreathed pearls her hair she *frees*.

5. A poet writing in 1920, 1980 or 2010 would most probably avoid archaic or archaizing words in writing a serious poem. He knows that the modern poetry-reading public dislikes obviously 'poetic' language, including attempts to revive old words beause they sound more poetic. This same public, however, cheerfully exempts long-dead poets from this stricture. For it is yet another fact of the aesthetic life that we flexibly adapt our receptivities to other times and other places. A volume rather than a footnote deserves to be written on this intriguing subject.

For even though the expression 'strip-tease' did not exist at the time, there could be no doubt in his mind that 'strips' sounded a trifle crude, a little rough in this context. It appears, as I remarked before, that Keats wanted his sensuality to remain exquisite.

This was not easy. The 'warmed' jewels seem to have come quickly to him, and Keats has been much admired for so intimately feeling this little truth in his imagination. But when the poet reached Madeline's bodice, his pen became almost frantic. He tried 'Loosens her bursting bodice,' then 'Loosens her bodice lace-strings,' then 'Loosens her bodice, and her bosom bare,' then 'Loosens her fragrant bodice and doth bare her...'—at which point he struck everything out! It is not hard to tell why. Keats was obtaining some most undesirable music hall effects, and guffaws were not what he was after. Still, the idea of fragrance survived. It, clearly, was in good taste, and harmonized with the warmed jewels.

The pangs were not ended, however. At one point, after the loosened bodice, he wrote:

<blockquote>
and down slips
Her sweet attire.
</blockquote>

This was not crude like the unfortunate 'bursting bodice'—yet Keats must have felt that it was too abrupt (like 'strips') and out of tune with the almost hothouse languor that pervades much of his poem. He dared to use the perilous 'creeps' by joining it to 'rustling' and achieved the desired slowness, along with an allusion to the sound the garment was making on its way down. And he dropped 'sweet' in favor of 'rich' with its more aggressive suggestions of abundance and princely quality.

Keats would also have known that 'sweet' was an overused word in comparison with 'rich'— a cliché, or commonplace.[6] The latter term speaks for itself. Words or phrases that are too common are as harmful to poetry as their opposites (so typical of our time), namely deafening innovations at every turn.

---

6.   See Chapter 11 n.7.

III

When we particularly admire a word or a phrase in a poem, when the choice seems especially brilliant, more often than not the reason is that it radiates strong implied meanings—that it speaks copiously in a very small space. Recall in this connection the 'flatness' of Eddie Guest's doggerel as against the richness and density of Milton's sonnet (Chapter 11). Here is a more focused example by John Dryden, who has an old poetaster by the name of Flecknoe making a speech on the occasion of handing over the throne of bad literature to Thomas Shadwell, a fellow-writer Dryden happened to dislike:

> Shadwell alone my perfect image bears,
> Mature in Dullness from his tender years:
> Shadwell alone, of all my sons, is he
> Who stands confirmed in full stupidity.
> The rest to some faint meaning make pretense,
> But Shadwell never deviates into sense.[7]

It is unlikely that a lesser poet would have hit upon that splendid 'deviates.' A mediocrity might have written (keeping the meter),

> But Shadwell never yet aspired to sense;

a tolerable line (I think), but one that we would have read without taking particular notice. *Deviating* into sense is brilliant because it is such a meaningful paradox. We expect people to deviate into *non*sense. But not fools like Flecknoe and Shadwell. For them nonsense is the norm, and writing sense would be a deviation. More: Dryden pretends he is paying Shadwell a compliment, for one usually praises people for not deviating. The irony (we will be discussing irony at leisure in a later chapter) is laid on with a vengeance.

---

7.   Lines 15–20 of *Mac Flecknoe* (1682). The actual text prints only the first two letters of Shadwell's name, with a long dash following, ostensibly to conceal the victim's identity. Dryden was using one of the 'related signs' of our definition for a little additional fun. The world of intellectuals was a small one in those days, and Dryden could be sure that his readers knew whom he meant.

Watch for the last line of the following poem by Emily Dickinson:

> A narrow Fellow in the Grass
> Occasionally rides -
> You may have met Him - did you not
> His notice sudden is -
>
> The Grass divides as with a Comb -
> A spotted shaft is seen -
> And then it closes at your feet
> And opens further on -
>
> He likes a Boggy Acre
> A Floor too cool for Corn -
> Yet when a Boy, and Barefoot -
> I more than once at Noon
>
> Have passed, I thought, a Whip lash
> Unbraiding in the Sun
> When stooping to secure it
> It wrinkled, and was gone -
>
> Several of Nature's People
> I know, and they know me -
> I feel for them a transport
> Of cordiality -
>
> But never met this Fellow
> Attended, or alone
> Without a tighter breathing
> And Zero at the Bone -[8]

'Zero' is a sharp metaphor, and 'Bone' a remarkable synec-doche—more topics I will be addressing presently. But we can

---

8.   This is one of a handful of Dickinson's poems published in her life-time, namely in 1866, but unbeknownst to her. When it appeared in the posthumous collection edited by Mabel L. Todd and Wentworth Higginson (1891), the editors, who had already 'cleaned up' Dickinson's peculiar grammar, spelling, punctuation, and so on, altered 'Boy' (in the third stanza) to 'child'. They naively failed to understand that the 'I' of a poem need not refer to the poet himself. They also 'corrected' Dickinson's 'Noon' to 'Morn' in order to obtain a true rhyme—something the sprightly poet must have consciously avoided, since it is so obviously available. The hand-written packets of Dickinson's poems were published by Thomas H. Johnson (Cambridge, MA: Harvard University Press, 1955). 'A Narrow Fellow' is number 986 in that edition.

examine them here simply as brilliant word-choices. A nonentity might have written:

> And Terror in my Soul-

which produces as good a near-rhyme (soul/alone) and as exact a rhythm as would have suited Dickinson. But both words are too lofty and featureless. They are abstractions and commonplaces at the same time. They are boring words. Dickinson would have laughed them away had they presented themselves briefly to her imagination. She, of course, chose hard, sharp words, with 'zero' suggestive of suddenness, cold (the cold blood of the snake), fear, stopping dead in your tracks ('I froze'), and the momentarily blank mind; and 'bone' suggesting death. Writers of the Eddie Guest variety simply lack the imaginative power to create language so compacted with meanings and suggestions.

Dickinson's line was in its time and remains for us today both original and fresh. Indeed, she in the United States and Gerard Manley Hopkins in England might be seen as opening the gate, in the nineteenth century, to the grand refreshing of language which has characterized poetry in the twentieth.[9] Posterity will pronounce its own verdict concerning our poets' indefatigable experiments with language. In principle, however, it can be stated that innovation works for us when it is especially vivid and/or dense with meanings, and not *merely* new. In other terms, since innovation ceases to be just that on a second reading (let alone a tenth), the new expression had better give us a pleasure more lasting than what is afforded by the impact of novelty alone.

Here is another poem by Emily Dickinson. She worked and reworked it, as we know from her papers, and one conventionally punctuated version was even published in 1862. Modern editors have had a choice as to which of her attempts they decide to print, and sometimes they publish a version that combines two of her drafts, thereby producing a very fine poem which does not, however, as far as we know, represent anything the poet herself ever put together. For my purpose her draft of 1861 will do:

9.   This is a general, international phenomenon, and each literature has its own pioneers. Note the cliché of 'opening the gate'. But clichés are useful in expository prose, where too insistent a search for 'brilliant' expressions would constitute an annoying affectation of misplaced artistry.

Safe in their Alabaster Chambers -
Untouched by Morning -
And untouched by Noon -
Lie the meek members of the Resurrection -
Rafter of Satin - and Roof of Stone!

Grand go the Years - in the Crescent - above them -
Worlds scoop their Arcs -
And Firmaments - row -
Diadems - drop - and Doges-surrender
Soundless as dots - on a Disc of Snow -[10]

Much can, should and has been said about the many virtues of
this small masterpiece. Observe for example, outside our immedi-
ate concerns, the poem's launch on a strongly accented word; the
rhetoric of repetition in the otherwise unremarkable second and
third lines; the music of alliteration in the fourth and fifth, and
then again in the last two lines; and the powerfully visualized
propositions of the penultimate line—those diadems dropping
and those Venetian heads of state vanishing without a sound. So
much, so fine. But let us pinpoint the innovative application of
the word 'members' in the fourth line, 'row' in the seventh and
'meek' in connection with the dead. There is grim humor here, as
there is in that 'safe' to which 'meek' is an echo. But the notion of
the dead as 'members' of some glorious and yet New England-like
club or lodge is especially innovative in its suggestion of an
attempt to domesticate the idea of death. Admirable too is the
picture of galaxies 'rowing' through space, because space becomes
for a moment, beautifully, a dark lake. And calling the dead
'meek' is both playful and touching. They are ever so humbly
waiting their turn to be called into life again, and yet, when we
read the second stanza, we do not find much hope of reward for
their humility in the poet's sense of vast time and space and
silence. Like Donne, Dickinson discovered that wit and solemnity

10. No. 216 in the Johnson edition. Although I have piously preserved
Dickinson's dashes, the reader should not feel obliged to hiccup his way
through the poem in obedience to these marks, most of which she would
surely have eliminated herself had she supervised the publication of a
volume of her poems. Many of the dashes in her manuscripts are in fact
nicks, notches, tittles and jots of varying fineness, which the medium of print
inevitably homogenizes.

make excellent bedfellows in art—as do stone gargoyles and saints set on the wall of an old church. What matters most, however, is that her innovations radiate meanings and feelings: they glow without being flashy.

Importantly, too, we observe that the quality of freshness (freshness in both its senses: newness and impudence) depends entirely on context. 'Members', 'row' and 'meek' are hardly unusual words. They are as common as words can be. Typically, freshness and surprise arise from context, that is to say from innovative juxtapositions, the words the words live with.

That is why, by the way, even commonplaces can look fresh: the right context makes them so. A poet may use a worn-out expression on purpose, in order, for instance, to characterize something or someone. Thus, when Yeats wrote:

> This man had kept a school
> And rode our wingèd horse,[11]

he was creating an implied proposition, namely that the man in question was a *very* minor poet, fond of the deadest stereotypes. But in the poem our *major* poet wrote, the dead sprang to life.

Uncertain of her effects, Dickinson scribbled, and then rejected, some alternatives to her second stanza. In this rejected material are such phrases as 'Hoar is the window / And numb the door'; 'Tribes of Eclipse'; 'Frosts unhook in the Northern Zones'; and 'Midnight in Marble Refutes the Suns'. In my opinion, Dickinson acted sensibly in turning these suggestions down. They seem strained, far-fetched to me—flashy, to use the word again; and I trust that she thought so too. All the same, while other bold women were pushing Westward across the United States, the Amherst-bound pioneer was vigorously prying open the language of English poetry. Poets on both sides of the Atlantic have continued to make innovation in language a major 'technique' for energizing their raw propositions, without always exercising the commendable self-censorship Dickinson imposed on herself.

11. In 'Easter, 1916', published in 1921 in *W.B. Yeats: The Poems, New Edition* (ed. R.J. Finneran; New York: Macmillan, 1983). The winged horse is the Pegasus of Greek mythology who, as a symbol of poetic inspiration, has had too many hundreds of poets since Antiquity riding him in their verses. By 'our' wingèd horse Yeats simply means that the poet was Irish.

It is no accident that this audacious renovation of poetic diction was carried out practically in secret by a marginal writer, distant from the mainstream, who had to be discovered after her death. Nor is it a queer coincidence that the other great renovator I have mentioned, this one in England, led an equally marginal artistic life and also had to die before his work was revealed to the world. With Hopkins we can take our next step, and cross from innovative juxtapositions to outright inventions: neologisms like 'unchilding', 'never-eldering', 'the inboard seas', 'lovescape', 'fall-gold mercies', 'the black-about air', 'down-dugged', 'the Yore-flood', 'the recurb of the gulf's sides'—all of these in 'The Wreck of the Deutschland' (1875)—not to mention his powerfully eccentric wrenchings of common English grammar like 'Let him easter in us' or 'the sodden-with-its-sorrowing heart'.

Neologisms may be strange indeed, and sometimes unintelligible to some, most, or all readers. However, in most instances poets who resort to them build their unknown squarely on the known, as Hopkins did; and do so, let me say it again, in order to bring new energies to bear on their overall subjects and themes, some of which (love, death, and the like) may appear to them dangerously time-worn and therefore in need of radical refreshment.

IV

The right word must also be in the right place. For example, it must not demolish a rhythm where a rhythm sounds right to us. Keats would have killed his first line had he chosen 'Presently' to launch it instead of 'Anon', chiefly because a dactyl here is musically intolerable.[12] But there are other dangers (dangers, as I said before, lurk on all sides of the aspiring poet). Consider a line by the same poet:

The poetry of earth is ceasing never.[13]

There is nothing wrong with its thought, nor with its rhythm. The three *s*-sounds and *e*-sounds of 'is ceasing' may be less than optimal in this particular context, but they do not positively

12. A dactyl is a rhythmic unit consisting of one strong sound followed by two less accented sounds: PREsently. See Chapter 15.
13. From the sonnet 'On the Grasshopper and Cricket' (1817).

poison the line. Why then is the line a dismal failure when that other verse, still by Keats, is so famous?

> A thing of beauty is a joy forever.[14]

For one thing, the progressive 'is ceasing' is an awkward and feeble distortion of normal English; still worse is the jarring word order. We are accustomed to a good deal of license with respect to word order in the poetry of our forefathers—shifts from ordinary prose sequences like Wordsworth's

> thy heart
> The lowliest duties on herself did lay;[15]

but we have our limits, and for most of us Keats's word order in his peccant line borders on, or falls into, the grotesque—where the grotesque is out of place.

Each word of a poem must do more than cohabit with all the others: it must serve the others, and receive service from them— an ideal marriage, in short. Hence the decision to choose one word over another is always made in light of the whole. Usually the poet will want all his words to belong to, or be consistent with, a range of diction that might be called a *lexical zone* of the language taken as a whole. Standard formal English, of the kind you are reading here, constitutes the major lexical zone of our and any language. Formal English spreads out on all sides, however, to penetrate and interact with other lexical zones; for example, a zone of colloquialisms and slang; or a zone that is strongly dialectal (like the Scots dialect of Robert Burns, or black ghetto American); or else, at the other pole, a zone of ennobled, lofty, monumental diction.

A contrasting of lexical extremes can be startling. We might return to Milton's sonnet, or the lines quoted from *Paradise Lost*, for sustained lofty diction at its best; or to Thomas Gray again:

> Say, Father Thames, for thou hast seen
> Full many a sprightly race
> Disporting on thy margent green
> The paths of pleasure trace,

14. The first line of Keats's long narrative poem *Endymion* (1818).
15. From his sonnet 'London, 1802', and referring to Milton.

Who foremost now delight to cleave
With pliant arm thy glassy wave?
   The captive linnet which enthrall?
What idle progeny succeed
To chase the rolling circle's speed,
   Or urge the flying ball?

And spring with a single leap to another planet of words:

MY MOTHER

My mother writes from Trenton,
a comedian to the bone
but underneath, serious
and all heart. 'Honey,' she says,
'be a mensch and Mary too,
its no good to worry, you
are doing the best you can
your Dad and everyone
thinks you turned out very well
as long as you pay your bills
nobody can say a word
you can tell them to drop dead
so save a dollar it can't
hurt—remember Frank you went
to highschool with? he still lives
with his wife's mother, his wife
works while he writes his books and
did he ever sell a one
the four kids run around naked
36 and he's never had,
you'll forgive my expression
even a pot to piss in
or a window to throw it,
such a smart boy he couldn't
read the footprints on the wall
honey you think you know all
the answers you don't, please try
to put some money away
believe me it wouldn't hurt
artist shmartist life's too short
for that kind of, forgive me,
horseshit, I know what you want
better than you, all that counts
is to make a good living
and the best of everything,

as Sholem Aleichem said
he was a great writer did
you ever read his books dear,
you should make what he makes a year
anyway he says some place
Poverty is no disgrace
but its no honor either
that's what I say,

love,
Mother'[16]

This is by no means the most extreme opposite in diction to Gray and Milton. I could have printed far less decorous language used by many a contemporary poet of the highest seriousness. But our two illustrations will do to establish the existence of widely different lexical zones in our language (in any language, for that matter), and the basic rule of consistency within each zone—one that begets a normally desirable 'unified emotional field'.

Like most rules, this one can occasionally be broken to good effect. Usually a flash of lexical inconsistency will create a moment of humor—for humor depends on sudden dislocations. Here is a portion of O'Hara's 'Poem' again:

Funny, I thought, that the lights are on this late
and the hall door open; still up at this hour, a
champion jai-alai player like himself? *Oh fie!*
for shame! What a host, so zealous! [Etc.]

'Oh fie! for shame!' is a deliberate momentary return to the dignified diction of a former age, like Keats's 'anon'. Were it not comical (grimly so, in context) it would be felt as amateurish and earn for its author the same rap on the knuckles teachers

16. In *White Blossoms* by Robert Mezey (West Branch, IA: Cummington Press, 1965). In Yiddish, the morally neutral German word for human being, 'Mensch', is often used to signify a full, warm-blooded and, particularly here, decent human being. Sholem (or Sholom) Aleichem (1859–1916) is the pseudomym of a famous Russian-born Yiddish story-teller. You might examine this poem for any number of implied propositions, including an implied theme that runs ironically counter to Mom's opinions and values. Incidentally, the commonplaces of lines 2-4 work exactly like the one Yeats wrote about the minor poet. For it too characterizes the mother rather than the poet. (For another debunking of mothers, re-read E.E. Cummings's 'my sweet old etcetera' in Chapter 10.)

administer to students who confuse formal and informal in their earnest compositions.

To conclude with an historical note: It is sometimes thought that in the twentieth century the entire vocabulary became at last available to the poet, as against the severe restrictions to which the Miltons and Grays conformed. But this is not quite true. With the decline of a culture in which the dominant class displayed itself in all but god-like attitudes and vestments (conquering monarchs sublime on their equestrian statues), a substantial fraction of the lofty vocabulary has become unusable in our times except for comedic purposes. For that matter, a great deal of Romantic diction of the ecstatic sort (another definable zone, perhaps) has also been tabooed by poets since the early twentieth century. However, by shifting downward to exploit a fully democratized diction, 'low' words, bad grammar and malapropisms, acceptable poetic diction has gained at one end what it has lost at the other. A similar shift, involving the same gain and loss, has occurred in the visual arts, where, for instance, assemblages made of the rubbish the artist has purloined from dumpsters are in, but potentates blessed by Zeus on ceilings of palaces are out. As my example suggests, art follows politics; and these shifts—shifts rather than net gains—show up among the interesting consequences of the historic changes in our culture that have occurred since the storming of the Bastille in 1789.

Chapter 14

The Sounds that Matter in Poetry

I

Of course all words make sounds, and poetry simply participates in that universal sound-making. When we read words in silence, these sounds are still alive; our tongues still move; and our brains still 'hear' the difference between *easy* and *pox*. Hence, as far as the sonics of poetry are concerned, we need not fret because once upon a time everything we call literature was delivered aloud to the audiences, whereas today we mostly read inaudibly to ourselves.

The study of the sounds and rhythms of poetry has preoccupied a large number of theoreticians over the centuries, and given rise to a daunting vocabulary in which terms like molossus, amphibrach and logaoedic keep common mortals at bay and properly impressed.[1] A treatise written by a certain Hephaestion in the second century AD examined Greek metrical systems in no fewer than 48 books. The good news is that they are lost. I intend to spare the reader all the pedantic minutiae and most of the technical vocabulary of this otherwise estimable branch of learning.

---

1.   Here, for instance, is a portion of the article under LOGAOEDIC in *The Princeton Handbook of Poetic Terms* (1986). 'Term invented by metricians of Roman imperial times as a general description of mixed anapaestic and iambic or dactylic and trochaic cola (ascending and descending rhythm respectively) in Greek Lyric verse. Logaoedic anapaestic cola may be composed of 2 or more anapaests followed by an iambic dipody catalectic or, more usually, by a single iambus, and logaoedic dactylic coda of 2 or more dactyls followed by a trochaic dipody (the last syllable being *anceps*), or by a trochaic dipody catalectic' (entry by Professor Robert J. Getty).

The axiom I want to stress above everything else in this chapter and the next is that the sounds and rhythms of poetry matter *more or less* along a gradient of possibilities. Matter in what sense? Matter, in our terms, as co-energizers, that is to say as contributing elements to the whole that must satisfy the reader in order to survive in the 'market-place' of Art. Our axiom states, in other words, that the poet can choose to what extent, *if at all,* he wishes to bring the special powers of sounds and rhythms into play in any particular poem. He can exploit this resource massively, moderately, slightly, or not at all. Harm is done only if, for lack of talent, he allows sound or rhythm to poison some other vital poetic element, or fails to use sonic possibilities that, in our opinion, he should have called upon.

Harmful or beneficent, the application of the musical possibilities of language simply does not enter into our definition of poetry.

It is altogether right and proper, in this connection, that while music is an optional resource for the poet, whose primary and indispensable resource remains language, for the composer the converse is the case: sounds are his primary and indispensable resource, and language an optional one.

Musical opportunities are in fact neglected in a great number of poems created since World War I, when something like a widespread aesthetic disgust with the intensely musical poetry of the preceding generations manifested itself. As a result, anthologies of modern poetry are full of poems whose sounds and rhythms do not draw our attention, thus remaining, for all practical purposes, 'out of the picture' with respect to any satisfaction these poems may produce. There is nothing wrong with this in principle: no artist is obliged to fire all the weapons available to his art. Here, for instance, is a little poem by Kenneth Rexroth entitled 'Trout' that (like several others we have read in previous chapters) seems to be indifferent to 'artistic' sounds and rhythms:

> The trout is taken when he
> Bites an artificial fly.
> Confronted with fraud, keep your
> Mouth shut, and don't volunteer.[2]

---

2.   From *Natural Numbers* (New York: New Directions, 1963).

Nothing prevents a new Hephaestion from placing the little marks over the syllables of this quatrain that signify stressed and unstressed syllables. And various observations might be ventured about the *t* sounds Rexroth used. However, as happens in numberless poems of our time, there is nothing here that you will not find in the most prosaic prose. And no clever remarks on sound and rhythm can mask the plain fact that the music in such a poem does not play a noticeable role in energizing the text: it does not *matter*. You may, of course, wish that Rexroth *had* infused his poem with noticeable music. As things stand, however, whatever energy the poem radiates is due to the force of the pre-poetic proposition illuminated by a strong image.

Indeed, in many modern poems, it is, if anything, the *absence* of significant sonics that matters, for this absence supports their characteristically dejected, defeated, disappointed and disgruntled themes. I will return to this idea in the next chapter, which deals with rhythm.

II

The term 'sonics' I have been using embraces the sounds in themselves *and* the rhythm or beat that can be applied to them when they are arranged so as to form symmetries of stress or duration. In the present chapter I propose to deal principally with sounds as such, and with rhythm only incidentally, although much of what I shall be saying pertains to both aspects of sound production. I urge you to read all the examples aloud and thus allow the printed matter to come alive.

Lacking the enormous range of pitches, chords, rhythms and timbres[3] available to the Beethovens of the world, the poet has to be content with drastically humbler means. The truth is that a musician may well scoff at what we literary people call the music of poetry. The most musical lyric poem in the world is still plain speech until some Schubert deigns to lift it into true music. Nevertheless, even in plain speech there is a marked difference between an *eeeee* sound (sense the tip of your tongue touching the base of your lower set of teeth) and an *ooooo* sound either as in *go*

---

3.   Timbre is the distinctive quality of each instrument. Obviously the poet has nothing like the contrast between, say, a trumpet and a violin.

or as in *goo* (feel the tip of your tongue sliding downward). There is a marked difference between the sound of *mmmm* and *p* or *k*—and observe that the first can extend in time like a vowel while the others must be separately repeated in order to endure. There is a marked difference between *zzzzz* and *sssss*. Besides, some sounds are short, others long: *bee* versus *bit,* for instance. Then again, some *sequences* of sounds are easy on the tongue, others hard. Compare *then again,* which is easily spoken, with *Josh hoists stones,* which is quite a mouthful.

The different qualities of sounds create, to some extent, different general fields of meaning-emotion. Note how prudently this is being asserted. To a limited degree, a few sounds, taken all by themselves, before they are attached to any intelligible words, *tend* toward certain moods or meanings. The *i* as in *flit* tends to intimate a lighter range of moods or meanings than your *oo* as in *doom.* The *k* and *sh* as in *crash* seem more violent than the *mmm* of *murmur.* The *sl* combination has a way of forming words like *slime, sludge, slush, slithe, slop, sleaze, slattern* and the like. But of course I am cheating a little. *Bloom* is a quite happy word, and *room* is a neutral one, even though both share that *oo* with *doom.* And *slim* and *slender* are perfectly pleasant words. Still, in English at any rate (far more so than in the Romance languages, among others) certain sounds and combinations of sounds (as in *crash*) do appear to have accreted to themselves a number of words that make use of certain very general tendencies; and poets have frequently taken advantage of these tendencies to support and promote the ideas and moods they want to create. In English, words of hard or sharp or rapid meanings have tended to gravitate toward hard, sharp, rapid sounds, for example, *kill, stab, jab, hack, bash, thump, hit, crack* and dozens of others, or *quick, hurry, run, hop, gallop* and the like; and words of slower actions have tended to gravitate toward slower-moving sounds, for example, our old friend *close* versus *shut. Sh* appears to invite distasteful words in English—though certainly not in French, where *chéri* and *charmant* show it off to everyone's satisfaction. Alongside *crash* we get *shame, sham, shit, shock, mash, mush, slush, rash, hash, trash, gnash*—even though *shimmer, shine, brush, flash* and *hush* are pleasant or harmless enough. *Ut* is no favorite either, for albeit words like *nut* and *cut* can radiate both good and bad connotations, most words ending in *ut* tend toward the bad: *gut, slut, strut, mutt, butt, rut, smut, glut, sputter, mutter, gutter.* This is, again, a purely English phenomenon; it does not operate in Swedish, for instance, where *sött* means sweet and *rött* means red; and even in English, we must not forget that *flutter* can be delightful and *hut* a welcome sight on a snowy mountain. It is all too easy, in this business of the intrinsic quality of sounds, to drift into *utter* nonsense!

Here are some lines by Tennyson:

> How sweet it were, hearing the downward stream
> With half-shut eyes ever to seem
> Falling asleep in a half-dream![4]

Sweet, hearing, stream, seem, asleep, dream: what can we say about these sounds? That all by themselves, to a stranger who knows no English, they suggest drowsiness? Nothing so definite. They might, for all we know, suggest something sinister and dangerous. Still, the stranger's ear would catch a slowness, relative to other English sounds he had heard—like Hamlet's 'A hit, a hit, a palpable hit!' *Sweet* is slower than *hit*: therefore we can say with some assurance that it works well as a co-energizer of propositions concerning drowsiness and the like.[5] However, to support a sinister meaning, we have Browning's description of a knight fording a fiendish-looking 'sudden little river':

> good saints, how I feared
> To set my foot upon a dead man's cheek,
> Each step, or feel the spear I thrust to seek
> For hollows, tangled in his hair or beard![6]

Now we have *feared, cheek, each, feel, spear, seek,* and *beard*—but with nothing like Tennyson's effect. And what about Hopkins's

> And all is seared with trade; bleared, smeared with toil,

4. From 'The Lotos-Eaters' (1842).
5. And why, in view of what we said in our last chapter, did Tennyson write 'half-shut' instead of 'half-closed'? We will never know; but I suspect that he overrode the possible objection that 'shut' is too hard and sharp in this context on the ground that the sequence 'half-shut' is smoother on the tongue than the sequence 'half-closed', and thus more in keeping with his overall tone of drowsiness.
6. From 'Childe Roland to the Dark Tower Came' (1855).

from 'God's Grandeur' again. Now we have disgust, even nausea expressed, some would claim, by the long-drawn-out *ee* sound! And remember, these are three poets writing in the very same Victorian England. So the only safe comment to make is that none of them is reporting on some light-hearted or swift-footed experience; the three passages have at least a negative in common. But the moral remains that we must not attach specific moods or meanings to sounds as such. The safe rule is that they work their effect (when the poet calls them in at all) when harnessed to the already known meanings of the words. Thus, when Browning, later in the same poem, makes the hills of his somber landscape seem to shout like giants:

> 'Now stab and end the creature—to the heft!'[7]

we are not surprised that most of the sounds in this line are short, though we know that short sounds, with plenty of plosives, can also co-energize a world of far other meanings than 'kill, kill!'

Can we surmise that certain universals exist as far as these general tendencies are concerned? Perhaps we can, even though they do not take us very far. The association of long sounds with slowness is an obvious illustration. Less certain but highly probable is the motion of a physically drooping tongue toward the *o* of *low* or the *oo* of *doom* where the meaning has also drooped. A Namibian native might realize, without knowing a word of English, that the following lines of Samuel Taylor Coleridge's *Rime of the Ancient Mariner* (1798) express something not very happy or wide-awake:

> Alone, alone, all, all alone,
> Alone on a wide wide sea!

When all is said and done, however, we had better believe that sounds play a role, 99 percent of the time, only when we already have the meaning of the words securely lodged in our minds. Let us look at the opening lines of a poem in Finnish—a drastically unfamiliar language for most of us:

> Miks' niin kiire kevähällä,
> Kesä miksei viivy sekään.
> Niin ma ennen mietin kysyin,
> Vastausta en ma saanut.[8]

7. 'Heft' is a variant of 'haft,' the handle of a dagger.
8. From 'Then I questioned no further' by the great Finnish poet Johan

Is it likely that a group of readers who cannot so much as say
'yes' and 'no' in Finnish will agree on the matter or mood of
these lines on the basis of the sounds they make? Can we even
speak of a general field of emotion and meaning in this instance?
The negative answer to this question should be enough to make
us look askance at large claims regarding the power of sound *as
such* in poetry—sound unattached to previously known meaning.

III

In general, we are musically pleased when a poet uses a variety of
vowels in a narrow space. Coleridge did so in the couplet just
quoted—and likewise Shelley in

> The keen stars were twinkling,
> And the fair moon was rising among them,
>   Dear Jane!
>   The guitar was tinkling,
> But the notes were not sweet till you sung them
>   Again.[9]

This is practically an anthology of vowels and diphthongs,
hence the lines make an attractive lyrical sound. Stubborn insis-
tence on a single sound would tire us after a minute or two. But
we should not forget that a dull business letter could easily exhibit
the same pleasing variety without attracting either the writer's or
our own notice. As does the sentence I have just written. It is safer
to say that a poet who wishes to write a musical poem, as Shelley
did, will dip amply into the supply of vowels, and will naturally
vary them in order to modulate his effects and avoid monotony—
unless, like Tennyson, he is attempting to create a very particular
atmosphere. Even children are sensitive to vowel variety. Note the
sound-curve of *eeny meeny miny mo.*[10]

Ludwig Runeberg (1804–77): 'Why is spring so quickly over, / why must
summer flee so soon? / Thus I used to wonder often, / and my mind could
find no answer.' Keep in mind that translations of lyric poetry usually sound
flat. The *ä* is sounded like the second letter in *letter*; the other letters carry
the ordinary sounds of European languages. Runeberg wrote in Swedish, but
was very soon translated into Finnish.

9.   This 'To Jane' poem was published posthumously in 1839.
10.   In the previously mentioned *Annotated Mother Goose* I find this written

Shelley's *tinkle* would usually be called an *onomatopeia*, as would several of the words we have been stringing along so far. This term refers to words like *tinkle* and *miaow* and a host of others that directly imitate the sounds that real things or creatures make.

Or give the illusion of doing so. For many such imitations are, in truth, partly or even wholly illusory. *Hiss* may come fairly close to the real sound made by certain snakes or by boiling water issuing from a tea-kettle, but does anyone believe that a robin goes *chirp-chirp* or *twit-twit*, that a rooster says *cock-a-doodle-do*, or that a dog barks *bow-wow*? It is instructive that the Japanese (I have been told) say *niao* for our *miaow*, but *wan-wan* for our *bow-wow*, *moh-moh* for mooing, but *boo-boo* for *oink-oink*. Oddly enough (for us) they snore *guu-guu*. The Chinese sound for a cat is exactly like ours. Their cows start out sounding like ours, but go on to say *maan*. *Di-da-di-da* serves in Japanese both for a clock and for water dripping. And for the Chinese, birds go *ji-ji-ji* or *zhe-zhe-zhe* (you can do the latter if you know how to say *je* —the first person singular in French—as in *je t'aime*). Conclusion? Some non-human sounds are physiologically more imitable by our human sound-making equipment than others, and those that are will tend to produce generally similar onomatopeias in most or all languages. Highly imitable are the *durations* of non-human sounds; hence it is not surprising that we and the Chinese both ascribe short sounds to most birds. On the other side, hard-to-imitate or downright inimitable sounds will produce thoroughly different attempts from language to language to render them—and this is where illusion prevails. In English, are words like *cackle, babble, crack, clatter, bang, growl, sludge, ding-dong, tick-tock, ping-pong, drip-drip, hush, buzz, shimmer, flicker, zoom,* and a hundred others true imitations of sound or motion, or do they merely take *focused* advantage of the very *general* tendencies I have mentioned before?

In any event, poets are sensitive to all these possibilities and do not care whether they are handling illusion, reality or a mixture of the two. For us, Keats's famous line in the 'Ode to a Nightingale' (1819), where he speaks of a beaker full of wine

> With beaded bubbles winking at the brim,

'eena, meena, mina, mo', which I take to be the 'authentic' spelling. But to my ears, the jingle sounds better the way I have written it down.

seems to render—almost render—the very sound tiny bubbles make. A close phonetic relative, *babble, seems* to sound a little like the thing itself to English-speaking persons. The truth may be, once again, that two syllables in descending stress, carrying two unassertive consonants, merely provide a general field on which a large number of particular games can be played. If we strummed a guitar to the Namibian tribesman, and asked him which English sound comes closest to the guitar, *tinkle* or *murmur*, I would not be surprised if he gave the first as his answer. For the falling of a mighty tree, he might think *crash* preferable to *tinkle*. But for all we know, he might deem a word like *hiss* an even better onomatopeia for a toppled tree.

IV

Having examined sounds in themselves, we are ready to take on *repetitions* of sounds. Repetition is of course the very phenomenon that defines rhythm, but rhythm is for our next chapter; here we are concerned only with repetition of sounds, regardless of rhythmical patterns.

Many kinds of repetition have been tried by poets; but most notably, as we all know, the poets of our particular civilization have exploited the manifold possibilities of rhyme. That children love it shows how deeply rooted is our satisfaction in this type of recurrence:

> Little Jack Horner
> Sat in a corner,
>   Eating of Christmas pie;
> He put in his Thumb,
> And pull'd out a Plum,
>   And said what a good boy was I.

In what does true and complete rhyme consist in English? We begin by separating all our words into two camps: those ending on a stressed syllable, like *adapt*, and those ending on an unstressed syllable, like *baby*.[11] In the group ending on a stressed syllable, there are words that end on a vowel or a diphthong (in fact, almost

11. A sexist terminology governs these two camps: in the first are the 'masculine' endings and rhymes, in the second are the 'feminine' ones.

all our English end vowels sound like diphthongs): *so, beau, grow*—
the spelling does not count. We get true and complete rhyme in
these words simply if those final vowel/diphthong sounds are
substantially the same. I say 'substantially', because phoneticians
manage to discriminate almost endlessly among similar sounds.
We, instead, can afford to be less precise because our interest is
confined to sounds that truly matter in poetry. *So* rhymes with
beau, beau rhymes with *grow* and *grow* rhymes with *so.*

Still in the group ending on a stressed syllable, consider words
that end on one or more consonants, as in *pat, adapt* or *firebrand.*
Now we feel true and complete rhyme only if the vowel + conso-
nant(s) are alike. The three words just listed do not rhyme per-
fectly. But *firebrand* does rhyme perfectly with *sand.*

We move to the second class: words that end on unstressed
syllables, like *sitting. Sitting* rhymes perfectly with *knitting,* on the
principle that now we ask for *three* recurrences: the vowel + conso-
nant(s) we had before + that final 'descending' sound. As you can
see and hear, the rhyme I have cited has its full complement of
three recurrences.

In practice, poets often make do with something less than such
perfect rhymes. They (and we) are happy enough with approxi-
mations like *pat, adapt* and *firebrand* in lieu of absolute repetition.
The main reason for this is that our language is relatively poor in
perfectly rhyming words. Witness the troublesome shortage we run
into when we try to find rhymes for 'love' in our amorous poetry.
The Romance languages rejoice in a vastly larger stock of rhyming
words than we do. No wonder it was *their* speakers who invented,
or popularized, rhyme as a major 'tool of the trade'. Nevertheless,
equipped with rhyme and approximate rhyme, English poets have
produced long works like *The Canterbury Tales* and translations of
Homer, Virgil and Goethe's *Faust*—all in rhyme. But they have
had to struggle for what is served on a platter in other languages.

What does rhyme *do* for us? To begin with, we take a sensuous
pleasure in these repetitions—a pleasure that, as we have seen,
goes back to our childhood and is surely rooted in our pre-verbal
physiological/psychological being. Infants respond with signs of
pleasure to such recurrences well before they can understand
speech—a point to be stressed in our next chapter, when we
speak of rhythm.

But children, and we who are, in a sense, children of these children, also embrace rhyme (and similar repetitions) because it makes remembering easier. Indeed, one of the chief functions of rhyme in the days of orally delivered poetry was to help the bards memorize their texts. In addition, we can detect in rhyme an element of reassurance and comfort, not unlike the pleasure of seeing an old face again, or the comfort of coming back to a place. Furthermore, since normal language does not rhyme, the sudden and unexpected difference may be received as seriously refreshing, or light-heartedly fun: how 'funny' is rhyming with 'bunny'![12]

However, rhyme also plays an important structural role. The recurring sounds seem to function as elements that hold the text strongly and tightly together. This is best felt in the so-called closed couplet, where the rhymes are bunched (*aa, bb, cc,* and so forth) and the meaning of the rhyming line comes to either a full stop or a lesser but still definite pause:

> And, spite of Pride, in erring Reason's spite,
> One truth is clear, WHATEVER IS, IS RIGHT.[13]

You could visualize the two lines as two horizontal bars clamped by 'spite' and 'right' to a vertical pole. Or, more nobly, to the twin steeples that form a rhyming architectural pattern on many a beautiful church—clamped, as one might put it, by the transverse mass of the body of the church. Or else rhymes can be compared to recurrent homecomings of the wandering text. We can also appeal to the psycho-physiological notion of *Gestalt*—a profound tendency of ours to look for completed structures. For, as the above example makes clear, rhymes can create an effect of closure, a sense of finality, even of confident authority. Moreover, rhyme is physically forceful. Repetitions reinforce. A crude but not inaccurate analogy is a hammer hitting a nail twice rather than once, 'just to make sure'.

Very close in effect to the couplet is the quatrain rhyming *abab,* as in

12. For reasons mysterious to me, 'feminine' rhymes are often humorous in English.

13. The concluding couplet of the first Epistle of Pope's *Essay on Man* (1733).

> With rue my heart is laden
> For golden friends I had,
> For many a rose-lipped maiden
> And many a lightfoot lad.[14]

I will risk one more analogy, and compare this form to that of a rectangular frame with its two sets of 'rhyming' sides.

The couplet and quatrain—the latter normally but not always rhyming abab—make up, together, the most frequently used forms of rhyme in English poetry, and, although no one has made a count, they have surely given us more memorable poems than any other pattern. They seem to provide just the 'tight little packages' that satisfy a deep need for easily-apprehended order.

Often, as I have said before, rhyme creates humor. A limerick would expire without its rhymes. Or else, consider again the little poem we read in Chapter 5:

> That poem is a splendid thing.
> I love to hear you quote it.
> I like the thought, I like the swing.
> I like it all. (I wrote it).

Clearly this depends for its life on the rhyme energizing the overall proposition, which, like all acceptable raw propositions, cannot become fine poetry unless energized. Imagine the text as follows:

> That poem is a splendid thing.
> I love to hear you quote it.
> I like the thought, I like the swing.
> I like it all. (I am its author).

This is very narrowly synonymous with the real thing. The theme is not in the least distorted. Only the music has failed. Having poisoned both the rhyme and the rhythm, I have murdered Armour's poem.

Note that Armour does not use humorous rhymes in this poem. The poem is funny, but its rhymes are straight-faced. Humor becomes more obvious when a poet makes the rhymes themselves amusing. Here is Byron's Don Juan as an adolescent prey to mysterious longings, upon which the poet comments:

---

14. From No. 54 of A.E. Housman's *A Shropshire Lad* (1896).

If *you* think 'twas philosophy that this did,
I can't help thinking puberty assisted.[15]

It is instructive to compare two translations of poetry, one of which uses rhymes while the other avoids it. Here, for instance, is how Jonathan Swift rendered a Latin poem by Catullus:

Lesbia forever on me rails.
To talk of me she never fails.
Now, hang me, but for all her art,
I find that I have gained her heart.
My proof is this: I plainly see
The case is just the same with me;
I curse her every hour sincerely,
Yet, hang me, but I love her dearly.

And now, a twentieth-century translation, namely by L.R. Lind:

Lesbia swears at me continually; she's never quiet
About me; damned if I don't think she's in love with me.
The proof? Because we are even: I swear at her in the same way
Day after day, but damned if I'm not in love with her.[16]

Granted, the startling difference between these two versions is due not only to the absence of rhyme but also to the very modern 'collapse' of rhythm in Lind's translation (similar in this to Kenneth Rexroth's 'Trout'). However, we readily detect the special beauty and force of rhyme in Swift's version: the music *per se*, and effects of firmness, completion, authority and humor. In spite of the repeated oath in the later version, it sounds singularly feeble in comparison with the master's work. The first one cleaves the waves; the second flounders.

V

Like all the other sonic effects available to the poet, rhyme can be ignored completely—neither the Hebrews, nor the Greeks, nor the Romans except very late in their history made use of it—or

---

15. From Stanza 93 of the First Canto (1819).

16. Swift's version was written in 1736. The modern one is in *Latin Poetry in Verse Translation* (ed. L.R. Lind; Boston: Houghton Mifflin, 1957). Catullus' poem is number 92 of his extant works, composed in the first century BC. The translators' degree of faithfulness to the original is not at issue here.

else deployed it with varying degrees of insistence. More than ignored, it can also be flatly rejected. No childish sing-song please! No tick-tock, tick-tock! Milton banished rhyme from his *Paradise Lost* as 'the invention of a barbarous age', as 'trivial and of no true musical delight', and as mere 'jingling sound'.[17] Can one, in English, sustain hundreds or thousands of rhyming lines of poetry of the highest possible solemnity and grandeur? I will let the reader decide—or not decide—while we go on to listen to degrees of audibility and insistence in rhyme.

Another, but quite minor open question—more a question of semantics than of substance—is whether an *aa* rhyme in which both members are precisely the same word constitutes a rhyme even 'more perfect' than the perfect rhymes we defined earlier in this chapter. Anyhow, the device is a rarity. Here is an instance of it—a stupendous virtuoso 65-line piece by Marilyn Hacker (b. 1942) in which five words are used as 'rhymes' throughout; I quote the first 14 lines:

CANZONE

Consider the three functions of the tongue:
taste, speech, the telegraphy of pleasure,
are not confused in any human tongue;
yet, sinewy and singular, the tongue
accomplishes what, perhaps, no other organ
can. Were I to speak of giving tongue,
you'd think two things at least; and a cooked tongue,
sliced, in a plate, with caper sauce, which I give
my guest for lunch, is one more, to which she'd give
the careful concentration of her tongue
twice over, to appreciate the taste
and to express—it would be in good taste—

a gastronomic memory the taste
called to mind, and mind brought back to tongue.[18]

17. He had, however, used rhyme like everyone else in his earlier, shorter poems.
18. In a private communication, Miss Hacker calls her poem an 'expansion' of the form known as the sestina, modelled by her on certain poems by Auden and Ashbery. Be that as it may, 'Canzone' ('song' in Italian) consists of five stanzas of twelve lines, each one using all five key words for its rhymes, but each stanza employing its own formula to sequence and repeat these key words, and each of the latter recurring twelve times in the five stan-

Next, we glance at another extremely insistent rarity, where the poet keeps going as long as he can on a single traditional rhyme—not unlike a lad hopping down the lane on one foot. Here is part of Thomas Hardy's 35-line tour de force, 'The Respectable Burgher' (1902):

> Since Reverend Doctors now declare
> That clerks and people must prepare
> To doubt if Adam ever were;
> To hold the flood a local scare;
> To argue, though the stolid stare,
> That everything had happened ere
> The prophets to its happening sware;
> That David was no giant-slayer,
> Nor one to call a God-obeyer
> In certain details we could spare
> But rather was a debonair
> Shrewd bandit, skilled as banjo-player;
> That Solomon sang the fleshly Fair,
> And gave the Church no thought whate'er,
>
> . . . .
>
> That Pontius Pilate acted square,
> That never a sword cut Malchus' ear;
> And (but for shame I must forbear)
> That — — did not reappear!
> —Since thus they hint, nor turn a hair,
> All churchgoing will I forswear,
> And sit on Sundays in my chair,
> And read that moderate man Voltaire.[19]

zas. The poem concludes with a five-line *envoi* (a terminal stanza much practiced in French and Italian medieval poetry) in which the five key words are repeated once again, once each, in a strict A B C D E order. 'Canzone' appeared in Hacker's *Taking Notice* (New York: Alfred A. Knopf, 1980). See section VI of this chapter for a brief discussion of pre-set forms.

19. 'Nor one to call' (line 9) is a syntactically compressed phrase of the kind we discussed in one of our practical pointers. A moment's thought tells us that it is the reader who is not calling David a God-obeyer. Solomon's 'fleshly Fair' refers to the passionate love songs in the *Songs of Songs*, which orthodox tradition interpreted allegorically as addressed to the Church. Malchus was the man whose ear Peter cut off in defending Jesus Christ from arrest (Matthew 26.51). The dashes for Jesus Christ belong to our 'related signs.' They are as pregnant with meaning as any words would be. For a naive reader they would indicate reverence; for the 'in' reader they are sarcastic as

It is no accident that Hardy's poem is serio-comic rather than simply serious, for the obsessive repetition of the rhyme is a dislocation, not only of plain speech, but also of normal rhyming; and dislocations, if not frightening, are typically perceived as amusing.

Interestingly, too, it demonstrates that music—even the narrow music of language—can produce meaning. In this instance the humor of excessive rhyme carries in itself the implied proposition that religion is bunk. You would obtain a similar effect if you played Handel's 'Hallelujah' chorus on a kazoo. We have seen that an 'inappropriate' diction achieves the same result. Hardy does not neglect the latter strategy either when he calls that stupendous event, the Flood, a 'local scare' and King David a skilled banjo-player. He thus combines debunking language with a suitably debunking music.

A more famous example of rhyme supporting or alluding to meaning, if not quite *producing* it, is Dante's use of a rhyme system called the *terza rima*, by means of which the Tuscan poet meant to invoke the Holy Trinity. Here, in Italian, are the opening lines of the final canto—canto 33 (another allusion)—of the *Paradiso*. Note the peculiar pattern in *aba, bcb, cdc,* and so on:

> Vergine, madre, figlia del tuo figlio,
>   umile e alta piú che creatura,
>   termine fisso d'etterno consiglio,
> tu se' colei che l'umana natura
>   nobilitasti sí, che 'l suo fattore
>   non disdegnò di farsi sua fattura.
> Nel ventro tuo si raccese l'amore
>   per lo cui caldo nell'etterna pace
>   cosi è germinato questo fiore.[20]

Dante's noble game with the number three in his rhyme pattern is fascinating, but it would be difficult to name a great

---

signs of pseudo-reverence. Voltaire (1690–1778) remained throughout the nineteenth century as the hero (or villain) of the grand battle against orthodox religions.

20. The *gl* sound is pronounced as in *miLLion*. The passage translates crudely as follows: 'Virgin, mother, daughter of your son, humble and high above any created being, final goal of eternal design, you are the one who so ennobled human nature that He who made it did not scorn to be made by it. In your womb was rekindled the love by whose warmth, in peace eternal, thus germinated this Flower.'

number of instances where rhyme as such creates or alludes to a distinct meaning.

Returning to normal English practice, we may note in passing a variant of the closed couplet, namely the triple rhyme (*aaa*), frequently found in seventeenth- and eighteenth-century poetry. John Dryden was very fond of it, as in this example among many:

> He is not now, as when, on Jordan's sand,
> The joyful people throng'd to see him land,
> Cov'ring the beach and blackning all the strand.[21]

The closed couplet, however, remains our true 'classic' of strong, insistent rhyme. Chaucer used it often, so did Shakespeare, then Dryden and Pope perfected it, and our contemporaries still turn to it now and then for the special *force* it exerts:

> 'Now lat us ryde, and herkneth what I seye.'
> And with that word we ryden forth our weye,
> And he bigan with right a myrie cheere
> His tale anon, and seyde as ye may heere.[22]

Or:

> Pity me then, dear friend, and I assure ye
> Even that your pity is enough to cure me.[23]

Or:

> A perfect judge will read each work of wit
> With the same spirit that its author writ:
> Survey the whole, nor seek slight faults to find
> Where Nature moves, and rapture warms the mind.[24]

Or:

> Full of her long white arms and milky skin
> He had a thousand times remembered sin.[25]

21. Lines 270-72 of the 1032-line First Part of *Absalom and Achitophel* (1681). The reference is once more to King David who in turn represents King Charles II. I have normalized Dryden's capitals and italics.

22. The last lines of the General Prologue to the *Canterbury Tales*. Geoffrey Chaucer wrote his unfinished masterpiece in the 1390s.

23. The closing couplet of Shakespeare's Sonnet 111. The *Sonnets* were published in 1609.

24. Lines 233-36 of Pope's *An Essay on Criticism* (1711). 'Wit' means, in this context, something like 'displaying real talent', not necessarily comic.

Or:

> If you were going to get a pet
> what kind of animal would you get.
>
> A softbodied dog, a hen—
> feathers and fur to begin again.
>
> When the sun goes down and it gets dark
> I saw an animal in a park.
>
> Bring it home, to give it to you.
> I have seen animals break in two.[26]

Not surprisingly, the couplet is the ideal—though not the only—vehicle for *epigrams*, short, witty poems that deliver a sting on a limitless variety of subjects. Here is a good example by Pope again:

ENGRAVED ON THE COLLAR OF A DOG WHICH I GAVE TO HIS ROYAL HIGHNESS

> I am his Highness' dog at Kew;
> Pray tell me, sir, whose dog are you?[27]

The audibility and hammer-force of the couplet diminishes dramatically when it ceases to be closed—when, instead of a sharp syntactical pause at the end of each line, we get what is called a run-on line or enjambment. Robert Browning's 'My Last Duchess' provides a fine example:

> Sir, 'twas not
> Her husband's presence only, called that spot
> Of joy into the Duchess' cheek: perhaps
> Frà Pandolf chanced to say 'Her mantle laps
> Over my lady's wrist too much,' or 'Paint
> Must never hope to reproduce the faint
> Half-flush that dies along her throat': such stuff

25. The first lines of 'The Equilibrists' by John Crowe Ransom, published in 1927. From *Selected Poems* (New York: Alfred A. Knopf, 1969).

26. The first half of Robert Creeley's 'If You', from *For Love* (New York: Charles Scribner's Sons, 1962).

27. Kew Palace on the Thames west of London was a royal residence. Note the difference between this simple factual piece of information and the general cultural 'off-stage' information about royalty and its entourage of lickspittles upon which a poem of this kind depends for its effect.

Was courtesy, she thought, and cause enough
For calling up that spot of joy.[28]

Browning deliberately avoided the assertiveness of the closed couplet; but he preserved the mild euphonies of open-couplet rhyming—almost a background music. So backgroundish, in fact, that we might well hear the poem read aloud to us—or even read it ourselves on the printed page—without noticing it. Sounds inevitably repeat themselves in our daily conversations, for the number of available sounds is finite, without being perceived as rhymes; and this is why 'run-on' rhymes can become, for all practical purposes, subliminal.

The same observation applies to the poem by Robert Mezey we examined a while ago:

be a mensch and Mary too,
its no good to worry, you
are doing the best you can
your Dad and everyone
thinks you turned out very well
as long as you can pay your bills,

and so on.[29]

And consider, climactically! the tricks Marianne Moore plays on the couplet in 'The Fish', from which I cite a few lines:

All
external
  marks of abuse are present on this
  defiant edifice—
    all the physical features of

ac-
cident—lack
  of cornice, dynamite grooves, burns, and
  hatchet strokes, these things stand
    out on it; the chasm side is

dead.
Repeated

---

28. Published in 1842. Frà Pandolf is a fictive painter.

29. The fact that 'well' and 'bills' are approximate rhymes causes a further diminution of the rhyme effect. See section VII below.

> evidence has proved that it can live
> on what can not revive
> its youth. The sea grows old in it.[30]

One would have to read these stanzas aloud in a very stagy manner in order to make the visual couplets *sound* like couplets.

In the English quatrain, the audibility and forcefulness of the *abab* or *abba* scheme can reach very nearly the level achieved by the closed couplet. Recall 'With rue my heart is laden' above, or else Shelley's 'Dirge':

> Rough wind, that moanest loud,
>   Grief too sad for song;
> Wild wind, when sullen cloud
>   Knells all the night long...

Once again, enjambment will bring a diminution:

> For three years, out of key with his time,
> He strove to resuscitate the dead art
> Of poetry; to maintain 'the sublime'
> In the old sense. Wrong from the start—
>
> No, hardly,[31]

And so on. This yields the same attenuation for the quatrain that we noted for the couplet in 'My Last Duchess'.

Gradually, as the rhymes move farther away from each other, we tend to lose contact. The following is from 'After Apple-Picking' by Robert Frost (1914). The poet tells us that in the morning he skimmed a thin pane of ice from the drinking trough.

> 1 It melted, and I let it fall and break.
> 2 But I was well
> 2 Upon my way to sleep before it fell,
> 2 And I could tell
> 1 What form my dreaming was about to take.

---

30. From *Collected Poems* (New York: Macmillan, 1951). I cite the last three out of eight stanzas, all in the same form, in which Moore allows herself one unrhymed line out of five at the end of each stanza. The quoted stanzas deal with an underwater cliff.

31. The opening lines of Ezra Pound's 'Hugh Selwyn Mauberley' (1920). In *Personae: The Collected Shorter Poems of Ezra Pound* (New York: New Directions, 1971).

3 Magnified apples appear and disappear,
4 Stem end and blossom end,
3 And every fleck of russet showing clear.
1 My instep arch not only keeps the ache,
5 It keeps the pressure of a ladder-round.
4 I feel the ladder sway as the boughs bend.
3 And I keep hearing from the cellar bin
5 The rumbling sound
3 Of load on load of apples coming in.[32]

Frost shows us quite a repertory in this passage: one triple rhyme (2); two instances of rhyme separated by one line (3); one case of rhyme separated by two lines (5); three rhyming words, each one separated by three lines (1); and two rhyming words, also separated by three lines (4). For most ears, rhymes are still audible—still play a role as energizers—across three-line separations. Thereafter the benefit becomes questionable. And yet, even at a five-line distance, a rhyme that strongly completes and closes a long sentence might still register more audibly than an enjambed *aa* couplet in the manner of Browning or Mezey:

> Alas! What boots it with uncessant care
> To tend the homely slighted Shepherd's trade,
> And strictly meditate the thankless Muse?
> Were it not better done as others use,
> To sport with Amaryllis in the shade,
> Or with the tangles of Neaera's hair?[33]

This is a charming example for us, since, in addition to a rhyme between our lines 1 and 6, Milton (as though teaching us a little lesson in audibility) offers us another between lines 2 and 5, and a third between lines 3 and 4. We can determine for ourselves at what distance if any the rhyme loses us.

The 'appear and disappear' in Robert Frost's poem introduces

32. In *The Poetry of Robert Frost* (ed. E.C. Lathem; New York: Henry Holt, 1970).

33. Lines 64-69 from Milton's 'Lycidas' (1637). 'What boots it' means 'what is the use?' The late Greeks invented the pastoral figures of shepherds as poets/musicians. The names of Milton's nymphs belong to the same tradition, of which poets tired at last toward the end of the eighteenth century. *A propos* of one of our practical pointers, note that we need to 'translate' the image of sporting with Amaryllis etc. into outer-ring language, for example, 'enjoying the pleasures of the flesh', a concept that Milton concretizes for us.

the subject of internal rhyme—words that rhyme in the body of the text rather than at the end of lines. When they occur in close proximity they are particularly forceful, like very strong repeats in music. Coleridge used the device to good effect in *The Rime of the Ancient Mariner*, writing, for instance, of the albatross:

> It ate the food it ne'er had eat,
> And round and round it flew.
> The ice did split with a thunder-fit;
> The helmsman steered us through!
>
> And a good south wind sprung up behind;
> The Albatross did follow,
> And every day, for food or play,
> Came to the mariner's hollo!
>
> In mist or cloud, on mast or shroud,
> It perched for vespers nine;
> Whiles all the night, through fog-smoke white,
> Glimmered the white Moon-shine.[34]

VI

Our concern in these pages is with the audibility and effectiveness of rhyme in general. But we should note, in passing, that certain types of fixed-pattern rhyming stanzas—that is to say the building blocks of whole poems—bear their own especial names. The *ottava rima* is an eight-line stanza, the strict rule of which is that it rhymes in the pattern of *ababab cc*. The *rhyme royal*, on the other hand, is a stanza of seven lines rhyming *ababbcc*. The practice of naming such systems—very much alive in southern France and Italy in the Middle Ages—has long since gone the way of the dodo bird; but modern poets sometimes enjoy showing their skill by writing contemporary poems in these bygone modes.

And also by imitating named, fixed-form types of *whole* poems that were current in the Middle Ages. The troubadours and trouvères invented set forms—rules of the game, we can call them—defining such parameters as rhyme schemes, number and

---

34. Lines 67-78. Note no fewer than four short *i*-sounds for the splitting ice in the third line. The *wind-behind* sequence of line 5 can be considered a visual rhyme (not a very satisfactory affair), although *wind* could be pronounced so as to rhyme with *behind* until the eighteenth century.

length of stanzas, repetition of words or whole lines in certain orders, meter, and anything else in the external form that could be manipulated. You will find descriptions of these fixed forms in all the handbooks of poetic terms—forms like the *sestina,* the *rondeau,* the *triolet,* the *villanelle* etc. For us, a single, typical instance will suffice. The triolet is a whole poem composed of eight lines using only two rhymes (say a rhyme in *-at* and another in *-ense*). One of these eight lines must be repeated *verbatim* three times, namely as the first, fourth and seventh lines of the poem; and another must be repeated twice, namely as lines two and eight. This leaves three lines free, provided they follow the overall rhyme scheme, which is strictly *ab* repeated four times. As you might guess, the bards who invented and practiced these fixed forms took pride in displaying their technical—I will even say their *acrobatic* skill with language when they made poems that obeyed these quite arbitrary rules. Modern poets (like Marilyn Hacker) occasionally take up the challenge and prove that they can play the game too.

Why did all these forms—save the *sonnet*—become poetic museum-pieces? In my opinion, this happened because, although the best medieval poets found it possible to speak seriously and passionately within these sometimes extremely complicated pre-set forms, as time went by poets became uncomfortable with the marriage of mere *tours de force* and deep seriousness of purpose; the blatant artificiality of the externally given form clashed with the passion that demanded its own individual ways of expressing itself. The sonnet may have survived because its rules were relatively uncomplicated and therefore allowed greater freedom of passionate expression.

Even so, poets were liberalizing or liberating the sonnet still further, and by the time Shakespeare came to write his series, three main types were already available, all in 14-line iambic pentameter (see the next chapter), but each with a different rhyme pattern. They were all legitimately called sonnets on the ground that they retained a strong family resemblance in spite of these variations. But the process of emancipation has continued to our own day: any rhyme scheme will do, and poets have even broken through the five-beat meter and either extended or shortened the standard line—all this within the precinct of what can sensibly be called the sonnet. Note in this connection how the final couplet in Shakespeare's sonnet 111, which was quoted in the present chapter, gives a more resonant and decisive closure than anything we find in Milton's softer 'Methought I saw my late espoused saint' (p. 137), where the poet chose an alternate sonnet form that deliberately avoids the couplet.

Be that as it may, what all the forms discussed in this section have in common is a determined if variable use of highly audible musicality as a paramount energizer of the raw propositions.

VII

Approximations to perfect rhymes compensate for the relative scarcity of rhyming words in English; but they can also be preferred by the poet and by the reader who favor less insistence on musicality. Let us look again at Yeats's 'The Mother of God':

> The three-fold terror of love; a fallen flare
> Through the hollow of an ear;
> Wings beating about the room;
> The terror of all terrors that I bore
> The Heavens in my womb.
>
> Had I not found content among the shows
> Every common woman knows,
> Chimney corner, garden walk,
> Or rocky cistern where we tread the clothes
> And gather all the talk?
>
> What is this flesh I purchased with my pains,
> This fallen star my milk sustains,
> This love that makes my heart's blood stop
> Or strikes a sudden chill into my bone
> And bids my hair stand up?

Analysis yields:

Perfect rhymes

room/womb   shows/knows   walk/talk   pains/sustains

Approximate rhymes

flare/ear/bore   knows/clothes   sustains/bone   stop/up

Inspecting the approximate rhymes, we note that in columns 1,

3 and 4, Yeats has repeated a consonant sound (if we call the characteristically weak English *r*-sound in the first column a consonant), while in column 2 he has maintained the vowel sound—along, as it happens, with the final consonant. The most interesting fact, however, is that approximations also range from more to less. *Stop/up* is very close to perfect rhyme. Many foreigners would not hear any difference at all. On the other hand, *sustains/bone* removes us so far that we could hardly be blamed for disqualifying the combination altogether—for asserting, in other words, that here is a repetition that does *not* matter.

I mentioned twin steeples a while ago as analogies to perfect rhymes. But quite a few famous Gothic churches—the cathedral at Chartres, for instance—are not ashamed to display a pair of steeples that do not match. These form, in effect, architectural equivalents to approximate rhymes. As we shall note again when we talk about rhythmic patterns, human beings love perfect symmetries and repetitions; but they also tire of them and want to roughen them. And later again they have enough of roughness and want to return to the harmonies. Artists often claim that only *their* way makes for good art. But in the long run, the public—sophisticated and simple alike—discovers that supposedly opposite ways can be delightful alternative ways.

VIII

Consider again Tennyson's

> How sweet it were, hearing the downward stream
> With half-shut eyes ever to seem
> Falling asleep in a half-dream!

Besides the perfect triple rhyme, we also hear plenty of sound-recurrences within the body of the text that do not form rhymes—notably the consonant *h* and the vowel *ee*. To name these internal recurrences, academic prosody introduces distinctions like alliteration, consonance and assonance. For us, the term alliteration suffices to name all non-rhyming sounds that are repeated within the body of a text. As before, it must be remarked that, inasmuch as our phonetic repertory is a limited one, alliterations are bound to show up anywhere; they do not put in 'limited

engagements' for the benefit of poetry.[35] Thus, once more, the
question is not merely whether alliterations occur in a poem (this
is almost unavoidable) but whether they play a significant role in
energizing meaning. Clearly they do so in the lines just quoted.
Here is Tennyson again, with passages of significant alliteration
and internal rhyme underlined:

> I will not shut me from my kind,
>   And, lest I *stiffen into stone*,
>   I will not eat my heart alone,
> Nor feed with sighs a passing wind;
>
> What profit lies in barren faith,
>   And vacant yearnings, tho' with might
>   To scale the *heaven's highest height*,
> Or *dive* be*low* the *well*s of *death*?
>
> What *find I* in the *high*est place,
>   But *mine* own phantom chanting hymns?
>   And on the *depth of death* there swims
> The reflex of a human face.
>
> I'll rather take what fruit may be
>   Of sorrow under human skies;
>   'Tis held that sorrow makes us wise,
> Whatever wisdom *sleep* with *thee*.

Once more we perceive that gradations occur. At lines 2, 7 and
11 the alliteration is very forceful. Furthermore, it would seem
that at line 7, Tennyson is finely suggesting the effort of scaling
the heights through the three-fold repetition of an *h* sound that
we commonly associate with physical effort ('heave-ho!'). Sonics,
we remember, can support and reinforce meaning. This *h*-set is
then contrasted against the two *d* sounds of line 8. Not that the
plosive sound of *d* is in some way 'contrary' to the fricative *h*; not
so; but it is very different; and when the two are repeated in prox-
imity to one another, a sense of contrast is created. Is this musical
effect essential to the success of the poem? That much may surely
be doubted. Does it heighten the poem's success? Surely, for most
of us it does.

35. Did the *prose* series 'dejected, defeated, disappointed and disgruntled'
in section I of this chapter catch your attention? If so, you found that allitera-
tion is not confined to poetry as an energizer of propositions.

The contrast between the rising effort of Tennyson's *h*-words and the sense of falling that is sometimes associated with *d*-words brings to mind again Dickinson's lyric that we read in the last chapter. I will underline the areas containing alliterations that matter, and at the same time, defying the diehard purists, exchange most of Dickinson's headlong dashes, meant for her own eyes in her private room, for minimal normal punctuation or none:

> Safe in their Alabaster Chambers -
> Untouched by Morning
> And untouched by Noon -
> Lie the *meek members* of the *Resurrection* -
> *Rafter* of *Satin* and *Roof* of *Stone!*[36]

> Grand go the Years in the Crescent above them,
> Worlds scoop their Arcs
> And Firmaments row;
> *Diadems drop and Doges surrender*
> *Soundless as dots on a Disc of Snow.*[37]

No better instance of the sheer music of alliteration could be found than this story-book 'diadems drop and doges surrender', although the full beauty of the line also depends on its rhythm. Like Tennyson, Dickinson uses *d*-words for falling. It is as though, in our language, words like *down, death, doom, damnation, decline, descent, depression, defeat* and the like exerted a stronger gravitational pull on the sound *d* than the contrary *delight, delicious, divine, distinguished*, etc.

There is no question of onomatopeia in these alliterations; whereas in Keats's

> With beaded bubbles winking at the brim,

36. The two 'untouched' can be classed under the rhetoric of word repetition, perhaps the most elementary, ancient, pre-literary rhetorical device—whether for poetry or for story-telling, painting, weaving, dancing and music—yet as effective today as it must have been among the Cro-Magnons, and as it is with children. In line 5, 'rafter of satin' and 'roof of stone' illustrate another figure, that of balance (the see-saw or weighing balance provide visual equivalents), with or without alliteration. These and other rhetorical maneuvers will be discussed in a later chapter.

37. Note also the much less 'active' alliteration on *c* in the first three lines of this stanza.

already quoted, I suggested that 'bubbles' all by itself may be a genuine onomatopeia, or close to one. So close, surely, that the *repetitions* of *b*—given the meaning of the words as such—create what might be called a *serial onomatopeia*, or *imitative alliteration*. For the series *b-b-b* seems to reproduce quite closely the non-human sound of a gas rising to the surface of a liquid like sparkling wine

The other repetitions in the stanzas I have quoted from Tennyson (aside from the true rhymes) are less audible. Presently we reach a point where differences in aural sensitivity come into play, and some readers detect and enjoy repetitions that others detect without particularly enjoying, and still others neither detect nor enjoy. No one can deny that, in line 3, Tennyson has used two *i* sounds (as in 'eye'), two *l* sounds and no fewer than three *t* sounds; and you can count repetitions in other lines as well. But do they matter? Do they support or create mood or meaning? Or are such repetitions merely the inevitable result of using language at all—whether for writing poetry or sending a memo to the boss?

In any event, the usual roles of truly audible alliteration seem to be, like rhyme, at times merely to tickle the child in us that responds to recurrences (*eeny-meeny-miny-mo* again), at other times to stitch elements together, at still other times to create force, and not infrequently to support meaning. Alliteration may have played *all* these roles, in addition to mnemonic facilitator, in the rhymeless poetry of the Anglo-Saxon bards. A typical line consisted of four stresses, two on each side of a pause in the middle of the line, with three of the four stressed syllables alliterated; for example,

Meotodes meahte and his modgethanc.[38]

The possibilities of playfulness should not be overlooked, as in these gaudily, exuberantly musical lines by Wallace Stevens:

Chieftain Iffucan of Azcan in caftan
Of tan with henna hackles, halt![39]

38. 'The Creator's might // and his mind-plans.' From Caedmon's *Hymn*, composed in the second half of the seventh century AD. Bards sang their poems with a harp accompaniment.

39. From the six-line 'Bantams in Pine-Woods' (1923). In *The Collected Poems* (New York: Alfred A. Knopf, 1957).

But we can best conclude with the tragic hammer blows of Hopkins (whose special prosody and diction owed a great deal to the Old English) as he harangues the figure of Despair:

> Why would'st thou rude on me
> Thy wring-world right foot rock? lay a lionlimb against me? scan
> With darksome devouring eyes my bruisèd bones?[40]

Powerful. Clenched. *Clinched.* And yet, when all is said and done, still appealing to the child in us.

IX

Even those who enjoy any or all strong musical effects in poetry may feel on occasion that they are overdone, and thus overwhelm instead of supporting. Normally, a degradation sets in when any sonic resource upstages meaning. This is not some law a critic tries to impose on you. It is a formulation of something that is generally, though not universally, felt. We have the art of music to cater to our needs in that area. From the art of poetry we usually ask for eloquent meanings, and many of us do not like these to be smothered by music. Or rather: from the art of *serious* poetry we are likely to want eloquent meaning not overwhelmed by sound. For, as we have seen, excess can spell success in the comic or serio-comic mode.

What is your opinion of lines 103-104 of *The Ancient Mariner*?

> The fair breeze blew, the white foam flew,
> The furrow followed free.

Too many *f*s? No! cry the enthusiasts; those *f*s beautifully render the sound of the sea! *Fffff* goes the ocean! Alas, say the others, Coleridge went too far that time, and gave us misplaced comedy.

But the invidious prize for excesses of music is traditionally bestowed on Edgar Allan Poe. Let the reader decide whether or not, in this opening stanza from 'The Raven' (1845), Poe drowned sense in a wash of sounds:

> Once upon a midnight dreary, while I pondered, weak and weary,
> Over many a quaint and curious volume of forgotten lore—

40. From an untitled poem usually called 'Carrion Comfort', probably written in 1885. We note the *d*-words again.

> While I nodded, nearly napping, suddenly there came a tapping,
> As of some one gently rapping, rapping at my chamber door.
> ''Tis some visitor,' I muttered, 'tapping at my chamber door—
>   Only this and nothing more.'[41]

Another unfavorite favorite is Algernon Swinburne, who wrote endless poems in the following vein:

> Wilt thou yet take all, Galilean? but these thou shalt not take,
> The laurel, the palms and the paean, the breasts of the nymph in the brake;
> Breasts more soft than a dove's, that tremble with tenderer breath;
> And all the wings of the Loves, and all the joys before death;
> All the feet of the hours that sound as a single lyre,
> Dropped and deep in the flowers, with strings that flicker like fire.[42]

This is a world of poetry away from Rexroth's poem, so typical for our times:

> The trout is taken when he
> Bites an artificial fly.
> Confronted with fraud, keep your
> Mouth shut, and don't volunteer;

but, as usual, there is no aesthetic police to oblige you to feel that in Swinburne the music blots out the sense, or that in Rexroth the sense obliterates music.

The music Swinburne makes (for better or for worse) involves even more emphatically than is customary a union of forceful sounds with forceful rhythms. His 'Hymn to Proserpine' thus provides us with a convenient bridge to our next chapter.

---

41. 'Napping' in the third line could serve as an illustration of inappropriate diction that creates unwanted humor and therefore damages (or kills) the poetry.

42. Lines 23-28 of the 110-line 'Hymn to Proserpine' (1866). Proserpine is the pagan queen of the underworld. The Galilean is Jesus Christ, whose victory over paganism Swinburne lamented in his poems, to the shocked thrill of his contemporaries.

Chapter 15

The Rhythms that Matter in Poetry

I

As the title of this chapter indicates, much that has been said in the previous chapter could be repeated in this one. Once more you are urged to read all the examples aloud. And let me repeat the central principle laid down there, namely that sonics may be deployed for aesthetic effect all along a curve, from 'very powerfully' to 'not at all'. It should also be remembered from Chapter 14 that the absence of music in poetry, and especially the absence of rhythm, may be eloquent. I suggested there that it might betoken those four *d*'s: dejected, defeated, disappointed and disgruntled. It could also be regarded as a subtle product of our casual, professors-in-blue-jeans democratic culture. In any event, what is so very important to keep in mind overall about the arts is that they have available to them an impressive panoply of 'weapons' for winning us over, not all of which are utilized in every campaign. As far as rhythm is concerned, this principle can be illustrated by a couple of examples from our last chapter, where I now capitalize the syllables our language makes us stress:

> The LAUrel, the PALMS and the PEAan, the BREASTS of the NYMPHS in
> the BRAKE;
> BREASTS more SOFT than a DOVE'S, that TREMble with TENDerer
> BREATH.

And:

> My MOther WRITES from TRENton,
> a coMEdian to the BONE

but underNEATH, SErious
and ALL HEART. 'HOney,' she SAYS,
'be a MENSCH and MAry TOO.

The first example offers stresses recurring at even (regular) time intervals to a *much* greater extent than what we hear in everyday prose discourse. It gives us a pattern—a waltz pattern, we could call it—in which a ONE-two-three beat prevails with enough insistence to justify our saying that rhythm is indeed one of Swinburne's weapons.

The other stanza starts out regularly enough with a line that goes one-TWO, one-TWO, one-TWO-one (the so-called feminine ending); and this is of course our basic iambic pattern. But thereafter the stresses show nothing that distinguishes them from everyday speech—even if we grant a half-stress or even a full stress to 'but' in line 3. Mezey, unlike Swinburne, is writing largely in 'free verse' and chooses not to use the weapon of rhythm. Perhaps he would argue, as military strategists do, that this particular weapon is inappropriate in that particular terrain. Democratic mankind slouches a great deal more than its ancestors.

So much by way of reminder that rhythm—using another metaphor now—may or may not be a significant 'actor' in poetry. Now for a few quick definitions. *Beat, accent* and *stress* are used interchangeably in these pages. Since English happens to be a strongly stressed language (a STRONGly STRESS'D LANguage), it follows that all discourse, spoken or written, sublimely poetic or crassly utilitarian, exhibits these emphases; they cannot be conjured away, whether in prose or in poetry. *Rhythm* is a term that refers to an organization of stresses, the latter typically random in normal prose discourse, into one or another regular formation— somewhat like a forcing of randomly scattered molecules into a crystal. A text is rhythmic when we feel that the stresses in it have been 'planted' at regular time-intervals, as occurs in simple music when we dance.

Of course, a text can be rhythmic in some parts and arrhythmic in others. The five quoted lines in our Mezey selection gave us a quick example. They also demonstrate that our language affords half-stresses, syllables that receive an in-between emphasis. We can indicate the three possibilities through lower-case type, small caps, and full caps. Note the small caps in lines 3 and 5:

My MOther WRITES from TRENton,
a coMEdian to the BONE
BUT underNEATH, SErious
and ALL HEART. 'HOney,' she SAYS,
'BE a MENSCH and MAry TOO.

To be quite truthful, these three levels of stress are no more than three convenient halting places that facilitate analysis. In actuality, stress runs along a seamless slope of force. Some words or syllables that any textbook will mark as fully accented are *more* fully accented in reality than others, usually because of their more emphatic meanings. For instance, both 'a thing of beauty' and 'to strive, to seek' carry two stresses, yet if we measured the true pressure we are likely to exert on the accented syllables, the result would show more power expended on the second phrase than on the first.

I say 'likely', because, in addition, we all emphasize words in our own personal ways. Frequently, a text cordially invites such differences. You might, for instance, disagree with my reading of Mezey's fifth line and wish to place a full stress on BE, in which case the line becomes quite rhythmic: DUM-di-DUM-di-DUM-di-DUM. My own way of reading that line is to deprive 'Be' of any stress at all and trot rapidly up to MENSCH.

Still, when all the possible refinements and variants are accounted for, we can return to a rough-and-ready view of rhythm as the regular recurrence of stressed and unstressed sounds in the language as normally and generally spoken.[1]

These recurrences appear either in addition to, or separately from, the recurrences of *sounds* which we discussed in Chapter 14. Obviously, a poet can choose to fire at us (I am sticking to the military imagery for the moment) with strong rhythms, assertive rhymes *and* emphatic alliterations. One overall effect of such poems will be a feeling of something intensely *organized.* Or else, he can decide that rhythm will do the job for him without rhyme. And so on.

The number of times a beat is heard in a given line yields the

---

1. 'Regular recurrence' by human standards of speech, not by metronome or atomic clock. We are interested here in macrophenomena like our *sense* of regularity, a sense that allows for considerable micro-irregularities.

meter in which that line is composed.[2] We will let meter refer to the number of stresses in a line *whether or not the latter exhibits rhythm*. When I say of a single line of poetry that it displays a regular meter, I mean that it shows x number of beats rhythmically arranged. If its beats are arrhythmic, it has an irregular meter.

But what about a stanza, or a whole poem? Suppose it exhibits five arrhythmic beats per line throughout, or almost throughout? In that case, we can speak of an irregular metrical *pattern*: the five beats make up the pattern, but since they occur in most lines without forming a rhythm, the pattern is irregular.

Perhaps a visual representation will help. Dots are unstressed, and exclamation points are stressed units.

Example of a line in perfectly regular meter:

..!..!..!..!

Example of a line in the same meter, but irregular:

!.!....!!..

Example of a two-line poem in nearly perfect regular meter:

..!..!..!..!
..!..!..!..!.

Example of a two-line poem with an irregular metrical pattern:

!.!....!!..
....!..!.!..!

Example of a two-line poem in free verse:

!.!....!!.!
....!...![3]

We always apply our nomenclature according to the effects that *dominate* the line or poem; we do not look for an absolute uniformity, which, as we shall see in a moment, good poets avoid anyway. Glancing again at the two lines by Swinburne, for instance, we see that they are quasi-regular hexameters, that is to say they display six beats each, predominantly but not entirely in a DUM-di-di rhythm. And a poem like Mezey's is apt to be called free

---

2. Meter means measure (*metron* in Greek).
3. An additional 'requirement' for free verse is that it must not rhyme.

verse even though it is occasionally rhythmic, and even though it occasionally rhymes.

Eccentricities aside, it is fair to say that every line in an English poem has a meter, since we are bound to stress something somewhere in it. This is true even in those rarities—poems written in monometer:

UPON HIS DEPARTURE HENCE

> Thus I
> Passe by,
> And die;
> As One,
> Unknown,
> And gone:
> I'm made
> A shade,
> And laid
> I' the grave:
> There have
> My Cave.
> Where tell
> I dwell,
> *Farewell.*[4]

However, eccentricities do crop up, and predictably so in the poetry of E.E. Cummings:

> un
> der
> fog
> 's
>
> touch
>
> slo
>
>   ings
>   fin
>   gering
>   s
>
> wli

---

4. In *Hesperides* by Robert Herrick, published in 1648.

whichs
turn
in
to whos

est

people
be
come
un[5]

What shall we do, prosodically speaking, about a line of poetry consisting of the letter *s?* Smile, and call it *ametrical.*

While we ponder this less than cosmic question, we can ascend from monometer to dimeter, trimeter, tetrameter, pentameter, hexameter, heptameter and octameter.[6] Theoretically, of course, we can keep going.

The accented sound and its surrounding unaccented sounds (e.g. di-di-DUM) form a mini-system called a *foot.* In English poetry we make do with six possibilities. The iamb: you SEE. The trochee: FASter! The dactyl: PAnama. The anapest: interFERE. The spondee: GO SLOW. And the pyrrhic, which we can define here as any two or more unaccented syllables not accounted for by the other units.[7] By the way, there is a tendency to grant the third syllable of a dactyl and the first of the anapest a semi-stress: PAnaMA and INterFERE.

If a given type of foot predominates in the line, it is turned into an adjective that qualifies the named meter, as in trochaic trimeter;

5.   Published in 1938. In *Complete Poems* (ed. George J. Firmage; New York: Liveright Publishing, 1991). Cummings enjoyed turning pronouns like 'which' and 'who' into nouns. 'Slowliest' can be read separately, but its elements can be inserted in different ways into the poem: 'slo(w)ings' and 'slowli whichs turn,' etc. Recalling the 'related signs' of our definition, we observe that the layout of 'slowliest' makes the idea of slowness visual and auditory as well.

6.   Pronounced dyeMEEter and tryMEEter, then teTRAmetter and likewise for the rest.

7.   This is an 'unauthorized' definition of the pyrrhic foot, the textbook definition of which confines the term to two and only two unaccented syllables, as in 'on the WARpath,' where a pyrrhic is followed by a trochee. But for us, 'HIGH over the WARpath' will *also* exhibit a pyrrhic followed by a trochee.

anapestic tetrameter; iambic pentameter; dactylic hexameter; iambic heptameter; and so on.

What we choose to define as a foot is not necessarily coextensive with a word. It is true that in PAnama, for example, the dactyl covers the whole word. But in the hexameter

> The LAU/rel, the PALMS /and the PEA/an, the BREASTS/
> of the NYMPHS/ in the BRAKE

we distinguish an opening iamb followed by five anapests, one of which blithely cuts a word in two.

A perfectly regular line of poetry is one in which only one type of foot occurs, since this will yield perfectly equal time between accents —provided we take a relaxed view of 'perfectly:'

> The force that drives the water through the rocks

is a perfectly regular iambic pentameter line.[8]

The presence and absence of stress have a significant effect on the rapidity with which we read a line. Spondees inevitably retard our pace, a fact Milton used to good effect in his description of that heaviest of places, hell, with its

> Rocks, caves, lakes, bogs, fens, dens, and shades of death.

But Dickinson, speaking of death, nevertheless urged our pace along in

> Safe in their alabaster chambers,

which *could* be read as

> SAFE in their ALaBAster CHAMbers,

with scarcely a swelling on *al* and *ba*. Of course, rapidity is also determined by the number of pauses, or *caesuras,* imposed by the meaning, and often, as in the Miltonic line above, marked by punctuation; and by the relative ease or difficulty our tongues experience in sliding from one sound to the next—a point I made in the previous chapter. If *then again* is much more rapid than *Josh hoists stones,* this is due in large measure to the sounds as such.

8. From 'The force that through the green fuse drives the flower' by Dylan Thomas, published in 1934. In *The Collected Poems of Dylan Thomas* (New York: New Directions, 1953). We can call this a perfect iambic line even though 'through' receives a bit less stress than the other accented syllables.

What we have been doing all this time to our quoted lines is to *scan* them. Scansion is the act of marking the stresses (mentally or by means of written signs), defining the feet, naming the meter, pointing out anomalies, variants and irregularities (if any), and noting the caesuras.

The combination of sounds, rhythms and pauses into an overall study of the sonic components of poetry constitutes the discipline of *prosody*. This is anything but an exact science, and many great minds that could perhaps be better employed fatigue themselves in quarrels over the right way of scanning this or that poem. Why, for instance, should we not scan Swinburne's line as follows?

The LAUrel, / the PALMS and / the PEAan / etc.

For indeed, there are daunting Greek names for this type of foot and any other combination you can imagine.

As a matter of fact, the prosodic system that has been summarily described so far is not the only one available to a given poet, or to a given poetic culture. The Anglo-Saxon bards, for instance, were not preoccupied with rhythm in our precise sense of the term. As mentioned before, they wanted, essentially, three or four beats per line (marked, perhaps, by striking the harp while chanting), with plenty of alliteration to reinforce the beats; but the beats did not need to recur at regular time-intervals—or, to put this differently, the number of unaccented syllables straying about did not strictly matter. So then, where we traditionally expect the unaccented syllables of a five-beat line (for instance) to measure out equal stretches of time between the beats:

di DUM	di DUM	di DUM	di DUM	di DUM
to STRIVE,	to SEEK,	to FIND,	and NOT	to YIELD,

another prosodic system could simply ask for five beats per line throughout the poem (along with other conditions involving pauses, rhymes, end-stops, alliteration, etc.) without counting syllables (durations) between them; for instance:

DUM di di di di DUM DUM di DUM di DUM di di di.

A prosody of this sort (which G.M. Hopkins practiced) is arrhythmic without being free verse, since it requires regularities—e.g. five beats in every line—as severely as our traditional prosodies.

The truth is that prosodic analyses can go on practically forever. Remember those 48 books by Hephaestion. They are probably at the source of a great deal of pedantic worrying of the subject ever since. The naive lover of poetry can easily be overwhelmed by seeing his dearest poems printed over with crabby little marks that tell him where the syllables are stressed, half-stressed and unstressed, where he is to pause, how regularities are subtly implied by irregularities, and how what seems a jumble is actually a splendid prosodic machine.

The reason I have given somewhat more attention to labels and tags in this chapter than in others is that when we speak of rhythm (and also of rhyme and other sonic effects) we are poking about furniture that is truly all but exclusive to the room, as I have called it, which poetry occupies in the house of Art. Ever so many other energizers of propositions—even some, like imagery, which many writers believe to be poetry's especial 'weapon'—poetry shares in fact with other types of literature. But where there is rhyme and meter, there is poetry, however incompetent, crude or childish—even though, as we have seen, where there is poetry there is not always rhyme or meter. Still, once we have absorbed the details of iambs and trochees, we can address ourselves to the fundamental issues. What deeply matters is whether or not a poem feels strongly rhythmic, weakly so, or not at all. And the deep question to ask is, What do various rhythms, pauses and the like do for us when they are present?

II

Our beating heart, our breathing in and out, our eyelids nictitating, our swallowings of saliva; the baby calmed as it is rocked in its cradle; a bird's wings flapping; the waves of the sea coming ashore line upon line; the sun that rises and sets and rises and sets; the recurring seasons; the earth repeating its oval journeys round the sun... More so than the sound repetitions we were studying in our previous chapter, rhythm is profoundly rooted in the nature of things, and specifically in our own biological, pre-literate, pre-intellectual lives. Therefore it is profoundly *satisfying*. It satisfies at the instinctual physiological level, and it satisfies at a somewhat higher level as an organizer of otherwise scattered materials: the band in the street going oom-pah oom-pah; dancers doing the waltz; the tom-tom in the clearing of a forest; the bang-bang of popular music; a grandfather clock ticking; church bells swinging ding-dong ding-dong; windows, columns and other architectural features evenly spaced (Figs. 8 and 9). And why is organization satisfying? Because the reduction of disorder to order means graspability, comfort, ease, security. It also underlies our sense of beauty; beauty begins in regularity.

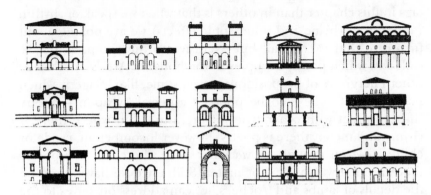

Fig. 8. Project for grand entrances, 1802. In *Daidalos*, March 1989

No wonder, therefore, that when a language happens to be strongly accented, poets will take advantage of this opportunity to order and organize into rhythm its otherwise random beats. In Wordsworth's 1802 Preface to his *Lyrical Ballads, with Pastoral and Other Poems*, the poet went so far as to declare that 'metrical arrangement' is the *only* element that distinguishes poetry from prose;[9] and indeed, nearly all the poetry written up to his time, and for several generations thereafter, obeyed one or another regular metrical pattern. But of course not all natural phenomena are rhythmic; to the image of ocean waves we can oppose that of a flowing river or that of jagged rows of mountain peaks. By the same token, architects (and interior decorators) eventually discovered that regular recurrence is not always the most desirable

9.   The term 'arrangement' corresponds to 'pattern' as I have used the word in this chapter; that is to say it refers to regularity of meter through the poem or parts of it.

organizing principle for their creations (Figs. 10, 11), and writers found out that poetry can be poetry even without a steady beat and without an overall metrical pattern. Wordsworth, it turns out, had mistaken *a* weapon for *the* weapon.

Fig. 9. Project for a store and apartments, 1927. In *Daidalos*, September 1989. The sameness, in both figures, of columns, windows and other elements can be thought of as the visual equivalents of rhyme, and their even spacing as the visual equivalent of rhythm.

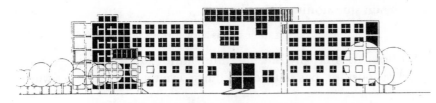

Fig. 10. A courthouse in Berlin, 1988–1990. A visual equivalent for approximate or 'imperfect' rhythm. In *Daidalos*, March 1989

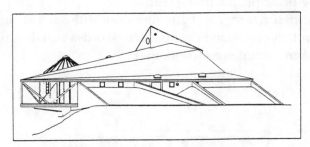

Fig. 11. A private house of the 1980s. In *Daidalos*, June 1989. An architect renounces 'regular beat'

But it was surely no accident that rhythm seemed indispensable to Wordsworth of all poets, for he often neglected the other weapons available to poetry, and in particular the highly imaginative metaphors and other tropes (figures of speech) that thrill us in the poetry of artists like Shakespeare and Donne. Consider this:

> Midway on long Winander's eastern shore,
> Within the crescent of a pleasant bay,
> A tavern stood; no homely-featured house,
> Primeval like its neighbouring cottages,
> But 'twas a splendid place, the door beset
> With chaises, grooms and liveries, and within
> Decanters, glasses, and the blood-red wine.[10]

You can feel that, in the absence of astonishing flights of the imagination and in the absence of rhyme, alliteration and other energizers of bare thought, the metrical regularity (with typical touches of irregularity) becomes a matter of life or death for these lines. In other words, in poetry so naked, 'metrical arrangement' becomes the one source of vitality that keeps it from expiring into prose. The same point can be illustrated by once again summoning Keats's

> A thing of beauty is a joy forever.

Without its mild rhythm, the line cannot survive. Its pre-energized proposition has stature, of course, even if one disagrees with

---

10. *The Prelude*, Book II, lines 138-44, composed between 1799 and 1805. A chaise is either a private horse-drawn carriage, or short for post chaise, a commercial vehicle for hire.

it, and it is composed in simple, unassuming English (so unassuming that it even dares to use the weakest of all words, 'thing'), while its sounds are unassumingly melodious—no sibilants, no krakky chuchy vocalizing! But whence does it truly draw its life? What has made it memorable? Surely, it owes its success to its rhythm, and specifically to the eleventh, descending syllable which ever so slightly lengthens the traditional ten-syllable iambic pentameter: a *lingering* sound that imitates, as it were, the meaning of 'forever' by lasting a little, by remaining overtime.

Imagine

> A thing of beauty is a joy forever

revised to

> A thing of beauty is a delight forever.

The rhythmic jolt kills the line at once.

What I have said about Keats's line yields the principle that rhythm can be not only pleasurable on the instinctual level, and then again as an organizer of materials, but also, on occasion, by supporting meaning: rhythm as such, like sounds as such, can be meaningful. Keats's lingering rhythm gently assists the feeling of foreverness. Many other thoughts and moods can be supported by rhythm. For instance, a heavy meaning can be reinforced by spondees, since these inhibit the forward movement. We have seen an instance by Milton. Here now is Pope's famous and witty

> And ten low words oft creep in one dull line

[and TEN LOW WORDS OFT CREEP in ONE DULL LINE]

and again (keep reading aloud!):

> When Ajax strives some rock's vast weight to throw,
> The line too labours, and the words move slow;

both in his verse *Essay on Criticism* (1709).

A strong iambic beat is useful for optimistic or martial poetry. Tennyson has already helped us to an example in 'Ulysses':

> To strive, to seek, to find, and not to yield—

every stress of which is like a drumbeat. Browning used dactyls to imitate galloping horses in 'How They Brought the Good News from Ghent to Aix' (1845). Three men have begun the urgent journey; two have fallen by the wayside; now only the speaker is left, riding furiously to deliver his message to the city at a steady Dum-di-di Dum-di-di equine clip:

> And there was my Roland to bear the whole weight
> Of the news which alone could save Aix from her fate,
> With his nostrils like pits full of blood to the brim,
> And with circles of red for his eye-sockets' rim.

Red-hot intensity in the language—in either emotional direction, exaltation or despair—is confirmed by a powerfully irregular beat, as in the opening lines of Hopkins's 'Carrion Comfort':

> I'll not, carrion comfort, Despair, not feast on thee;
> Not untwist —slack they may be—these last strands of man
> In me ór, most weary, cry *I can no more*. I can;
> Can something, hope, wish day come, not choose not to be.

Such lines can be scanned in several ways, because aside from the 'or' that Hopkins himself has accented for us, we can decide for ourselves whether or not we want to stress certain words—like the second 'not' of line 1, or 'may' in line 2. The essential rhythmic fact of the poem is that the latter delivers a powerful jostle of shocks, which reinforces the jostled syntax, and then, together with that, the extreme agitation in the pre-energized meaning, the fundamental theme of the poem. A rhythmic strategy that would have been fatal to the Keatsian line we examined brings about an aesthetic triumph here.

But beware! A jostle of beats can support many other states of mind. As for Browning's dactyls, while it is true that they invigorate the subject-matter of the galloping horses, Swinburne, in the very same epoch, used dactyls, as we have seen, for a hothouse effect. The moral is one we have encountered before, to wit, that sonics do not in themselves make meanings. Meanings are made by words, and sometimes by the arrangement imposed on the words. Sounds and rhythms can support these meanings. They are, by themselves, too versatile to determine a single meaning or even a category of meaning. It can never be said, for instance, that iambs or short *i*-sounds produce merriment. But if we see a merry poem, we may be persuaded, in some instances, that the iambs and/or the short i-sounds support the merriment.[11]

III

Historically speaking, it can be argued that the widespread disuse of metrical regularity since the years around World War I reflects an equally widespread loss of the several fervors that once animated the elites of the Western world: belief in the power and goodness of God and the grandeur of Man, patriotism, the exaltation of noble blood and warlike acts, pride in empire and dominion over other nations, worship of Womanhood, passionate trust in romantic love, a sense that mourning and despair matter in the universe, veneration of Virtue, belief in the domestic bond of family, and so on. I also mentioned, at the beginning of this chapter, the probable connection between casual democracy and dissolution of 'stiff' meter. I am not passing judgment here on the profound changes our civilization has undergone in a hundred years. I am saying only that firm rhythm does seem appropriate to strong beliefs and high confidence, even in tragic circumstances:

> Suffolk first died; and York, all haggled over,
> Comes to him, where in gore he lay insteeped,
> And takes him by the beard; kisses the gashes
> That bloodily did yawn upon his face.
> He cries aloud, 'Tarry, my cousin Suffolk!
> My soul shall thine keep company to heaven;
> Tarry, sweet soul, for mine, then fly abreast,
> As in this glorious and well-foughten field
> We kept together in our chivalry!'[12]

11. The article on meter in the *Princeton Handbook of Poetic Terms* (a work I quoted in the previous chapter) interestingly suggests some other possible effects of (regular) meter: 'It often establishes a sort of 'distance'...by interposing a film of unaccustomed rhythmical ritual between observer and experience...It reminds the apprehender unremittingly that he is not experiencing the real object of the 'imitation'...[It] also tends to suggest (since ordinary people don't speak in meter) the vatic role of the poet.' I have my doubts, however, about 'ritual' and 'vatic.' The writer himself—Professor Paul Fussell—comes down a peg when he goes on to refer to 'the strange power of meter to burnish the commonplace'. It might be added, in any case, that these remarks could be applied to rhyme and, of course, to the fundamental strangeness of discourse by limited verbal quanta.

12. Shakespeare's *King Henry the Fifth* (1599), Act IV, Scene vi. Haggled =

While disillusionment and cynicism are supported by slack or
absent rhythm. Remember E.E. Cummings on the subject of war:

> my sweet old etcetera
> aunt lucy during the recent
>
> war could and what
> is more did tell you just
> what everybody was fighting
>
> for,
> my sister
>
> isabel created hundreds
> (and
> hundreds) of socks not to
> mention shirts fleaproof earwarmers
>
> etcetera wristers etcetera, my
> mother hoped that
> i would die etcetera
> bravely of course my father used
> to become hoarse talking about how it was
> a privilege and if only he
> could meanwhile my
>
> self et cetera lay quietly
> in the deep mud et
>
> cetera
> (dreaming,
> et
> cetera, of
> Your smile
> eyes knees and of your Etcetera)[13]

Modern cynicism has flattened out the ancient proud rhythms
of war poetry.

Even in the past, however, perfect regularity was usually avoided.
In order to stay in the mainstream of the prosodic world, I opened

hacked. The action concerns the victories of the English over the French
from 1415 to 1420. Here the deaths of the Earl of Suffolk and the Duke of
York are reported to the king.

13. The war is World War I (1914–18), precisely half a millennium off in
time *and* spirit from Henry V's invasion of France as seen through Shake-
speare's eyes.

this chapter with a quotation from Swinburne that tended toward regularity without espousing perfect symmetry. Scanning Shakespeare's lines in *Henry V* would also show a number of irregularities within the metrical pattern. Of course, excellent poems of perfect metrical regularity do exist. But they are few, because absolute symmetry quickly becomes monotonous, vapid and infantile, revealing too openly the roots of rhythm in our baby-life. No wonder, then, that rudimentary art is often highly regular: geometric patterns on pots and rugs, for instance, or the easy steady beat of most pop music and disco or ballroom dancing. So-called 'serious' music (which is often quite light-hearted) tends to be complex in its rhythms and durations, as do the dance steps and motions devised by elite choreographers. Note the all too perfect metrical pattern in the hapless doggerel verse I have been persecuting in this book:

> The DEAD friends LIVE and ALways WILL;
> Their PREsence HOvers ROUND us STILL.
> It SEEMS to ME they COME to SHARE
> Each JOY or SORrow THAT we BEAR,

and so on—which can be contrasted with the sophisticated pattern of a Shakespearean sonnet, whose basic scheme is the iambic pentameter:

> Where ART thou, MUSE, that thou forGET'ST so LONG
> To SPEAK of THAT which GIVES thee ALL thy MIGHT?
> SPEND'ST thou thy FUry on some WORTHless SONG,
> DARK'ning thy POWer to LEND BASE SUBjects LIGHT?[14]

Here the first line is *almost* regular, for its second 'thou' leaves us, once again, free to choose between a pyrrhic and a half stress, and either way provides a continuity for the iambic beat. The second line boasts five pure iambs. In the third line a classic reversal occurs: the line opens on a trochee instead of an iamb. Opening with a stressed syllable naturally lends emphasis to a line. After FU, an indisputable pyrrhic replaces the iamb. And we can see by now that the swift pyrrhic is as 'popular' an alternative for the iamb as is the momentary reversal occasioned by a trochee. Interestingly, the fourth line (which also opens with a trochaic substitute for the iamb) seems to compensate for the pyrrhic above it by

14. Sonnet 100: see Chapter 4.

adducing a spondee. Was Shakespeare performing this elegant maneuver consciously? We shall never know. What we do know is that we are worlds away from the primitive satisfactions of rock-a-bye-baby motion.

Chapter 16

Poetry without Figures

Mostly we think of poetry as 'appealing to the senses', and appealing to the senses especially through metaphors, similes, symbols and the like that illuminate and enchant. But in the present chapter we are going to consider—before shipping out on the sea of metaphor—that poetry can excel without appealing directly to the senses; and furthermore, that when it does appeal directly to the senses, it need not do so through figures of speech.

I doubt whether we can find many *extended* passages of successful poetry that do not evoke what is seen, heard, touched, smelled or viscerally felt. Sooner or later, and usually not *much* later, a writer will be using some of the 'first-ring' words we were discussing in Chapter 6—the words directly threaded to our pre-verbal and non-verbal existence: our *physical language*. You have had many illustrations of it throughout these pages, like this from Yeats:

> Chimney corner, garden walk,
> Or rocky cistern where we tread the clothes
> And gather all the talk;

or, a few pages back, Wordsworth speaking:

> Midway on long Winander's eastern shore,
> Within the crescent of a pleasant bay,
> A tavern stood; no homely-featured house,
> Primeval like its neighbouring cottages,
> But 'twas a splendid place, the door beset
> With chaises, grooms and liveries, and within
> Decanters, glasses, and the blood-red wine.

We have no trouble, however, citing brief or not-so-brief passages that have become memorable without physical language, namely through a judicious use of what we have called collector words. 'A thing of beauty is a joy forever' might be summoned again. Or Hamlet's

> To be or not to be, that is the question;

Or Milton's

> That, to the height of this great argument,
> I may assert Eternal Providence,
> And justify the ways of God to men.

We could also quote a few more lines that precede Pope's famous aphorism:

> All Nature is but art, unknown to thee;
> All chance, direction which thou canst not see;
> All discord, harmony not understood;
> All partial evil, universal good:
> And, spite of pride, in erring reason's spite,
> One truth is clear: WHATEVER IS, IS RIGHT.[1]

And, more recently, here is a Tempter speaking to Thomas Becket in T.S. Eliot's *Murder in the Cathedral* (1935). But note where, finally, three specific physical words appear (I have italicized them) amidst the second-ring or third-ring collector words:

> You know and do not know, what it is to act or suffer.
> You know and do not know, that acting is suffering,
> And suffering action. Neither does the actor suffer
> Nor the patient act. But both are fixed
> In an eternal action, an eternal patience
> To which all must consent that it may be willed
> And which all must suffer that they may will it,
> That the pattern may subsist, that the *wheel* may *turn* and still
> Be forever *still.*[2]

Our cooperative dog of Chapter 6, where we glanced at the meaning of meaning, possesses knowledge and ignorance ('not-knowledge'), acts, suffers, displays patience, consents, understands

---

1.   See Chapter 14. The copulative 'is' must be supplied in lines 2, 3 and 4; a simple but apt illustration of one of our practical pointers.
2.   In *The Complete Poems and Plays* (New York: Harcourt, Brace, 1952).

immobility and, of course, perceives a wheel as well as you and I do. But knowledge-in-general, action-in-general and so on: these are collector words, generalities, abstractions beyond the power of animal and infant. Even more remote is the idea expressed in these lines by the unspoken but extremely present word 'paradox'. Except, then, for the still or turning wheel, these lines, which have proved very successful (in our noble sense of this word), are about as non-sensuous as it is possible to be. In short, great poetry can be 'colorless'.

A point made in our last chapter bears repetition and expansion here. When a poet writes a line, or a stanza, in that the language is predominantly general, he places himself in a more vulnerable position than a colleague whose imagination provides him with an abundance of startling figures—like Eliot's memorable

> I have measured out my life with coffee spoons.

Such a poet finds himself under strong pressure to make the ideas that his rather colorless language conveys particularly impressive. Or let me state this in reverse: the poet who is about to convey a highly significant idea may not feel the need to enrich— say through resonant metaphors—what is already rich in itself. Be that as it may, colorless language in the best poetry tends to utter thoughts like

> To be or not to be, that is the question,

in preference to some trivial

> To bet or not to bet, that is the question.

When Sophocles' Antigone disobeys the laws of the State in order to obey the gods, the thought is so impressive that it can afford to express itself in the simplest, most colorless of statements, relying only on meter as an energizer. Antigone is addressing Creon, the ruler of Thebes:

> I do not think that you, a mortal man,
> Can by a breath annul and override
> The immutable unwritten laws of Heaven.
> They were not born today nor yesterday;
> They die not; and none knoweth whence they sprang.[3]

3. *Antigone*, lines 453-57 in the translation, slightly modified, by F. Storr (1912); in the Loeb Classical Library's *Sophocles*, vol. I. *Antigone* was produced

However, since pure intelligence, you will recall, is not enough to beget great poetry, the composer of an abstract passage, no matter how intelligent in its raw, paraphrased state, must levy *some* other weapons from the arsenal—choosing whatever he wishes, say rhyme, rhythm or other sonic resources, or anything from a panoply of rhetorical figures we have not explored as yet: exclamation, hyperbole, irony, balance, climactic or anti-climactic structure, repetition, and so on. In the passage taken from *Murder in the Cathedral*, we can observe especially the figure of repetition, which eloquently supports the concept of the turning wheel, almost to the point of hypnosis. If the poet ignores these weapons, or wields them badly, mere intelligence will not save his poetry, and we may feel that he could have spared himself the trouble of delivering his message in verse form (limited quanta). Shall I dare quote Eliot again for an illustration?

> This is the use of memory:
> For liberation—not less of love but expanding
> Of love beyond desire, and so liberation
> From the future as well as the past.[4]

If this passage seems as dreary to you as it does to me, the reason is that Eliot failed here to *do* anything with his propositions: he had meaning, and plenty of it, but failed to energize it, while the mere quanta that define poetry were insufficient to infuse a charge.

As soon as we have acquiesced in the idea that fine poetry *may*, for a while at any rate, dispense with physical language, we can allow ourselves to return to the well-founded belief that poetry often thrills us by evoking, through language, pre-verbal and non-verbal physical experiences. The poet knows that man lives chiefly by his senses and viscera. He realizes that people are more likely to be *stirred* by the sensory impact of objects and events (e.g. the sight of a beautiful woman or handsome man, the noise of an incoming shell) than by general ideas. A paradoxical situation ensues. We set out in infancy as sheer creatures of the senses and

in Athens around 441 BC. Here, of course, the meter is that of the English language.

4.   From 'Little Gidding', Part III. 'Little Gidding' is one of the sections of *Four Quartets* (1944). In T.S. Eliot, *The Complete Poems and Plays*.

slaves to our viscera. We grow up, and presently, rising above even
the highest animals, we proudly acquire language, which opens
the possibility of forming and communicating an endless series of
conceptions derived from the senses and viscera, but no longer
representing things directly perceived. (This last sentence is an
elaborate example.) And when that is done, we run to poetry
(and the other literary arts) in order to stir up, in fancy and
memory, the life of the senses again—by means of that very lan-
guage that allowed us to escape from it! The beauty of this situa-
tion is that it enables us to combine or fuse the physical with the
conceptual/abstract.

Why we should want to and need to return to the sensory-vis-
ceral is no mystery, but the myth of the Lybian King Antaeus
offers us an allegorical view of the matter.[5] Antaeus was a gigantic
son of Mother Earth and a mighty wrestler. He ate the flesh of
lions and slept on the bare ground in order to husband his
strength. If he was compelled to rise off the ground while
wrestling, he regained his power by touching the earth again.
Challenged by Hercules, who was unaware of this magic, Antaeus
held out against the hero by landing on the soil as often as he
could and coming up reinvigorated. Finally Hercules caught on to
the trick. He held Antaeus aloft, cracked his ribs and killed him,
to the great chagrin of Mother Earth.

In this little allegory,[6] Antaeus represents, for us, the language
that remains in direct touch with and gains its power from the
vital visceral/sensory/emotional pre-verbal and non-verbal core,
while Hercules stands for Abstraction, so often the enemy of
poetry. For by and large, we are more powerfully aroused by 'a
tidal wave of terror' than by 'immense terror'. And remember
Blake's 'The Sick Rose', where rose, storm and flying worm gave
physical shape to highly abstract ideas. Antaeus-like, poetry keeps
returning to the physical ground of our being: sights and sounds,
anger and love, cuts and caresses, a pain in the chest, water when
we are thirsty, blood on the pavement, a daisy in a child's hand.

5.   The legend of Antaeus is told by Apollodorus of Athens (c. 140 BC) in
his *Biblioteca*. (The true authorship is in doubt.)

6.   Allegory is a narrative mode that can manifest itself in prose as well as
in poetry. We can define it, most simply, as a series of symbols in symbolic
action (see Chapter 18).

In practice, to be sure, poetry usually weaves back and forth between the abstract and the physical, taking advantage of the power of language both to generate large ideas and to evoke fancies and memories of physical experiences. Note this weaving in a poem by William Carlos Williams:

PASTORAL

When I was younger
It was plain to me
I must make something of myself.
Older now
I walk back streets
admiring the houses
of the very poor:
roof out of line with sides
the yard cluttered
with old chicken wire, ashes,
furniture gone wrong;
the fences and outhouses
built of barrel-staves
and parts of boxes, all,
if I am fortunate,
smeared a bluish green
that properly weathered
pleases me best
of all colors.
           No one
will believe this
of vast import to the nation.[7]

The poet begins and ends with abstractions, and puckishly inserts one in the middle ('if I am fortunate').[8] These abstractions are physically grounded and exemplified. Why is it fortunate to find an old crate smeared bluish green? ('Smeared': Williams uses a word bearing unlovely associations in order to make his statement as extreme as possible.) The answer is an implied proposition about the nobility of humble, even broken and abandoned

---

7.   In *Al Que Quiere* (1917). From *The Collected Earlier Poems of William Carlos Williams* (New York: New Directions, 1951).

8.   'To make something of oneself' collects a limitless number of possibilities, as does 'being fortunate', while 'nation' is a more specific huge collector.

things.[9] Furthermore, Williams seems to be sarcastic about the large claims he made when he was young. Older, he has realized that true wisdom finds happiness in lowly rejects (a fine Franciscan view, we might call it). Paradoxically, he *has* made something of himself. Like the mystics, he has gone up by going down. And finally, such wisdom *is* important to the nation (mankind); but 'we' are too blind to believe it. See incidentally how, in voicing this implied theme, Williams has energized it by the rhetoric of sarcasm, which we shall be considering in a later chapter.

All this time I have been speaking of the physical experiences *evoked* by language, and not about the physical sound-experiences *made* by language that were our subjects in Chapters 14 and 15. The word 'thunder' sends a given sound to our ears, with a trochaic beat; but what we are talking about in this chapter is the memory or imagination of the actual noise in the sky that the word stirs up in us. Neither are we talking about the visual experience of seeing the print- or quill-marks on the page, although in some languages—Chinese and Arabic come to mind—these can be so beautiful in themselves, regardless of what the words are evoking, that people hang up on their walls poems they cannot even read.

You may have noticed my avoidance all along of the term 'imagery', which most writers use in lieu of my 'physical language'. There are two reasons for keeping 'imagery' at bay. First, 'imagery' has two meanings that are too easily confused. In 'the tidal wave destroyed six houses on the beach' the images are 'absolute'—that is to say, they are not figures of speech; they are straighforward, literal descriptions. In that application I have chosen the term 'physical language'. But in 'a tidal wave of longing came over me', image means figure of speech; there is no tidal wave at all (as there was in the first application); only an emotion that seemed to have something in common with a tidal wave. And in such cases, I speak of figures or tropes—metaphors, similes, and others.

The second reason for making a detour around 'image' and 'imagery' is that these terms pay too great a compliment to our

---

9. We remember that 'The Red Wheelbarrow' proposed the same theme.

dominant visual sense, and thus blur the fact that both physical language *and* tropes often involve the other senses. Writers on the art of poetry find themselves enlisting as 'imagery' lines like:

> The trumpet's loud clangor
> Excites us to arms

and:

> The double double double beat
> Of the thundering drum.[10]

By using the expression 'physical language' we open the door democratically to all the senses alike.

Just as it is difficult to remain for a long time on a purely abstract linguistic level, so it is hard to compose in physical language without sooner or later roping in (this is a metaphor) a metaphor or other figures. But it can be done. Poets have written very effective physical poetry without resorting to *energetic* figures—I mean, figures of speech that energize the raw propositions and are thus aesthetically operative. Descriptive poetry often confines itself to such plain, literal physical language:

MEETING THE MOUNTAINS

> He crawls to the edge of the foaming creek
> He backs up the slab ledge
> He puts a finger in the water
> He turns to a trapped pool
> Puts both hands in the water
> Puts one foot in the pool
> Drops pebbles in the pool
> He slaps the water surface with both hands
> He cries out, rises up and stands
> Facing toward the torrent and the mountain
> Raises up both hands and shouts three times![11]

And here are a few illustrative lines from Robert Frost's classic 'Mending Wall' (1914):

---

10. From the third stanza of Dryden's 'A Song for St. Cecilia's Day' (1687). The three 'double' in sequence constitute a striking example of onomatopeia.

11. Gary Snyder, in *Regarding Wave* (New York: New Directions, 1970). Note the word repetitions as super-perfect rhymes.

Something there is that doesn't love a wall,
That sends the frozen-ground-swell under it,
And spills the upper boulders in the sun;
And makes gaps even two can pass abreast.
The work of hunters is another thing:
I have come after them and made repair
Where they have left not one stone on a stone,
But they would have the rabbit out of hiding,
To please the yelping dogs. The gaps I mean,
No one has seen them made or heard them made,
But at spring mending-time we find them there.
I let my neighbor know beyond the hill;
And on a day we meet to walk the line
And set the wall between us once again.
We keep the wall between us as we go.
To each the boulders that have fallen to each.
And some are loaves and some so nearly balls
We have to use a spell to make them balance:
'Stay where you are until our backs are turned!'
We wear our fingers rough with handling them.
Oh, just another kind of out-door game,
One on a side. It comes to little more:
There where we are we do not need the wall.[12]

Why have I italicized two of the lines? You will have guessed the reason: they are the only lines where physical language is used to create active figures of speech. Literally, Frost is lying to us in these two lines. He knows, we know, and he knows that we know, that the boulders are not loaves, as he says they are, and that he and his neighbor do not cast a spell, as he says they do. But let us leave these figures for other chapters and survey the rest of the quotation. Aside from a couple of quite lifeless metaphors, Frost has written his lines with a remarkable simplicity of physical diction: the groundswell toppling the stone wall; gaps in the wall; hunters; rabbits; dogs; the acts of seeing, hearing, pleasing; a neighbor and notifying him; mending the wall by walking each on his own side; handling things; wearing fingers rough; playing games; feeling the uselessness of an action... And from these 'primitive' resources, avoiding any trope that would have made the thick-skulled neighbor stare and shrug his shoulders, Frost

12. In *The Poetry of Robert Frost* (ed. E.C. Lathem; New York: Henry Holt, 1970).

managed to compose one of his most enduring poems; one in which, in a process I have described before, we 'translate' the first-ring language into abstractions—namely, in this instances, impressive thoughts about human relationships and Nature.[13]

For one of the sublime moments in literature, we turn, in conclusion, to the *Iliad*. Achilles has killed Hector, the leader of the Trojan army, and grossly defiled his body. Hector's father, the aged king Priam, is reduced to begging the Greek hero to allow him to take his son's corpse home for burial. Achilles, we know, has killed several of Priam's sons before this. Now the old king kneels before grim Achilles and supplicates him, saying:

> I have gone through what no other mortal on earth has gone through;
> I put my lips to the hands of the man who has killed my children.[14]

The raw idea here and the picture it produces in our 'visual cortex' are so powerful (for many or most of us) that the lines stand as great poetry without figures of any sort. Rhythm is the only energizer the poet (and his translator) needed to apply. Of course, he was careful to avoid any word whose unwanted connotations (of levity, for instance) would have poisoned the raw proposition. But he looked for no interesting comparisons, and did not try to draw words into unexpected meanings. He had a grandly moving thing to say, and saw that the simplest way of speaking was the best.

13. In this way, 'Mending Wall' becomes an allegory. Note, in the first line, the reversal of ordinary word order that gives importance to the 'Something' in the cosmos. The trochaic beat of 'Something' enforces its conceptual importance. After this grab for attention Frost can allow the line to become smoothly iambic. Negatively, you will feel at once that 'There is something that doesn't love a wall' would have poisoned the line; and yet the raw proposition is the same.

14. Book 24, lines 505-506 in Richmond Lattimore's translation (Chicago: University of Chicago Press, 1951).

Chapter 17

Energetic Metaphor: The Major Trope

I

After King Antaeus and Hercules, let us imagine Adam and Eve living in their orchard east of Eden by a jolly stream full of fish under a sun never too hot and rain never too wet. One day Adam, seduced by the serpent's propaganda, ate the forbidden apple, much against his wife's advice, for Eve did not like snakes, even snakes that talk. God sent down an angel, who told the pair that they must quit the Garden and *work* for a living for the rest of their lives. At this bad news, Adam sat down and did what neither he nor Eve had ever done: he wept buckets of tears, as we might put it nowadays. Of course, he had cried a little now and then when Eve would not play with him or when he stubbed a toe on a stone. But never so much as now, not by far, and Eve, who tried to be stoical and not belabor her husband with bitter reproaches, was astonished at the quantity of tears she was seeing for the first time in her life. That night, in the foul world outside the Garden, sitting by their first campfire (after expelling them, the angel had left them his smoldering brand as a parting gift), and mulling over the day's cruel events, Eve heard herself saying, among other things, 'And then, pet, I saw a stream of tears flowing down your cheeks.' With this, the first postlapsarian metaphor had been invented (buckets would come much later). I hope that it impressed Adam, and distracted him a little from his gloom.

What Eve had done was to use her God-given *imagination* (which is the power to bring to one's consciousness things and combinations of things that are not physically present) to realize that two quite different phenomena, a stream and weeping, have one or more attributes in common. Their realities—or rather, to be punctiliously philosophical, their *perceived* realities—overlap. Both are wet, both flow, and both can be abundant. Having imagined this overlap in a fraction of a second, Eve could both define and characterize, in a single word familiar to her and Adam, a phenomenon altogether new to her.[1]

In pre-historical fact rather than my pretty story, metaphors must have sprung up spontaneously among all the creatures who were using language, and must have appeared very quickly after language took its first tottering steps. For, needless to say, language was not born a seasoned adult. It began by coping with the limited social and natural phenomena of early communal life. It grew as new phenomena demanded attention—and of course still grows for the same reason: coping with new situations. Whenever something new and unfamiliar appeared to the mind, the easiest and therefore most natural strategy was to apply to it a word or a phrase signifying something already familiar to the community: usually something clear and communicable to the senses (like 'stream')—something physical whose special feature was that it displayed—was thought or perceived to display—a significant connection (usually a partial similarity, an overlap) with the hard-to-express new phenomenon.

This sort of lexical activity was especially useful when it came to finding words for vague, hard-to-define yet important phenomena. Think, for instance, how difficult it would have been to avoid metaphors when people tried for the first time to name the kinds of persons we call 'deep' or 'shallow'.

Since the real or imagined universe offered endless possibilities of perceiving similarities and interconnections, every language found itself in possession of as many metaphors as there are waves in the ocean (but this is not a metaphor; it is a simile—a hyperbolical one—that must be despatched to another chapter).

Indeed, after looking at Eve in some bewilderment, Adam proved himself capable of rising to the occasion by assuring her, 'I see what you mean'; and then, fibbing a little, as was natural after the Original Sin: 'In fact, my dear wife, I grasped your invention

---

1. And with the same stroke of the imagination, she invented the figure of hyperbole.

of metaphor at once,' thus providing mankind with two basic metaphors for understanding.

While this mental procedure for naming new things or making unfamiliar things familiar is in one sense gloriously creative, and of course unique to *homo sapiens*, viewed from another angle it seems downright lazy—a case of taking the line of least resistance, which is what living beings typically do. The mind boggles at the hardship of minting a brand-new name for each new experience. For that matter, the mind is *unable* to create what would amount to an infinite lexicon, where each object or experience would receive its own discrete term. Metaphors make it possible for mankind to augment the language 'organically', the new and unfamiliar getting linguistically grafted on the old and familiar.

In our own times, this primordial function of metaphor subsists and thrives. Whoever gave the name *mouse* to the instrument I am using at this very moment to move the cursor to and fro upon the screen of my word-processor drew upon a familiar, physical creature to designate an item quite new to the universe. He was poetically inspired to find an amusing if somewhat farfetched overlap between the rodent and the grey box that dashes about the pad under my hand.[2]

But why was our Adam taken aback for a split second by Eve's metaphor? Because in the instant before informing her that he had 'seen' and 'grasped' what she was doing, he had thought, 'A stream of tears? Why did she say a stream? As if there were fish swimming in my tears!'

What Adam had realized is that even though metaphors are based on perceived similar attributes among things, the things themselves retain their own essential beings: the mouse remains a *Mus musculus* and the little electronic box remains a little electronic box. In other words, the metaphor-maker also *excludes*; in fact, he normally excludes much more than he includes. For instance, when Donne tells his ex-mistress that she will be 'bath'd in a cold quicksilver sweat' (see Chapter 7), it is not recommended that we import into our enjoyment the fact that mercury

---

2. The mouse was invented in 1964 by the computer genius Douglas Engelbart, working at that time for the Stanford Research Institute. I don't know whether Mr Engelbart also invented its name.

is a good conductor of electricity or that it forms alloys called amalgams.

The fact of exclusion helps explain why metaphors can be obscure, even unintelligible, to the hearer. Had Adam been less perceptive, Eve would have been obliged to explain what she had included and excluded from her metaphor: 'It was not because of any fish, darling, but because of the quantities of water that were coming out of your eyes.' By the same token, when I remarked that the similarity between a live mouse and the electronic cursor-guidance unit is far-fetched, I implied that some persons, hearing 'mouse' in this context for the first time, would need a brief explanation.

II

At this point, we can walk away from the usefulness of metaphors in naming new things, or making the unfamiliar familiar, in order to examine other significant and significatory work they do for us.

Of the mouse metaphor I said not only that it was helpful though a bit farfetched, but also that it was amusing. Metaphors, it turns out, are created not only because they help us grasp new or difficult situations, but also because they are, or at any rate try to be, more *interesting* (in some particular context) than the already familiar names of the objects or events they replace. If they are indeed interesting, this is because (1) they are new; (2) they are vivid; (3) they contribute their own 'cargo' of implied propositions, values and emotions. Any of these powers will do, or a combination of two or all three of them.

Since these are indeed powers (potentially so, at any rate) and not neutral characteristics, it is understandable that poets are not the only active people who try to invent strong metaphors—and other tropes (figures of speech). Powerful tropes are effective; effective for the poet in producing aesthetic pleasure, but effective as well for people who are after very different goals: selling more cars, winning a case before a jury, getting a candidate elected, arousing the public against an enemy, and so on.

Thus calling the computer thingamajig a mouse instead of sticking to 'Handheld Input Device' or HID was not only amusing; it was also brilliant salesmanship. The metaphor was new; it was vivid; and it sucked into the thingamajig certain implied values concerning those tiny, cuddly and active creatures. You might argue that many potential customers are afraid of mice. I believe I would have brought up this argument myself at the conference where the name was adopted. I would have suggested some other metaphorical name out of fear of losing a large number of customers. But it seems that I would have been mistaken. 'Rat' was of course out of the question. Public disgust is invincible vis-à-vis rats. But 'mice' turned out to be a hit. The attributes of 'scary' and 'repellent' were successfully excluded, as they are for Mickey Mouse.

Newspapers are a good source for mere vividness. Sportswriters, for instance, draw upon an army of metaphors ('army' is a metaphor, of course) in order to replace the tired verb 'defeat'. Teams seldom merely defeat other teams. They clobber, swamp, clip, blank, blitz, whip, stun, etc. Note, however, how easily *mere* vividness becomes flashy (another metaphor, but not a flashy one).

Vividness is usually produced by drama or by physical language—the immediate appeal to our senses we discussed in our previous chapter. 'Bath'd in a cold quicksilver sweat' substituting for 'extremely frightened' is typical. First-ring physical language excitingly replaces, in the guise of metaphor, language that is general, abstract, vague, private/internal (my thoughts, for instance), emotionally neutral, or simply hackneyed. If Eve had remarked, 'You cried with many, many, many tears,' using Basic Humanese, Adam might have paid no attention. Inasmuch, however, as abstract language can also be highly effective in poetry (so we demonstrated in Chapter 16), it follows that it too can exert its power in the guise of metaphor. We might, for instance, speak of 'a democracy of wavelets on the lake', using a highly abstract collector word as a dramatic metaphor for perfectly visible things. So then: although metaphors *usually* exploit physical and communicable immediacies (with pride of place, as always, to the visual), brilliantly dramatic metaphorical effects can sometimes be elicited from abstract language.

A point worth noting is that the metaphor that donates its services can easily be a physical impossibility in our non-verbal world of experiences. Two instances come to mind, both from Chapter 6: Herbert's 'Thy rope of sands' in 'The Collar', and, from

Tennyson's *In Memoriam,* 'I will not eat my heart alone.' As an action, eating one's own heart is no more real than the Gorgon or Medusa; but it works so nicely as a metaphor—'eat your heart out, buddy!'—that it has long since become a cliché.

For artists, the most important power of significant as against flashy metaphor derives from the implied propositions and values, with their attendant emotions, that are instantaneously drawn into the thing to which the metaphor is being applied, provided the listener or reader knows what to exclude as well as what to include. Since the included ideas, values and emotions can be abundant and complex, metaphors often *encapsulate*, that is to say, they do a great deal of work briefly. And we enjoy brevity: the power of compressed things.

Consider these two simple sentences:

> Innovative practices blossomed in the Church;

and:

> Innovative practices infected the Church.

In the first, I have raided the agreeable realm of springtime flowers, captured the emotion of approval that pertains to them, and injected the whole, instantaneously, into a series of complex events that occurred in the Church. For the second sentence, I have dipped into the world of disease and, instantaneouly, injected its bacteria into the self-same events. Briefly much is said. But the illustrations I have chosen also afford us an incidental glimpse into the more dangerous work that metaphors can do in the practical world. In a poem the successful metaphor is one we absorb with a jolt of pleasure. But when the politician, advertiser, journalist, lawyer (and so on) use expressions like 'Innovative practices blossomed in the Church' or 'Innovative practices infected the Church,' they measure success by the ability of these metaphors to persuade the public without logic, arguments or troublesome presentations of evidence.[3]

---

3.   Remember, however, that words need not be used as metaphors in order to have all sorts of power, including the power to make insidious propaganda. We covered this subject in our chapter on implied propositions; but here, from the daily newspaper, is an instance of propaganda without metaphor: 'Thatcher shrieks that the poll tax is more fair than the rates' (*Los*

III

Insidious though they may be in their psychological power to sway the unaware, as far as literature is concerned my two metaphors—'blossomed' and 'infected'—can hardly be called remarkable. They are unremarkable because they participate in the destiny of most metaphors created by mankind either to name the new or refresh the old, which is to decay. What I mean by this is that in the course of time most metaphors become ex-metaphors. We no longer *feel* them as metaphors; and our dictionaries cease to treat them as metaphors. As metaphors, 'to see' and 'to grasp' have lost their power to innovate, startle or enrich. 'Shallow' and 'deep' have long since become the plainest of plain words. And our dictionaries ratify the decay by giving such words the very same definitions, among others, that they give to the words that had undergone the metaphorizing in question. Thus, see and grasp have become synonyms of understand instead of enjoying the privileged status of metaphor.

Some metaphors remain energetic indefinitely, as we shall see. For those that decline from metaphor to ex-metaphor, the move is a gradual one of variable velocity. As a result, all of us encounter many metaphors that retain part of their power—an in-between of vividness or propositional richness. Illustrations are hazardous, for a metaphor that may sound fairly fresh to me might have lost any power to wake *you* up, or vice versa. But let me try anyhow. In one of the preceding paragraphs I remarked that 'metaphors must have *sprung up* spontaneously', namely after 'language took its first *tottering steps*'. Both italicized phrases are characteristically physical metaphors for the general idea of beginning. The first, however, is surely an ex-metaphor that never will be fresh again; the second seems to me somewhat dog-eared (a metaphor), yet still a going concern (a metaphor again)— somewhere between fresh and wilted.

Angeles Times, 1 April 1990; the poll tax is a flat tax on each voter; rates are property taxes). It is highly improbable that the British Prime Minister was literally shrieking. Nevertheless, the nasty disvalue we attach to 'shrieks' does its underground work of condemning in advance, without the hard work of producing evidence. All these ploys, so dangerous in the 'real world', are happy potential energizers for the artist.

Here is the first stanza of 'Mirror in February' by Thomas
Kinsella (b. 1928; italics mine):

> The day dawns with scent of must and rain,
> Of opened soil, dark trees, dry bedroom air.
> Under the fading lamp, half dressed—my brain
> *Idling* on some compulsive fantasy—
> I towel my shaven lip and stop, and stare,
> *Riveted* by a dark exhausted eye,
> A dry downturning mouth.[4]

Here too, I think, it can be said that for many of us *riveted* in
this context is practially an ex-metaphor, while *idling* is somewhat
fresher as an image borrowed from motor cars (where it was itself
originally a metaphor!) and applied to a human brain. But is it
always a mistake to make use of a worn-out metaphor? By no
means. I would suggest that *riveted* still works, in that, together
with *idling*, it subtly and successfully conveys a notion and feeling
of man in our industrialized age, a fellow decidedly less glam-
orous than the weary Romantic of a former age.

A very common phenomenon is the nesting of metaphor inside
metaphor. This occurs all the time in ordinary speech, but the
opening stanza of an ode by Richard Crashaw (c. 1613–49) in
honor of Saint Mary Magdalene's tears provides an apt poetic
illustration :

> Hail, sister springs!
> Parents of silver-footed rills!
> Ever bubbling things!
> Thawing crystal! Snowy hills,
> Still spending, never spent! I mean
> Thy fair eyes, sweet MAGDALENE![5]

4.   From *Nightwalker and Other Poems* (New York: Random House, 1967).
Note also the 'fading lamp' of line 3. The poet is not trying to tell us that the
lamp as such is doing the fading, like Lewis Carroll's Cheshire Cat, which
vanished, leaving only its grin behind. Obviously the lamp is not fading; it is
the light *of* the lamp that fades. The source of the effect is substituted for the
effect. This species of trope will be discussed in the next chapter.

5.   This 186-line hymn first appeared in 1646. The story of the weeping
'woman who was leading an immoral life' can be found in the seventh chap-
ter of Luke. Although she remains nameless in the Gospel, tradition
confused her with Mary of Magdala, who is mentioned in Luke 8.2, and as

Within three lines, the saint's eyes are called springs, snowy hills and thawing crystal; but note how metaphor is nested into metaphor: the springs are parents, the hills are spending and the rills have feet. In short, metaphors can breed their own metaphors.

Because Crashaw—though secure, it would seem, in the established canon—can be and has been accused of extravagance, let us turn to a few less dubious poetic instances of thrilling novelty, vividness, drama and richness of implications. Here, to begin with, are some daring and astonishing lines by Yeats:

> A woman can be proud and stiff
> When on love intent;
> But Love has pitched his mansion in
> The place of excrement;
> For nothing can be sole or whole
> That has not been rent.[6]

We are going to devote our attention to lines 3-4. Line 3 can be paraphrased as 'The location of the organs for sexual intercourse is.' We pause briefly at the capital-lettered Love, noting that this is a common personification—a trope we will treat in due time— and proceed to the metaphorical 'pitched his mansion'. To begin with, we get the powerful physicality of this strange metaphor, in sharp contrast to the anemic abstraction of my non-metaphorical paraphrase. For most readers this makes for an immediate leap from boredom (the neutral state) to excitement.

But the metaphor also concentrates and donates rich implied propositions. Metaphor for metaphor, why did Yeats not write 'built his house' or 'built his mansion' or the expected 'pitched his tent'? An easy first answer is that 'pitched his mansion' has the advantage of novelty. Unlike the other phrases, this one has never been heard before. Therefore it jabs us awake. But novelty alone does not make for greatness. Mere novelty is flashy. So then, where else are the merits of Yeats's metaphors? For one thing, thanks to the phrase 'pitch his tent', which any English-speaking person overhears (or underhears!) in Yeats's phrase, Love appears as a captain on the march, bivouacking for the night, rather than

such she became the prototype of the tearful, penitent sinner who is saved because of her faith in Christ.

6.   From 'Crazy Jane Talks with the Bishop' (1933). In *The Poems of W.B. Yeats* (ed. R. J. Finneran; New York: Macmillan, 1983).

showing up as an honest but unexciting carpenter building a house; an obvious gain in power and a highly dynamic view of Eros. But beyond this, the meaning of 'pitch' as a smeary substance all but demands admittance in view of the shocking line that follows. True: I have warned against indiscriminately admitting any and all meanings and sub-meanings of a word as you read a poem; but this time there is strong textual pressure to deal with this 'dirty' meaning that seems to contradict conquering Eros, yet accords with Yeats 'place of excrement'.

This conquering captain does not, however, pitch an ordinary tent in a miasmal place, he pitches a mansion! He chooses the pitchy place to construct neither a flimsy, temporary tent, nor even a solid house, but a rich, grand, proud, important, permanent dwelling. It dawns on us that, while we may have been tempted to think that Yeats is disparaging love by associating it with excrement, he is in fact glorifying it by declaring its ability to shine in the lowliest of places. One does not become a Mother Teresa by attending to tycoons, but by comforting starving Indians. Thus, while pursuing full honesty and fighting the sentimentalities often associated with Cupid, Yeats is also asserting the tremendous power of love, for it survives the pitch-worst that can be said to denigrate it. Survives and conquers. And all this is conveyed as implied proposition through metaphor: physically, dramatically, and perhaps (by way of our subconscious) instantaneously.

We can call metaphors that say so much so compactly *illuminating*, an ex-metaphor that contrasts effectively with 'flashy'. Of course these are judgments, and you need not approve of my particular example. But here is a passage—one I came across in a literary quarterly some years ago—which will leave most of us shuddering and laughing at the same time, and which few of us will call illuminating:

> I know it's morning by silk
> straining small gold curds of sun
> into the black borscht of my slumber.

After this horror, we thankfully return to a true poet, and listen again to Emily Dickinson's illuminating tropes when she speaks of seeing a snake:

But never met this fellow
Attended or alone,
Without a tighter breathing,
And zero at the bone.

In an entirely different mood, watch John Dryden giving advice to the despised Thomas Shadwell:

Leave writing Plays, and choose for thy command
Some peaceful Province in Acrostic Land.[7]

The metaphor is playfully martial: Dryden orders the hapless general of literature to take charge of a province in an extremely unimportant country, for an acrostic is a trivial verbal game, whereas the Drama is a high form of art. But that is not insulting enough. The province to which this general is being sent is safely at peace. Judge how his abilities are rated by headquarters. Playful but deadly; for a humorous metaphor can be as illuminating as a tragic one.

An entire existence can be encapsulated in a single metaphor. Recall Eliot's

I have measured out my life with coffee spoons.

A person could read this single line of *The Love Song of J. Alfred Prufrock* and draw an accurately complex portrait of Eliot's anti-hero without reading a single word of the rest of the poem.[8]

Remarkably, not one of the metaphors I have drawn from Dryden, Dickinson, Yeats and Eliot has decayed over the years. Each one has retained its freshness, originality, and therefore its full power to thrill.

IV

I conclude with an historical observation. Some poems abound in fresh metaphors; some, as I showed in our previous chapter, make do without them. Some poets keep returning to this particular means of energizing pre-poetic propositions; others prefer other means. For we must remember that a poet need not use all the

---

7.   Lines 205-206 of *Mac Flecknoe* (1682). See Chapter 13.

8.   There would have been nothing wrong with 'tea spoons'—except that it would have destroyed the beat, and thus killed the line.

aesthetic weapons available to him. However, besides these indi-
vidual variations, large-scale historical alternations have occurred.
English poetry has prospered alike through periods in which
innovative metaphors (and related tropes) were in fashion, and
others in which they were not only less in demand, but positively
ridiculed. Metaphor-making was singularly active in the first half
of the seventeenth century (the high age of baroque art), and has
been extremely active again in ours. As a result, both epochs can
furnish us with marvelous metaphors on the one hand, and trivial,
absurd, farfetched, and even monstrous figures on the other.
Crashaw on Mary Magdalene is representative for his time. Later
in the same poem, he refers to the penitent's weeping eyes as

> Two walking baths; two weeping motions;
> Portable and compendious oceans.

Metaphors so bizarre (our Eve would have been hard put to
invent them!) were called 'conceits'—a term related to 'concept',
not to self-regard—and remained current in Italian, Spanish,
German, French and English until the fashion was displaced by a
so-called 'neo-classical' ideal of simple grandeur and encompass-
ing abstraction (e.g. 'Whatever is, is Right').

In the twentieth century we have seen once again—what shall
we call it? an epidemic of metaphoritis? a flowering of metaphors?
Choose your metaphor; I mean: many, many, many metaphors. I
will leave the 'black borscht of my slumber' alone, however, and
rather quote a more respectable passage from early in the cen-
tury, namely in Hart Crane's 'The Tunnel', with eleven metaphors
and conceits italicized:

> A tugboat, *wheezing wreaths* of steam,
> *Lunged* past, with one *galvanic* blare *stove* up the River.
> I counted the echoes *assembling,* one after one,
> *Searching, thumbing* the midnight on the piers.
> Lights, *coasting* left the oily *tympanum* of waters;
> The blackness somewhere *gouged glass* on a sky.[9]

What an amazing contrast, is it not, with that characteristic

---

9. Hart Crane (1899–1932). This is one of a series of poems called *The
Bridge*, published in 1930. In *Collected Poems* (New York: Liveright Publishers,
1933).

neo-classical effusion of Pope's, utterly uninterested in 'grabbing' us with metaphor:

> All Nature is but art, unknown to thee;
> All chance, direction which thou canst not see;
> All discord, harmony not understood;
> All partial evil, universal good:
> And, spite of pride, in erring reason's spite,
> One truth is clear: WHATEVER IS, IS RIGHT.

Poetry swings between these two extremes. Our individual tastes may run to one or the other; but the amassed judgment of the centuries is unequivocal—namely (to re-use a metaphor) that the room of poetry in the house of art is a large one that accommodates furniture in a surprising variety of styles.

Chapter 18

Synecdoches and Symbols

Here again are the lines in Emily Dickinson's poem we were inspecting a while ago:

> But never met this fellow
> Attended or alone,
> Without a tighter breathing,
> And zero at the bone.

'Zero' is a true metaphor, because what enables it to substitute for 'a chilling dread' (or some such phrase) is a perceived area of similarities—perceived by the poet, who then attempts to transmit her perception to the reader. But besides similarity or shared attributes among phenonema, mankind perceives many other types of connections (relationships). And often, when we perceive a connection between phenomenon A and phenomenon B, we are capable of making our language say B and yet be understood to mean A. We might call B the donor and A the recipient. Naturally, as is the case with metaphor, writers do not perform this act of linguistic acrobatics just to keep their brains and ours busy; they have the very same purposes in mind as those I have described in the last chapter.

What are some of the connections among phenomena other than perceived zones of shared attributes? I might exclaim: what are they not! We perceive connections between part and whole, cause and effect, container and thing contained, individual and group, past and present, concrete and abstract, product and producer-of-the-product, and so on practically without limit—and any of these in either order, that is to say x can be donor to y and y can behave as donor to x.

Terms like 'metonymy' (from the Greek for 'a change of names') and 'synecdoche' ('simultaneous comprehension') divide these possibilities between them. But I propose that we coolly drop half the baggage and allow 'synecdoche' (pronounced siNEKdokee) to serve as an umbrella for all figures of substitution other than metaphor—until, that is, we come to the topic of symbols.[1]

I remarked that the purposes, or functions, of synecdoches are identical with those of metaphor. That is why, in Chapter 13, I was able to consider the two figures of Dickinson's 'zero at the bone' together, even though 'zero' is a metaphor while 'bone' is a synecdoche. And why is 'bone' a synecdoche? Because the clearest connection between bone and the entire human being is not one of shared attributes or resemblance. The clearest relationship is that of part to whole: a bone is one part of the body. Nevertheless, the force of this figure springs from the same sources as that of the metaphor 'zero'. Dickinson said 'bone' instead of, for example, 'flesh', because 'bone' brings with it hard intimations of 'skeleton' and therefore death.

For a typical example of an attribute substituting for the owner of the attribute, we listen again to Anne Sexton describing the denizens of a mental institution:

> and this is the gray dress next to me
> who grumbles as if it were special
> to be old...

The poet knew by instinct that the long-winded and everyday '[woman in] the gray dress' would have diluted the force she achieves by concentrating on the gray dress. We keep returning, in fact, to the aesthetic principle that compression is a major

---

1. I am tempted, indeed, to drop both 'synecdoche' and 'metonymy' and allow 'metaphor' (from 'metapherein', meaning 'to transfer') to carry the entire load of figures of substitution—always excepting 'symbol'; and so place a check on the multiplication of distinctions that professionals in every human discipline love to create. But the half-measure I propose is at any rate a half remedy, which is better than none.

source of force or energy for the poet's raw propositions; as it is, remarkably, for the physical matter science and engineering deal with.

We can hardly cover our subject without quoting Christopher Marlowe's classic lines:

> Was this the face that launched a thousand ships
> And burnt the topless towers of Ilium?[2]

While it is plausible that Helen of Troy's face was the young lady's most attractive feature, surely if it had been attached to a deformed body, Paris would have declined to abduct her from her husband, and we would have had no Trojan War to furnish poets with tales, allusions and tropes. *All* of Helen must have been ravishing; and we can suppose that the real Marlowe and his created Faust took that for granted. In short, 'the face' is a synecdoche for the whole beautiful girl. Like the rest of Marlowe's couplet, it shows his concern for dramatic concreteness and compression.

Furthermore, it is neither the face nor the whole Helen who literally launched those ships. Helen was the cause, the motivating force for the launching. And to top things off, the point of the story is not the launching, but the war of which the launching was an essential part. Nothing but synecdoches!

As an interesting companion to Marlowe's lines we might cite the first stanza of a poem by Dylan Thomas (1914–53):

> The hand that signed the paper felled a city;
> Five sovereign fingers taxed the breath,
> Doubled the globe of dead and halved a country;
> These five kings did a king to death.[3]

Unlike Marlowe's 'Was this the face', Thomas's 'The hand' does not begin as a trope, since the hand is what actually does the signing, but it turns into a synecdoche as it fells, taxes, etc. by means of its equivalent, the five fingers in the second line. The third line (by the way) is a fine example of hyperbole. And the fourth line gives us one more example of nesting of figures: the synecdoche of five fingers encloses the metaphor of five kings: the

---

2. *The Tragical History of the Life and Death of Doctor Faustus* (c. 1592), Act V, Scene i. Ilium is another name for Troy.

3. In *Collected Poems 1934–1953* (New York: New Directions, 1953).

five-fingered hand, which stands for the powerful man, is as powerful as five kings vanquishing a single one.

Even more striking is the phrase 'A grief ago', which opens another poem by Dylan Thomas. Now the content, grief, is substituted for the container, time. To express himself without trope, the poet would have been obliged to write something like 'Sometime ago, in the course of a time so full of regular-coming griefs that I measure time by these griefs...' There is simply no forceful way of saying literally what Thomas managed to compress into his explosive figure.

Synecdoches are extremely common in ordinary discourse, out of which the kind of discourse we call literature gently grows. 'Have you read Dickens?' 'He lives from his pen.' 'A genuine Ming.' 'The greybeards are in charge.' 'The German eagle triumphed.' 'A wicked tongue.' And here is a headline in a December 7, 1990 newspaper:

'THE MAN MUST LEAVE KUWAIT', BUSH INSISTS.

'The man' was Saddam Hussein, dictator of Iraq. However, Saddam Hussein could hardly have been asked to leave Kuwait, since he was not in Kuwait to begin with. 'The man' was running the show in Baghdad. But the compression of the president's synecdoche gave dramatic power to his discourse by focusing our attention on the center of power, substituted here for the tool wielded by that power, namely the army. Needless to say, there was no danger that any reader would be naive enough to misunderstand the American president, or the headline writer.

II

Now that we have inspected metaphors and synecdoches as figures of connection and substitution, what space, one might wonder, remains for symbols? What are symbols anyway? How do they relate to metaphors and synecdoches? Do they perform some function peculiar to themselves?

One point that can be made immediately is that 'metonymy' and 'synecdoche' remain foreign terms, active only in the service of specialists. But even 'metaphor' is not a word that leaps easily from Everyman's lips. The word 'symbol', instead, is universally known and used as a matter of course by the educated and uneducated alike. As a result, even if it gives us a mite of trouble when we try to apply it to literature, we can hardly ignore it and must certainly not try to suppress it from our vocabulary, like the unfortunate 'metonymy'.

Why is 'symbol' such a common word? After all, it is as Greek as our other friends. It was the name given to the round metal token that allowed Athenians entry to their amphitheaters, which were the all-in-one equivalents of our playhouses, movie theaters and concert halls. Inasmuch as this copper token 'stood for'—symbolized—the people's right to see the play or dance (like today's paper ticket), it is not surprising that its name, *symbolon*, eventually became the word that denotes *any* object that 'stands for' something else.[4]

And here, perhaps, is the reason the word is so common. Unlike metaphors, synecdoches, similes and other tropes, which are manipulations of verbal representations of reality, the symbol starts out by being a piece of that reality itself, that is to say a physical, three-dimensional object or event or condition—or even four-dimensional, if we include time. In other words, the symbol begins its life (so to speak) not as a figure of speech (trope) at all. When, on a holiday in New York, you climb the stairway inside the Statue of Liberty, you are not working your way up a metaphor; you are perspiring inside an extremely solid symbol. At this point, however, a minor technical problem arises for the writer of a book. How can he evoke a physical object on a flat sheet of paper (like this one) without metamorphosing the object into a word or a drawing? I cannot show you an actual token, or cross, or flag or Statue of Liberty. The best I can do is to use **bold** letters every time I mean such a **physical reality**. Here then we have a **flag** or, passing in a parade, **a cardboard dragon**. The world is full of such **real** symbols, either invented and made by people or borrowed from Nature: a particular kind of **hat**, a **donkey** or a **flower**, a special **gesture of the hand**,[5] a **crown**, etc. As I said before, this may

---

4. True, nowadays we would call the *symbolon*, as we do the theater ticket, a 'token' rather than a symbol. This is because, like so many words, 'symbol' evolved and, in this instance, magnified its stature (as we shall see presently) above and beyond such a humble object as a permit to enter a theater.

5. For instance, the real-life human action of symbolizing unity or accord

well be why the term 'symbol' is so very current in our languages.

Incidentally, a related term, namely 'sign,' is another reality mostly encountered 'in the street', and not a figure of speech. Literally in the street: for instance a **green light** or a peculiar **design** at a street corner signifying, respectively, 'your turn to go' and 'one way street'; or the **pattern** over a laboratory door signifying 'danger: radiation'. You can call them 'symbols' too if you wish; but we seem to prefer the term 'sign' when the item is a directive, a finger pointing you sharply at what to do, avoid, say or even think.

Language itself, which is often called symbolic in its nature, can be more clearly understood if it is called, instead, a system of signs. Thus, when I write the following letters: S-t-a-t-u-e o-f L-i-b-e-r-t-y, I call them signs that point to a manner of speaking these words aloud (quite different, for instance, from 'Shashu off libbu-tah'), *and*, at the same time to an image in my mind of the **Statue of Liberty** as it looks over the harbor of New York. In this second role, we see that words are signs that have the ability to point to **symbols**.

And what are 'emblems'? A **crown**, for instance, is a symbol of royalty; but it can be called an **emblem** of royalty as well. An **emblem** is usually an important and pointedly pictorial **symbol**. In literature, we speak of 'an emblematic poem' when its lines are so arranged as to form a rudimentary drawing on the page, for instance of a wing, which imitates, flat on the page, what would be an **emblem/symbol** in three-dimensional reality.

III

We can leave the world of **symbols** now and devote our attention to the verbal signs pointing at them. This is inevitable, since our concern in this book is with one of the verbal arts. Considering, however, that the clause 'this is a sign pointing to a **symbol**',

by means of **hand holding hand** is signed or signaled by Milton when, at the end of *Paradise Lost*, he quietly reconciles Adam and Eve:

> The World was all before them, where to choose
> Their place of rest, and Providence their guide;
> They hand in hand with wand'ring steps and slow,
> Through Eden took their solitary way.

though perfectly correct, is also painfully clumsy, we will adopt the generally accepted short-cut, and refer to these verbal signs as 'symbols' without worrying about the deleted intermediary. Thus, we say that William Blake's worm, in the 'The Sick Rose', is a symbol (no **bold** letters) for destructive love or some such generalization, instead of saying that it is a verbal sign pointing to a **worm** that is a symbol, for Blake, of destructive love.

Most symbols seem to us 'natural'; that is to say, the donors appear to participate in some way in the life of their recipients. Since, however, this is true of metaphors and synecdoches as well, a great deal of overlapping and interchangeability occurs. More about this in a moment. Right now we should observe that the most natural symbol of all occurs when, synecdochically, an important single specimen of a class is named as 'an example of', thus standing for, representing, acting as an ambassador for the class. 'Vincent van Gogh,' writes a newspaper book-reviewer, 'has been picked over by so many biographers, art critics, psychologists, neurologists, song-writers, amateur sleuths and historians that he's become perhaps the leading symbol of the suffering artist of all time.'

However, countless symbols that are not 'examples of' also seem entirely natural. The cross as symbol for the Church is an obvious candidate, since the Second Person of the Trinity was nailed to its 'objective' original. One person's hand in another seems like a natural symbol of agreement or love. Or take the hat as a symbol of authority. In the story of Wilhelm Tell, the fictitious hero of Swiss independence, the citizenry are forced to salute their tyrannical governor's hat perched on a pike. The hat that belongs to the governor synecdochically and symbolically represents the governor himself, who in turn synecdochically and symbolically stands for the Habsburg king in Vienna. Because stars, as popularly viewed, are noble and beautiful and bright, they make fine metaphors and natural symbols to decorate the American flag. As for the dove that stands for peace, it is at any rate a harmless beast—at least as compared to a hawk—and thus makes for another metaphor and natural symbol.

It looks very much as though what we call a natural symbol is either an *outstanding example* or a *promoted metaphor or synecdoche*. Clearly, too, it can be a *promoted sign*. We will have to ask, a bit later, in what this promotion consists. For now, the point is that so long as we can detect any metaphorical or synecdochical nature in the word or words under inspection, their symbolic function appears natural to us. When we fail to detect these connections, we speak of the symbols as arbitrary. Flags with certain colors and designs are in many or most instances arbitrary symbols for the nations they represent. And speaking of colors, if you think that green is a natural color for hope, then why is it also a symbol of envy? And does red, which is our normal symbol for danger, play the same role for a woman when she applies it to her lips?

Consider, next, those well-established sign-symbols for male and female:

I confess that I keep forgetting which is which—evidence that for me, at any rate, these are absolutely arbitrary symbols. What happens, however, is that many arbitrary symbols gradually take hold and thus become *traditional.* For many of you the male and female symbols may have become 'second nature', which is, in fact, a fine way of saying 'traditional'. For me this has yet to happen. But when the process is complete, and we are as much at home with more or less arbitrary as with more or less natural symbols, the distinction loses its importance. For the poet, certainly, it is of no consequence whether green as a sign for 'go' or symbol for hope or envy is more or less arbitrary or more or less natural.[6] What matters to him is that it is understood and endowed with a given potential aesthetic energy.

To natural and arbitrary/traditional symbols we need to add *private* symbols, especially important in modern poetry: things, situations, events that have either not existed as symbols before, or else have stood in the past for different things. Creating symbols in a poem is neither good nor bad in itself; the proof, as they

6.   Arbitrary does not mean causeless. All sorts of motives, reasons and causes can come into play in the assignment of a symbolic value to a thing or a representation. Arbitrary simply means that the observer fails to see a real-life connection between donor and recipient.

say, is in the pudding: how satisfying is their taste?

IV

We have seen that certain metaphors and synecdoches can easily turn into symbols in our minds. In other words, something that is in some way *like* something else might also *stand for* that something else. Or: something that is a *part* of something larger might also *stand for* that something larger. And I have called this alternative a kind of promotion. Why so? Because a (textual) symbol is an entity that seems to be endowed with a (textual) life of its own (like a non-textual **symbol**); it is or at least seems capable of being a character or agent in a narrative.[7] Furthermore, it points to some phenomenon we believe to be very significant and long-lasting (e.g. a moral force, a nation, a human discipline). Hence symbols often become long-lasting themselves—they become traditional. Metaphors and synecdoches, instead, tend to act like passing and localized figures in a text, however powerful. All the same, the distinction is not always clear-cut, and what feels like a symbol to one reader may feel like a metaphor to another.

Consider the following section from George Herbert's 'The Collar', a poem we read in its entirety in Chapter 6:

> Shall I be still in suit?
> Have I no harvest but a thorn
> To let me blood, and not restore
> What I have lost with cordial fruit?
> Sure there was wine
> Before my sighs did dry it; there was corn
> Before my tears did drown it.
> Is the year only lost to me?
> Have I no bays to crown it,
> No flowers, no garlands gay? all blasted?
> All wasted?

These lines hold a veritable throng of metaphors, synecdoches, and/or symbols. And/or, because it seems impossible to legislate. Thorn, fruit, wine, corn (wheat), bays, flowers, garlands—do these

---

7.   That is why I have called an allegory a system of symbols in a narrative. Colors, of course, can lead a life of their own in a narrative only as carried by objects like flags, shields, bodies, etc.

have the stature and independence of symbols? Or are they (or some of them) ad hoc images, that is to say metaphors and synecdoches? Bays and garlands, at any rate, have Greek tradition behind them, while the thorn rests on Christian tradition—the crown of thorns set on the head of Jesus and drawing his blood. Most of us, I believe, are likely to call all these images symbols, especially after considering 'Is the year only lost to me?' where 'year' is so very clearly a temporary, ad hoc synecdoche.

What about T.S. Eliot's

I have measured out my life with coffee spoons,

spoken by the anti-hero of *The Love Song of J. Alfred Prufrock?* Coffee spoons could be private and new symbols—and very effective ones. But the image as a whole seems too localized, however powerful, to be called a symbol. It cannot live a life of its own and is unlikely to become traditional.

Contrast this with Blake's flying worm, which is a living character and could easily turn into the serpent in the Garden, if it is not already that as the poem stands. However, if someone tells you 'You're a worm, my boy, when you talk to your teacher,' you feel that the figure, however dramatic, has been chosen to make an immediate and localized description of your behavior—and there metaphor strikes us as the better name for this unfriendly observation.

All the same, a degree of uncertainty remains perforce. Words are like searchlights in the night, sometimes aiming their beams separately, but frequently criss-crossing one another and blending. This is so because they are born and they grow in multiple circumstances without being ordered and given specific assignments by some Commission of Rational Sages. Fortunately, though, in the literary arts the names of things have little importance. After debating whether we should call Eliot's line an instance of this or of that, we conclude, far more importantly, that it gives us a deeply imaginative heightening of ordinary language.

V

At this point I propose that we do a little hands-on work with symbols to supplement our chapter on Practical Pointers, and to complete the interpretation of a few texts we have left unresolved.

As I remarked earlier, behind the many natural and traditional symbols that everyone recognizes—everyone in a given culture, that is—are ranged a multitude of others, from widely but not universally recognized symbols all the way to symbols invented, privately, for the occasion of a single poem. As a result, we may find ourselves hesitating as to the significance of certain symbols; and if so, we must, as always, launch tentative hypotheses to elucidate them.

For example, Robert Lowell (1917–77) has a well-known poem titled 'Skunk Hour', published in 1959, the first four stanzas of which deal with decay, failure and death in a seaside resort in Maine. This done, the poet shifts to a two-stanza scene of watching cars in a lovers' lane on the *skull* of a hill, near a *graveyard*. Within these two stanzas, the poet abruptly remarks that his mind is going, and that he is hell to himself. Suddenly, in the final two stanzas, a family of skunks emerge,

> that search
> in the moonlight for a bite to eat.
> They march on their soles up Main Street:
> white stripes, moonstruck eyes' red fire
> under the chalk-dry and spar spire
> of the Trinitarian Church.
>
> I stand on top
> of our back steps and breathe the rich air—
> a mother skunk with her column of kittens swills
> the garbage pail.
> She jabs her wedge-head in a cup
> of sour cream, drops her ostrich tail,
> And will not scare.[8]

Now, skunks have a bad name; hence if we decide that these particular skunks, brought in to climax so ponderous a poem, surely stand for something, our inclination must be to interpret them as symbolizing Lowell's generally 'smelly' world that he cannot rout ('And will not scare'). But why might not these humble animals, despised by respectable folk, symbolize something that *contrasts* with the depressing human world instead of, as it were, summarizing it? Here are indomitable children of nature ('And will not scare'), serenely indifferent to Main Street and the

8.   In *Selected Poems* (New York: Farrar, Straus & Giroux, 1976).

Trinitarian Church (more symbols!); close-knit families (versus the cheap lovers in their cars); turning the refuse we produce to good account.

Which is the better of these opposite readings of Lowell's symbols? Perhaps the answer must be sought off-stage; and indeed, one editor who reprints the poem in his anthology refers the reader to certain published comments on it by the artist himself. For us, it is sufficient to note that non-traditional, ad hoc symbols are not always as lucid as Eliot's coffee spoons.

It will be instructive, I think, to re-read the New Testament parable we examined in Chapter 7:[9]

> Listen! A sower went out to sow. And it happened that as he sowed, some seed fell along the footpath; and the birds came and ate it up. Some seed fell on rocky soil, and it sprouted quickly because it had no depth of earth; but when the sun rose the young corn was scorched, and as it had no root it withered away. Some seed fell among thistles; and the thistles shot up and choked the corn, and it yielded no crop. And some of the seed fell into good soil, where it came up and grew, and bore fruit; and the yield was thirtyfold, sixtyfold, even a hundredfold.

Surprisingly, perhaps, the symbolism here turns out to be as questionable as Lowell's. You will remember that the apostles were puzzled by it. Consider the birds that ate up the seed. Birds are usually as likable as skunks are not. We can assume that the apostles enjoyed their company—centuries before Saint Francis sang their praise. When they are used symbolically/metaphorically, they tend to stand for desirable things like freedom, happiness and beauty. In Christ's parable, however, it appears that they represent Satan! No wonder the Lord was obliged to explain his quite original symbolism.

A little later we hear of thistles choking the young corn. What can these thistles symbolize? Satan has already been disposed of. Do they represent evil priests? This would work; but Jesus has something else in mind. He explains that the thistles stand for

---

9.   A parable might be thought of as an allegory (a set of symbols fashioned into a narrative) that is always short and extremely pointed to a definite moral meaning. But terms like parable, fable and allegory criss-cross like searchlights and often blend.

wealth and glamor. Thistles for wealth and glamor? Hardly self-evident! The Son of Man was obliged to act, in effect, as his own literary critic, seeing that the apostles were experiencing the same trouble as many a reader of poetry today.

Of course, the reader must decide whether a particular 'scene' in a poem is symbolic to begin with. Did Lowell by any chance mean nothing in particular with his skunks? That is doubtful. But some readers go too far and nervously look for symbols in every other word the poet has set down. Instead, I recommend a degree of tact. The best strategy, generally speaking, is to read a poem without hunting for symbols until it seems to *insist* that we interpret a passage symbolically (or metaphorically or synecdochically) if we are ever to take possession of the text it lives in.

Most readers will feel that a poem like 'The Surprises of the Superhuman' does so insist.[10]

> The palais de justice of chambermaids
> Tops the horizon with its colonnades.
>
> If it were lost in Uebermenschlichkeit,
> Perhaps our wretched state would soon come right.
>
> For somehow the brave dicta of its kings
> Makes more awry our faulty human things.

But again, the symbols here are distinctly less than universal or traditional; they are invented for the occasion. How obscure or equivocal are they? Would you not agree that Stevens's 'palais de justice' is rather easily interpreted as a symbol/synecdoche for any and all major institutions of government? The chambermaids, on the other hand, are less transparent. What and whom might they symbolize? We shall hardly rest content with the easy supposition that they are nothing *but* chambermaids. Like Blake's rose and worm, they are too odd to mean nothing beyond themselves. They seem to aspire to rise in the world as symbols. A hypothesis is summoned. Shall we bid them stand for all of us ordinary people governed from afar? You may feel that a strain is placed on these worthy creatures, and therefore on the poem as a whole; but I know of no better hypothesis. As for 'topping the horizon',

---

10. We have looked at this little and not in itself very important poem in Chapters 4 and 9.

whether we call it a metaphor or an integral part of the palais de justice symbol, either way this action smoothly translates as 'commanding awe' or 'exercizing great power' or some similar proposition. Finally we can take Stevens's kings to stand for any powerful rulers, and here, of course, Stevens is using an easily understood natural symbol.

With these symbols firmly grasped, we should be able to complete our exegesis (explication), for the rest of the poem seems to validate our hypotheses. It appears that our ruling institutions are failing to set right 'our wretched state' ('condition', with the political meaning thrown in as a useful flavor). If human institutions could go higher than merely topping the horizon—if, in a word, they could be superhuman, then *perhaps* (Stevens is not sure), the crooked could be made straight. We notice, incidentally, that Stevens does not speak, as Nietzsche does, of the Super*man*, that is to say of some individual Hero, but of the super*human*. This leaves us free to interpret the poem as wondering, not whether a Hero might set things right, but whether mankind needs more inspired institutions (religions, we surmise) for its salvation.[11]

Reading Stevens's magical 'Disillusionment of Ten o'Clock', we feel at once, do we not? that there is more to it than basic physical language:

> The houses are haunted
> By white night-gowns,
> None are green,
> Or purple with green rings,
> Or green with yellow rings,
> Or yellow with blue rings.
> None of them are strange,

11. If we now add the off-stage information mentioned earlier, namely that the poem was written during the First World War (as one of a series called *Lettres d'un soldat*), our hypothesis becomes all the firmer. This would have been an apt time for mulling over the notion that human institutions, however mighty, are still thoroughly earthbound and therefore unable to bring about human perfection. The one remaining trouble spot is the title with its surprising 'surprises'. Does the word anticipate the 'perhaps' we have just looked at—we do not really know what the superhuman might hold in store for us? Or is this too strained an explanation? If so, perhaps the entire hypothesis collapses, and a new explanation must be found for the symbols.

> With socks of lace
> And beaded ceintures.
> People are not going
> To dream of baboons and periwinkles.
> Only, here and there, an old sailor,
> Drunk and asleep in his boots,
> Catches tigers
> In red weather.[12]

A plausible hypothesis is that the poet has promoted a series of newly minted hence private synecdoches and metaphors into a little allegory—a set of symbols in action—that speaks to us of blank, routine, unimaginative existence. If this hypothesis is correct (however flatfooted), the drunk sailor readily becomes a symbol (a promoted synecdoche) for the poet or any other imaginative hero.

The scene of Auden's 'A Misunderstanding' also presents a highly symbolic appearance. We asked a number of questions of it in Chapter 8. You are now invited to read it once more. Who and what are Auden's riddling characters? Does each of them stand for a category of persons—say a distinct social class? Or do they all together (except for the visitor) represent a certain kind of humanity? Is the chateau itself a symbol? Why is it green? Is green a symbol too, though not the same as Stevens's? Is the meal symbolic? Is the deafness symbolic? Are the flowers symbolic? Is the garage symbolic? Is the whole visit symbolic? And if so, are these symbols so private that we can reach them only through off-stage illumination, if at all? Or have the characters and place been picked by the poet at random for a theme, as yet mysterious to us, which would have allowed him a quite different cast, set in a different place—a pub, for instance, where the visitor meets a businessman, a typist and a carpenter? After all, Stevens could have chosen a purple lion instead of a red tiger!

If, reading a biography of the poet for off-stage light, we discover that at the time he was writing his sonnet, Auden seems to have experienced urges to save the world (or at least England); and if we happen to know, in general, that he was rummaging in the writings of both Marx and Freud (each with his own recipe,

---

12. In *Harmonium* (1923). In *The Collected Poems of Wallace Stevens* (New York: Alfred A. Knopf, 1957). *Ceinture* is French for a belt.

one public and the other private, for making us happy); we can, more easily than if we have nothing beyond the poem itself, interpret the latter as a self-doubting piece—a commendably modest poem in which the savior discovers (as he has foreseen, according to the first line) that perhaps he needs saving as much as his 'patients' do: healer, heal thyself! Saviors are, of course, in part 'incendiaries', whether they are of the Marx, Freud—or Christ persuasion; so this explains the last line. And now, with the theme possibly in hand, we can indeed surmise that, although the grimy boy might symbolize the working classes, the deaf girl—who knows?—perhaps all those who are handicapped, and the professor the class of intellectuals, Auden could have chosen other symbols. Neither does the castle appear as a necessary symbolic setting. Let us say that it symbolizes a land, or a world, that is still prosperous, tradition-bound and at peace ('green')—well then, Auden could have chosen a grand hotel at the seashore. Then again, the chateau need not be a symbol at all. It will do as an enjoyable setting for the theme. We do not need to press for more symbols in any given poem than are required for a fulfilling sense of essentially possessing it.

The interpretation of metaphors, synecdoches and symbols takes us back to a vital process that I described in Chapter 6, where I pointed out that in poetry we typically 'translate' difficult first-ring (physical) language 'either into slightly different first-ring language that threads cozily to the core...or into outer-ring language (a generalization) which then returns upon the puzzling images and threads them cozily to the core'. Neither a scientist nor a philosopher would ever have written 'People are not going to dream of baboon and periwinkles.' Both would have said something like 'People will remain boring.' But then, neither the philosopher nor the scientist is in the business of giving shocks of delight.

Chapter 19

Similes

Similes are expressions of partial but effective resemblances the writer has perceived between apparently unrelated phenomena. *Presumed* effective, of course; presumed effective because intelligent, suggestive, sensitive, powerful, tender, amusing, etc.; and perceived whether or not the truth/validity of the perception can be sworn to before an assembly of the gods. All this means that similes too are obviously akin to metaphors, since the latter also depend on a perception of similarity and ground their effectiveness in the same conditions. But whereas metaphor is, so to speak, a transplant of language, simile keeps language in place, merely yoking two elements together because of the perceived similarity without in any way altering either one of the elements. To say 'I grasp your idea' is to raid, capture and transplant the word 'grasp' from its native habitat ('I grasp this branch') to a new setting, where it momentarily ousts its presumably tired host ('I understand your idea'), takes on the meaning its host possessed, and substitutes for the host's pallor its own presumed youth and vigor. Simile does not perform any of these operations. In Robert Burns's well-known stanza:

> O, my luve is like a red, red rose,
>   That's newly sprung in June,
> O, my luve is like the melodie,
>   That's sweetly play'd in tune,

'my love' is a synecdoche—a substitute for 'the girl I love', but the rose remains a rose, and the melody remains a melody.[1] For these,

---

1. 'Luve' is Scottish dialect; pronounce as in '*souvenir*'. The poem

there is no substitute, there is no transplant, the two elements remain intact, retaining their own initial vitality, whatever that may be.

We saw that new metaphors play a vital role in making language grow. Similes do not play this role. When the entomologist Edward O. Wilson remarked that destroying a rain forest for economic gain is like burning a Renaissance painting to cook a meal,[2] or when the social philosopher Camille Paglia writes that 'Leaving sex to the feminists is like letting your dog vacation at the taxidermist,'[3] nothing new is added to the English language, nothing like what was done by the inventor of the computer's 'mouse'. And yet the effectiveness of Wilson's and Paglia's wittily 'loaded' similes is of the same order as what is produced by good metaphors.

Hence as far as the poet is concerned, the difference is of less than primordial importance. His business with either metaphors or similes is, I repeat, to get them to energize his raw propositions by the drama, fantasy, merriment, poignancy, fervor, and especially the conceptual alterations and enlargements they can bring onto the scene of his text. However, since we quoted Emily Dickinson for metaphors and synecdoches, let us solicit from her a brilliant simile as well:

> I'm Nobody! Who are you?
> Are you - Nobody - too?
> Then there's a pair of us!
> Don't tell! they'd banish us - you know!
>
> How dreary - to be - Somebody!
> How public - like a Frog -
> To tell your name - the livelong June -
> To an admiring Bog![4]

appeared in 1796. Remove one 'red' from the famous first line and read aloud: the rhythm collapses and the line is ruined.

2.   *Time Magazine*, 3 September 1990, p. 78.

3.   Quoted in the *Times Literary Supplement*, 8 January 1993, p. 4, from Paglia's *Sex, Art and American Culture* (New York: Viking, 1992).

4.   Number 288 in the 1955 edition prepared by Thomas H. Johnson (see Chapter 13). The poem was written around 1861. It should be remembered that the dashes and capital letters represent Dickinson's manuscript, not necessarily her wishes for a published version.

Animals have furnished mankind with countless similes and metaphors (you will find about ten of them in this chapter alone); but Dickinson, as usual, managed to contribute a fresh one by bringing in the mindless repetitious unlovely croaking of the clammy little beast as a likeness for the seeker after popularity. We might call her tactic the insult indirect. She provokes laughter at her victim without doing any arguing: simply by brandishing the ridiculous image of a frog. This is intelligence, drama and wit. But, as if this were not enough, she finds a rare rhyme for 'frog'— just the rhyme she needed, yielding the 'bog' (a synecdoche, you will have observed) that is ecstatic at the frog's serenading. The theme—to desire fame is to crave the admiration of ninnies— remains unstated but visibly and audibly implied by the simile.

But—again—metaphor can work the same magic. Here is a virtuoso passage of invective by Alexander Pope against incorrigible poetasters, one that stretches an animal metaphor over six lines:

> Who shames a Scribbler? break one cobweb through,
> He spins the slight, self-pleasing thread anew;
> Destroy his Fib, his Sophistry; in vain,
> The Creature's at his dirty work again;
> Throned in the Center of his thin designs;
> Proud of a vast Extent of flimsy lines.[5]

And then, back again to simile, and this time a sweet one. We listen to Robert Frost extending a figure over an entire one-sentence sonnet of perfect 'classical' purity, in which he praises a lady: a *lady* in the fullest, most ethical, Henry Jamesian meaning of the word:

THE SILKEN TENT

> She is as in a field a silken tent
> At midday when a sunny summer breeze
> Has dried the dew and all its ropes relent,
> So that in guys she gently sways at ease,
> And its supporting central cedar pole,

---

5.   Lines 89-94 of the 419-line *An Epistle from Mr. Pope, to Dr. Arbuthnot* (1735). English poets of the baroque and neo-classical ages liked to dignify their works by capitalizing many of the nouns (German capitalizes all of them to this day for no good reason). Emily Dickinson went farther and capitalized anything she felt like capitalizing.

That is its pinnacle to heavenward
And signifies the sureness of the soul,
Seems to owe naught to any single cord,
But strictly held by none, is loosely bound
By countless silken ties of love and thought
To everything on earth the compass round,
And only by one's going slightly taut
In the capriciousness of summer air
Is of the slightest bondage made aware.[6]

One lesson—a purely technical one—to be drawn from this poem is that the two elements of a simile can be of very unequal length and energy. Here, on one side of the scale, we find nothing but 'She', and on the other the entire poem, except for that little 'is as' which signals the presence of a simile.

Frost's extended comparison is a conscious renewal of the so-called epic or extended simile that delights us in the *Iliad*, where it often creates an oasis, a moment of peace and respite in the midst of all that goring, gashing and hacking of flesh in which Homer's heroes revel:

As when some stalled horse who has been corn-fed at the manger
breaking free of his rope gallops over the plain in thunder
to his accustomed bathing place in a sweet-running river
and in the pride of his strength holds his head high, and the mane floats
over his shoulder; sure of his glorious strength, the quick knees
carry him to the loved places and the pasture of horses;
so from uttermost Pergamos came Paris, the son of Priam,
shining in all his armour of war as the sun shines.[7]

Extended similes of this kind (and they can be much longer than the one I have quoted) become in effect little poems in their own right. Beginning readers are sometimes baffled by them at first, because they go on and on like riddles before they yield their explanation, precipitated by a most welcome 'so' or its equivalent: 'so from uttermost Pergamos came Paris'. How best to take possession of them? Keep reading until the 'so' or its equivalent

6. First published in 1942. In *The Poetry of Robert Frost* (ed. E.C. Lathem; New York: Henry Holt, 1970).

7. Book 6, lines 506-15 in Richmond Lattimore's translation (Chicago: University of Chicago Press, 1951). Pergamos is yet another name for Troy. Note that the grand horse simile concludes with a modestly routine sun simile.

clicks the meaning in place; then start again from the top (hurry
is a deadly foe to poetry); that second reading, meaning in mind,
can now be serenely loved, and new details pleasantly explored.

The epic simile was perpetuated by later writers, among them
Virgil, Dante and Milton. Here is an instance from Dante's *Inferno*:

> In the turning season of the youthful year,
>> when the sun is warming his rays beneath Aquarius
>> and the days and night already begin to near
>
> their perfect balance; the hoar-frost copies then
>> the image of his white sister on the ground,
>> but the first sun wipes away the work of his pen.
>
> The peasants who lack fodder then arise
>> and look about and see their fields all white,
>> and hear their lambs bleat; then they smite their thighs,
>
> go back into the house, walk here and there,
>> pacing, fretting, wondering what to do,
>> then come out of doors again, and there despair
>
> falls from them when they see how the earth's face
>> has changed in so little time, and they take their staffs
>> and drive their lambs to feed—

Well, we say, what has that most authentic-looking cameo of
pastoral life in Italy to do with the damned in Hell? The hoar-frost
lies on the ground in the last days of winter or first days of spring;
the peasants mistake it for snow; they fret; and then they happily
discover that it wasn't snow at all, spring *is* here after all. We pick
up the text again:

> and drive their lambs to feed—so in that place
>
> When I saw my Guide and Master's eyebrow lower,
>> my spirits fell and I was sorely vexed;
>> and as quickly came the plaster to the sore:
>
> for when we had reached the ruined bridge, he stood
>> and turned on me that sweet and open look
>> with which he had greeted me in the dark wood.[8]

---

8.   The opening lines of Canto 24 in John Ciardi's translation (New York:
New American Library, 1954). Dante and his guide, Virgil, are crossing the
concentric trenches of hell from outer to innermost circle by stepping over
bridges; they have now run into a collapsed one; Virgil has a moment of per-

Virgil, in his noble, godlike equanimity, is both sun and frost; Dante, humble before his master, likens himself to a naive, easily frightened and ignorant sheep-herder; and all this is developed at leisure in what is almost a scenario for a short film. This takes us a considerable distance from the concentration of *most* metaphors; a fact we are reminded of in the second stanza, where Dante activates a fine metaphor (in which a second one is nested) within his ample simile.[9]

I remarked that in 'The Silken Tent' Robert Frost made his own bow to the tradition of the epic simile. At the same time, however, he tipped his hat to another, later tradition—that of the 'conceit', which is a figure noteworthy for its boldness, its power to astonish, even its extravagance. We looked briefly at Crashaw's metaphorical conceits in 'St. Mary Magdalene' (Chapter 17); but a guidebook like ours cannot be allowed to overlook everybody's favorite simile-conceit, namely the passage in John Donne's 'A Valediction: Forbidding Mourning' in which a husband goes on a journey, leaving his faithful wife at home. Husband and wife are one, according to the poet; but now, he adds, suppose for a moment that they are two:

> If they be two, they are two so
>   As stiff twin compasses are two;
> Thy soul, the fixed foot, makes no show
>   To move, but doth, if th'other do.
>
> And though it in the center sit,
>   Yet, when the other far doth roam,
> It leans, and hearkens after it,
>   And grows erect, as that comes home.
>
> Such wilt thou be to me, who must,
>   Like th'other foot, obliquely run;
> Thy firmness makes my circle just,
>   And makes me end where I begun.[10]

plexity that alarms his apprehensive pupil. The last quoted line refers to the original meeting between Dante and Virgil when the former was lost 'in a dark wood'.

9. Note, as well, the metaphor in 'as quickly came the plaster to the sore'.

10. Though widely known in his lifetime, Donne's poems were published two years after his death, namely in 1633.

Donne and Frost imagined extremely different analogies for
steadfastness; but both similes lie beyond the inventive power of
ordinary mortals. They are fetched far without being farfetched.
Reading them—especially the first time—most of us register sur-
prise, followed by understanding, followed by admiration. Donne
in particular earns our admiration because he has made some-
thing utterly fresh out of that most timeworn husband-and-wife-
are-one commonplace, and forced a cold geometrical tool into
the service of warmest love. But both poets succeed; and they
succeed, perhaps, by being clever without sacrificing a deep ten-
derness. Of course, neither conceits nor plainer figures need to
be elaborately developed in order to succeed, but it so happens
that both Donne and Frost, leaving behind the simple simile of
the 'My luve is like a red, red rose' species, impress and delight us
by venturing on a detailed and point by point set of correspon-
dences. 'How unexpected and yet how apt!' they invite us to
exclaim.[11]

A simile might be aborted and still be a simile, as in the follow-
ing, where 'the other shoe' is simply not dropped on the reader:

HOMERIC SIMILE

> Like a dog and his master:
>   both burly but of course the master burlier
>   still the dog tugs on the leash
>   the backward way he wants to go
>   where a bunch of mutts and pups are frolicking
>   and he wants to fool around with them
>   or bite their ears off
>   or pop a little sex
>   or just smell them under the tail
>   fun all the way
>   but the master is yanking and yanking hard
>   and of course the master wins
>   but the dog has to be dragged
>   wrenched head bruised neck yelping

11. Not to be forgotten, in the meantime, are the other, simultaneous,
contributions to success—among them, most obviously, rhyme and rhythm—
which we have discussed throughout this book. We keep in mind that analy-
sis separates for consideration what the reading experience fuses.

paws trenching four streaks in the gravel:
So mankind (you fill in the rest).[12]

A strategy contrary to the elaboration of a single simile is the mobilization of a troop of short ones. This is how Ben Jonson (1572–1637) proceeded in the third and last stanza of a lyric for one of his plays, *The Devil Is an Ass* (1616):

> Have you seen but a bright lily grow,
>   Before rude hands have touched it?
> Have you marked but the fall o' the snow,
>   Before the soil has smutched it?
> Have you felt the wool o' the beaver?
>   Or swan's down ever?
> Or have smelled o' the bud o' the briar?
>   Or the nard i' the fire?
> Or have tasted the bag of the bee?
> O so white! O so soft! O so sweet is she![13]

However, similes are not what they are, and do not do what they do, just because a 'like' or 'as' or 'so' or 'as though' is popped between two or more juxtaposed elements. In fact, they live and breathe as soundly without these articulations as with them. Comparing a new model of a Lamborghini sports car to an older version called the Countach, a journalist writes: 'Gone are the edges, angles and appendages that gave the 20-year old Countach the stance of a mantis sniffing for sirloin.'[14] Here is a sensational and funny conceit without benefit of 'like' and 'as.' For a poetic instance of *implied simile* we can recall Kenneth Rexroth's 'Trout':

> The trout is taken when he
> Bites an artificial fly.
> Confronted with fraud, keep your
> Mouth shut, and don't volunteer.

12. By Oscar Mandel, in *Prairie Schooner*, Summer 1995, p. 124. You may recall at this point the idea that not saying may say a great deal.

13. 'Rude', as in Marvell's 'The Garden' (Chapter 10), means coarse. 'Nard' is an aromatic ointment. Besides the array of similes, Jonson makes use of the rhetoric of questioning and the rhetoric of repetition—both fundamental energizers and known to every orator since Antiquity (see Chapter 21).

14. *Los Angeles Times*, 6 February 1991, p. E4. Journalists pride themselves on their inventive images, but it might be argued that most of them are flashy rather than illuminating, more ingenious than penetrating—like some

In other words: 'If you volunteer, you will be *like* the trout.'

If we prefer, we can call the implied simile an *analogy*. Examine in this connection three of the 32 stanzas of Thomas Gray's *Elegy Written in a Country Churchyard* (1751), where the poet speaks of the humble folk who might have dazzled the world if circumstances had but favored them:

> Perhaps in this neglected spot is laid
> Some heart once pregnant with celestial fire,
> Hands, that the rod of empire might have sway'd,
> Or wak'd to extasy the living lyre.
>
> But Knowledge to their eyes her ample page
> Rich with the spoils of time did ne'er unroll;
> Chill Penury repress'd their noble rage,
> And froze the genial current of the soul.
>
> Full many a gem of purest ray serene,
> The dark unfathom'd caves of ocean bear:
> Full many a flower is born to blush unseen,
> And waste its sweetness on the desert air.[15]

This famous last stanza contains two implied similes or analogies juxtaposed to the thought that came before. 'Some of the humble dead are *like* gems and flowers no one has ever seen.'

Similes can also be negative. There are times when the poet believes that an *un*likeness will be more striking than a similarity. In Pope's mock-heroic *The Rape of the Lock* (1712–17), where the poet applies Homeric and Miltonic grandiloquence to a silly baron who snips off a girl's lock of hair during a card game, the offended Belinda meditates revenge:

> Not youthful kings in battle seized alive,
> Not scornful virgins who their charms survive,

of the conceits of seventeenth-century poetry.

15. A couple of the practical pointers from Chapter 9 need to be applied, namely an imaginary restoration of prose word order, and syntactical analysis. The latter reveals, to our surprise, that the first quoted stanza is grammatically defective, for it says that hands (plural) that might have ruled a country *is* laid in a humble grave! Genius and perfection are not the same thing. The 'rage' of line 7 is simply passion, ardor, force. In the next line, 'genial' is to be read as the adjective for 'genius' (which makes more sense anyway than its current meaning). 'Serene', in the line following, includes, if one wishes, the Latin meaning 'bright'.

Not ardent lovers robbed of all their bliss,
Not ancient ladies when refused a kiss,
Not tyrants fierce that unrepentant die,
Not Cynthia when her manteau's pinned awry,
E'er felt such rage, resentment, and despair,
As thou, sad virgin! for thy ravished hair.[16]

From the negative simile we move easily to comparisons of more or less, which can be endowed with the same dramatic and conceptual force as similes of likeness and unlikeness. We can listen to Pope again, describing Belinda just after the baron has committed his 'rape' by means of an obliging pair of scissors (called 'a two-edged weapon', 'a little Engine' and, in sonorous Latin, 'the glitt'ring Forfex'). Belinda lets out a series of epic screams ('Screams of Horror rend th'affrighted Skies'):

Not louder Shrieks to pitying Heav'n are cast,
When Husbands or when Lap-dogs breathe their last,
Or when rich China Vessels, fall'n from high,
In glitt'ring Dust and painted Fragments lie![17]

Things can be larger, more visible, louder, more abundant, more important—more anything than others, or less anything than others. We might quote Dante again for another noise-comparison. The poet and his mentor are being escorted along one of the pits of Hell by a rabble of uncouth devils. Their Captain trumpets his 'Forward, boys!' with a most indecorous rearward noise. The poet is taken aback, but does not lose his grim sense of humor:

16. Canto IV, lines 3-10. Line 2 in our selection expresses in highly compressed shape a thought common in elegant society before the French Revolution but frequently puzzling to the video-cassette adepts of our times. Pope is talking about ladies who refused to have lovers while young and now have lost their charms. The 'ancient ladies' two lines down are still peppy enough to be angry when a beau refuses to kiss them. Cynthia is any fashionable girl, and 'manteau' is 'a loose upper garment'. The humor of this passage depends, of course, on forcing together two incompatible worlds, that of the epic battlefield and that of drawing-room card-playing and flirtation. The odd result is that *both* worlds seem to be mocked.

17. Canto III, lines 157-160. The implied proposition in the second line is that in elegant circles marriage is taken *very* lightly. One is equally sensitive to the loss of a poodle, the breakage of a china vase and the demise of a husband.

> I have seen horsemen breaking camp. I have seen
>   the beginning of the assault, the march and muster,
>   and at times the retreat and riot. I have been
>
> where chargers trampled your land, O Aretines!
>   I have seen columns of foragers, shocks of tourney,
>   and running of tilts. I have seen endless lines
>
> march to bells, drums, trumpets, from far and near.
>   I have seen them march on signals from a castle.
>   I have seen them march with native and foreign gear.
>
> But never yet have I seen horse or foot,
>   nor ship in range of land nor sight of star,
>   take its direction from so low a toot.[18]

And to conclude on a whimsical note, we go to Cummings—two stanzas will do:

> love is more thicker than forget
> more thinner than recall
> more seldom than a wave is wet
> more frequent than to fail
>
> it is most mad and moonly
> and less it shall unbe
> than all the sea which only
> is deeper than the sea.[19]

Some of which may be nonsense; but a savory proof all the same that a simile need not say, exactly, that A is like B.

---

18. Canto 22, lines 1-12, in John Ciardi's translation. The Aretines are the citizens of Arezzo, south of Florence.

19. Published in 1940. In *Complete Poems, 1913–1962* (ed. George J. Firmage; New York: Liveright Publishing, 1991).

Chapter 20

Irony

(1) Irony in a literary text is a rhetorical maneuver stage-managed by an author and offered to our perception in the expectation that it will arouse our interest and admiration—in short, that it will contribute to the hoped-for success of the text. The maneuver consists—I shall put it as neutrally and coldly as possible—in offering data on the page to which a plus or minus feeling is attached by the writer or by a character in the text (or both), and simultaneously, or else gradually, or else eventually, making us perceive that the plus or minus conveys or all along conveyed something to which the reader attaches the opposite value. The plus in question may be a sense of correctness, effectiveness, goodness, nobility, luck, beauty, bigness, youth, relief from pain, enjoyment of life—anything whatsoever—and the minus, obviously, will be the opposite. Here is a quick and basic example. You look out the window into a snowstorm and exclaim to a friend: 'Fine weather we're having today!' Your statement is a plus intended to convey a minus to the recipient. But note that although your words are meant ironically, they will *work* as irony only if the recipient receives them as intended. Otherwise, upon looking out the window himself, he will conclude that you are mad.

In 'real life' (the point of departure for art) irony is very often created, not by a person speaking or acting, but by brute Reality itself. Take the weather again. We consider it ironical if, having spent a great deal of money to escape from the chill of winter to some tropical resort, we run into an untimely frost there, or a destructive hurricane. The plus offer of relief from bad weather turns into the minus result of running into awful weather. Here then, unlike the ironies we encounter in texts, the irony is a perfectly unintended effect due to what we call by such names as Fate, Reality, Life, Nature, Circumstances, Satan or God.[1]

Not, of course, that the ironies of brute Reality are confined to natural phenomena. If the friend you trusted betrayed you while your supposed enemy came to your rescue, this is still 'one of life's ironies'. The interesting point, however, is that the abstract agencies of irony that we call Reality, Life and so on, as well as gods and devils, saints and witches, are the real-life equivalents of the literary person who fashions ironical texts. In a text, it is the author who creates the friend who turned out to be an enemy. In a life situation, the maker of this irony is God or Life, or whatever we care to name.

(2) Even elementary irony—as exemplified by the cry 'Fine weather we're having today!'—requires a degree of mental and cultural development, first in the sender for thinking up the possibility of this trope—plus or minus conveying the opposite—and then in the receiver who must learn not to take the discourse at face value. Beyond these rudimentary manifestations, when irony becomes more subtle or complex, the players on both sides of the game must keep matching one another at an ever higher level of sophistication. No wonder, therefore, that the earliest texts we possess—for example, the oldest parts of the Old Testament for the Near East, Homer's epics for Greece, *Beowulf* for the European North—display very little consciously applied irony. Literary irony—irony as a trope—grows into a favored tool in mature societies, where *indirection* is often prized for its way of tickling the intellect.

---

1.   A discussion of irony is bound to stress the ostensible plus value that conceals and reveals an actual minus value. This reflects our normal linguistic practice, itself based on the original Greek meaning of 'irony', namely 'deception' or 'dissimulation'. But when Emily Dickinson wrote 'I'm Nobody! Who are you? / Are you Nobody too?' (see Chapter 19) she showed that a full view of irony has to include the reverse movement, a movement upward from pseudo minus to intended plus. Obviously Dickinson's Nobodies are better Somebodies than the 'official' Somebodies in her second stanza.

Sometimes it is not naiveté that prevents transfer of information but cultural difference. The more sophisticated ironic contrivances are likely to depend on a cultural community in order to work, that is to say in order to be understood and therefore interest and excite. An irony may be clearly understood and appreciated by the members of an 'in-group' (one that may be extremely broad or quite narrow); less clearly by neighboring groups; and not at all by distant groups—distant in time, place or both. When Jonathan Swift published his *Modest Proposal for Preventing the Children of Poor People in Ireland from Being a Burden to their Parents or Country, and for Making them Beneficial to the Public* (1729)—where he suggested with a straight face (so to speak) that unwanted babies in a famished land be processed into high-quality meat— we can suppose that all but a naive few among his Irish readers understood that what he truly advocated lay somewhere at the opposite pole of his zealous advice. But an audience residing in— well, I shall be prudent and say 'in some distant land'—might have taken him at his word, and manifested either shock at the revolting idea, or wise assent at the excellent suggestion. At a critical cultural distance, the outsider, however sophisticated a denizen of his own group, reverts in effect to the stage of infancy: he is a baby vis-à-vis the foreign group or culture into which he has fallen.

(3) Just as in 'real life' Fate, or God, or Whatever can be imagined as contriving one of 'life's ironies', so in a text irony is consciously activated by its writer and aimed at the reader. Now, ironical discourse can be either *local* or *pervasive*. By local irony I mean pinpointed irony—a sentence in a larger text, or a word in a sentence, or even a 'related sign'. The larger text, in this case, remains straightforward, but the poet (or any writer) resorts here and there to the rhetoric of irony, just as here and there he may use a provocative simile.

Pervasive irony, on the other hand, suffuses an entire text, or at least a substantial block of it—for example, a scene in a play. Of course, if an entire text consists of something like a single sentence, the two terms simply fuse. But the essence of pervasive irony is that the plus-minus or minus-plus rhetoric is textually encompassing.

A representative example of local irony occurs in the first of the two stanzas of a poem by Yeats called 'The Scholars':

> Bald heads forgetful of their sins,
> Old, learned, respectable bald heads
> Edit and annotate the lines
> That young men, tossing on their beds,
> Rhymed out in love's despair
> To flatter beauty's ignorant ear.[2]

Most of this is a straightforward, that is to say non-ironical attack on professors of literature. But within this general attack the word 'respectable' occurs as a local irony. The scholars may indeed be respectable as citizens—and Yeats does not obliterate this meaning—but his 'in-group' will understand that the poet is chiefly conveying *dis*respect, and doing so as the very consequence of the esteem in which the scholars are held by the Establishment.

For a pervasively ironic poem, we might return to Richard Armour's funny little poem, which we already called ironic in Chapter 5:

> That poem is a splendid thing.
> I love to hear you quote it.
> I like the thought, I like the swing.
> I like it all. (I wrote it).

Here was my comment: 'Parentheses mean "not very important", or "not the main point at all", and Armour utilizes that meaning to play an ironical game with us, since in fact "I wrote it" is very much the main point.' We can now expand this observation by noting that the seemingly unimportant final remark turns the plus value of a compliment to a fellow poet into the minus value of partisan self-love, and then compounds and reverses the ironic movement by calling for our approval of the speaker's candor. He has admitted being a cheat; but the admission shows that he is laughing at himself: the intelligent 'I' as berater peeps ironically out from behind the ironically berated 'I'.

But why would we call this poem pervasively ironic, since the

---

2.   From *The Wild Swans at Coole* (1919). In *The Poems of W.B. Yeats* (ed. Richard J. Finneran; New York: Macmillan, 1983). Note the synecdoche of 'bald heads'—obviously better targets of satire than 'men' or 'scholars' and the like would have been.

only ironic element in it is a three-word statement enclosed in a pair of curved signs? The answer is that a local irony—even one as minute as this—can act retroactively and suffuse the entire text. We are right to consider Armour's whole poem as ironic—something we cannot say of Yeats's mordant stanza. *A fortiori*, when several local ironies are scattered over a poem, they will in all probability spread an ironical 'color' over the whole once we have read it through.

We also learn from Armour's quatrain how essential context is for all local ironies. Armour's send-off is ironical only within the context of the other lines; not in itself; and not in any number of other imaginable contexts.

In a mock heroic poem like Pope's *The Rape of the Lock*, the irony is systematic and unremitting. Pope pretends to trumpet the business of Belinda's lost curl as an event of heroic magnitude. Only a reader excessively stupid—or, if intelligent, living at an immense cultural distance from Pope—could be taken in and accept this judgment without mentally reversing it. Let us look at a passage where the irony is created by a couple of heroic similes—if only to demonstrate that tropes do not necessarily appear one by one. After a game of cards, while an elegant company is seated round the coffee table, a foppish baron (you will remember) has succeeded in applying his scissors to one of Belinda's locks. Could it have been otherwise, muses the poet:

> Steel could the labor of the gods destroy,
> And strike to dust th'imperial towers of Troy;
> Steel could the works of mortal pride confound,
> And hew triumphal arches to the ground.
> What wonder then, fair nymph! thy hairs should feel
> The conquering force of unresisted steel?[3]

'The steel of the baron's scissors,' says Pope in effect, 'destroyed an object as grand as Troy and the triumphal arches in antiquity.' Namely? Belinda's curls. These are only six lines; but Pope renders the entire scene in this extravagant manner, ridiculing the

---

3.   Canto III, lines 173-78. At the end of *The Rape of the Lock*, Pope announces that the lock has risen into heaven to become a star. At that final point the narrative reenters the realm of fantasy, fairy tale and the like (it had entered there in a previous section), where 'the opposite is being meant' does not apply, for we are invited to join the narrator in the world of magic.

petty drawing-room quarrel pervasively and consistently by pretending to exalt it.

(4) Needless to say, Pope is having delicious fun with his Belindas and his barons, and so are we. Irony can be all pretense and play, just as it can be tragic and occupy every stage in between. For it refers to a positive-negative manipulation of data, not to the mood which that manipulation evokes in the reader.

(5) The pervasive irony of a text is often attached to a character who speaks, acts, believes or expects something in a plus direction, where the truth or the outcome is revealed to the reader (and sometimes to the character himself) as lying in minus territory.[4] 'A character' can turn into many characters, of course; and, more interestingly, the character can be the pretended 'I' of a text. The *persona* of Swift in the *Modest Proposal* is a superb example; and so is Arthur Hugh Clough (1819–1861)—or shall we say 'The fictive speaker'—offering the following recommendations:

THE LATEST DECALOGUE

Thou shalt have one God only; who
Would be at the expense of two?
No graven images may be
Worshiped, except the currency.
Swear not at all; for, for thy curse
Thine enemy is none the worse.
At church on Sunday to attend
Will keep the world thy friend.
Honor thy parents; that is, all
From whom advancement may befall.
Thou shalt not kill; but needs't not strive
Officiously to keep alive.
Do not adultery commit;
Advantage rarely comes of it.
Thou shalt not steal; an empty feat,
When it's so lucrative to cheat.
Bear not false witness; let the lie
Have time on its own legs to fly.
Thou shalt not covet, but tradition
Approves all forms of competition.[5]

4.   Again, the opposite movement is also a possibility.

5.   This poem exemplifies the possible force of poetry essentially devoid of figures and images, and the importance of sheer intelligence for such poems.

Like Swift, Clough presents himself to us as a character advocating a good that the perceiver understands to be evil.

In Chapter 13 we examined a clever staging of irony in Robert Mezey's 'My Mother'. As the mother speaks, we silently and gleefully reverse her contention that she knows what is right and good. No, we retort, she does *not* know what is right and good, she is a prosaic philistine.

Or so she appears to the in-group readers who understand Mezey's wink. This in-group may be surprisingly narrow. A great number of Americans (to go no farther afield) might well side with the practical mother, condemn like her the rebellious artist-son, and thus turn a blind eye to the irony. Irony, we see again, is a perception. If we side with the mother, the poem simply ceases to be ironical.

However, for a classic of staged irony, we return, all but inevitably, to Robert Browning's 'My Last Duchess', the most famous of the *Dramatic Lyrics* of 1842. The setting of this monologue is Ferrara, a city-state in sixteenth-century Italy. The duke, its ruler, is speaking throughout the poem. He is addressing the emissary of a nobleman from another city-state whose daughter he wishes to marry. With greater affability than would be expected toward a mere envoy (though a gentleman), the duke is giving the latter a private tour, as we would say today, of the art collection in his *palazzo*. They stop, as if by chance, before a particularly lovely painting of a young woman. The duke condescends to explain that the young woman was once his wife. Everyone, it seems, who gazes at the painting marvels at the sweetness of expression which the painter caught. It was not, alas, a sweetness the duke relished:

> Sir, 'twas all one! My favor at her breast,
> The dropping of the daylight in the West,
> The bough of cherries some officious fool
> Broke in the orchard for her, the white mule
> She rode with round the terrace—all and each
> Would draw from her alike the approving speech,
> Or blush, at least. She thanked men,—good! but thanked
> Somehow—I know not how—as if she ranked
> My gift of a nine-hundred-years-old name
> With anybody's gift.

As for giving the girl lessons in decorum, the duke would have none of it; it would have meant stooping—admitting that his pride was hurt—

                                        and I choose
              Never to stoop.

Instead, he 'gave commands'—

              Then all smiles stopped together.

That is all we find out; the duke evidently feels that a word to the wise (especially among diplomats) is enough; so now he invites his guest to rejoin 'the company below'; and, presumably while they are stepping through the gallery toward the staircase, the duke intimates that he looks forward to a suitable dowry from the count. Glancing at another work of art, he remarks that it is a precious bronze Neptune, cast especially for him. And there Browning ends the poem.

Let me digress for a moment and revert to the topic of implied propositions that we have treated rather fully before, but about which it would be difficult to say too much. 'My Last Duchess' abounds in such between-the-lines propositions: that is part of its greatness. One of them, which readers often miss, is that the tour, the 'incidental' stopping before the painting of the dead wife, the intimate revelations dropped with such surprising familiarity to a stranger and commoner, all constitute an *innuendo,* which we can think of as a proposition that masks and yet delivers an aggressive one, whether serious or humorous. In Browning's poem, the innuendo's extremely serious message is: 'Tell the count to instruct his daughter to mind her behavior with me, so *she* doesn't come to a sorry end!' So important is this concealed message that we can call it one of the several subjects of the poem—an implied one, of course.

Another innuendo, this one immediately apparent, is created by the duke's reticent

                    I gave commands;
              Then all smiles stopped together.

We are left at liberty to choose what happened to the unfortunate girl. Since she is dead, however, and obviously died young, the meaning is hardly in doubt.[6] A third innuendo is provided by the poet himself, who seems to be saying, mainly through the final remark about the bronze Neptune, that the duke is more sensitive to beautiful art than to beautiful human beings.

This brings us to the main subject of Browning's poem, namely a character study, or a double character study, conveyed through a pervasive irony, devoid of local ironies, embodied in or carried by a personage. Like Mezey's mother-figure (but in a more sinister key) the duke believes he is good and right and his wife deficient and wrong, while we the readers are expected to read the characters in reverse. But once more, it must be emphasized that without cultural collusion between author and reader the irony will not be operative. An Italian reader *in* the sixteenth century could easily have sided strongly with the duke and against the young goose who failed to appreciate him. By 1842, however, Browning could count on a high estimate of the humane, egalitarian, liberal duchess and a thorough dislike of snobs who make more of their pedigree than of their own merits. And yet even today—as any literature teacher will attest—some beginning readers naively miss the irony and remain puzzled as to whether or not they are supposed to sympathize with the duke.[7]

(6) Pervasive irony is usually called 'dramatic irony' when the poet chooses to make his fictive character unaware of the reverse spin, from plus to minus or minus to plus, that the poet intends to convey to the reader. This blindess may persist to the end of the text, or, alternatively, the deluded personage does finally recognize the reality *we* see. The classic here is Sophocles' *Oedipus Rex*. Oedipus has launched an enthusiastic inquiry into the identity of a murderer, expecting enhanced power and glory for himself. At the climax, however, the truth is revealed to him that he himself

6.   Browning himself left open, in a letter, the possibility that the duke had his wife shut up in a convent. If so, we still have to imagine her as dying long before her normal life-span was over. Aesthetically, the text demands that we ascribe her death to her husband.

7.   This happens in part because naive readers regularly expect the speaker, the 'I' of a narrative, to be the 'good guy'; but Browning slyly helps them, besides, through the ambiguity of 'I gave commands'. Maybe he only told her to cease and desist!

was the murderer, and thus he has in effect worked at procuring his own destruction.[8]

Instead, for Mezey's mother and Browning's duke the delusion persists to the end of the text. It does so as well for Shelley's 'Ozymandias':

> I met a traveler from an antique land
> Who said: Two vast and trunkless legs of stone
> Stand in the desert. Near them, on the sand,
> Half sunk, a shattered visage lies, whose frown,
> And wrinkled lip, and sneer of cold command,
> Tell that its sculptor well those passions read
> Which yet survive, stamped on these lifeless things,
> The hand that mocked them, and the heart that fed:
> And on the pedestal these words appear:
> 'My name is Ozymandias, king of kings:
> Look on my works, ye Mighty, and despair!'
> Nothing beside remains. Round the decay
> Of that colossal wreck, boundless and bare,
> The lone and level sands stretch far away.[9]

Obviously, the tyrant died without realizing that his plus vision of eternal glory was destined for the minus of wreckage.

In other texts, however, the pervasive irony which is created by the artist and perceived by the reader is *also* experienced throughout by one or more fictive characters. For example, in Edwin Arlington Robinson's 'Richard Cory' (1897) a first-person speaker tells us in three quatrains how rich, gracious and accomplished Richard Cory appeared to everyone in town:

> In fine, we thought that he was everything
> To make us wish that we were in his place.

This leads into the fourth and last quatrain:

> So on we worked, and waited for the light,
> And went without the meat, and cursed the bread;
> And Richard Cory, one calm summer night,
> Went home and put a bullet through his head.

8.   For the first-time reader or spectator the irony is perceived more or less at the same time as it dawns on Oedipus; but for those already familiar with the text, it works as a rhetorical maneuver from the start.

9.   Line 8 remains obscure. Whose hand mocked Ozymandias's passions, and why?

It can be assumed that, within the fiction, Cory recognized for a long time that he was living out an irony: happy in show, wretched in reality. This would be a case of a fully self-conscious irony staged by the poet—and I suppose that it should not be called 'dramatic' irony (not, however, that the terminology matters). In any event, standard 'dramatic irony' appears in this particular poem with respect to the long-deluded speaker and the towns-people ('I' and 'we' in the poem) whose eyes were opened only at the end.[10]

(7) The ironic act of pulling down is sometimes confused with sarcasm. The Oxford English Dictionary defines the latter term as 'a sharp, bitter, or cutting expression or remark'. But while many sarcastic remarks are indeed ironical ('That's just what I needed!' you exclaim when a friend spills some catsup on your dress), they can also be direct, literal, straightforward—as in Pope's

> My Lord advances with majestic mien,
> Smit with the mighty pleasure, to be seen;[11]

or as in the piece by Cummings we have met before:

> my sweet old etcetera
> aunt lucy during the recent
>
> war could and what
> is more did tell you just
> what everybody was fighting
>
> for,
> my sister
>
> isabel created hundreds
> (and
> hundreds) of socks not to
> mention shirts fleaproof earwarmers
>
> etcetera wristers etcetera, my
> mother hoped that
> i would die etcetera
> bravely of course my father used

---

10. We might consider the *calm* summer night a local irony. To be sure, the night may have been outwardly calm (just as Yeats's scholars are literally respectable); but it was inwardly stormy.

11. *Moral Essays*, Epistle IV, lines 127-28. Pope's devastatingly sarcastic epigram quoted on p. 185 is equally devoid of irony.

> to become hoarse talking about how it was
> a privilege and if only he
> could

and so on. No ironies in sight, but plenty of sarcasm.

In 'The Latest Decalogue,' on the other hand, sarcasm is transmitted through irony. The poet insults people-in-general by telling them the true reasons why most of them obey the Ten Commandments. But this sarcastic message is transmitted to us by means of statements that pretend to *recommend* these reasons. To make a long story short, irony and sarcasm are like overlapping circles, where part of each circle remains free of the other.

While sarcasm is often ironical and therefore apt to be confused with irony, outright invective stands out as quite distinct from the latter, even though local ironies may occur in the course of its utterance. Here is Swift's 'A Satirical Elegy on the Death of a Late Famous General' dated 1722.[12]

> His Grace! impossible! what, dead!
> Of old age too, and in his bed!
> And could that mighty warrior fall,
> And so inglorious, after all?
> Well, since he's gone, no matter how,
> The last loud trump must wake him now;
> And trust me, as the noise grows stronger,
> He'd wish to sleep a little longer.
> And could he be indeed so old
> As by the newspaper we're told?
> Threescore, I think, is pretty high;
> 'Twas time inconscience he should die!
> This world he cumber'd long enough;
> He burnt his candle to the snuff;
> And that's the reason, some folks think,
> He left behind so great a stink.
> Behold his funeral appears,
> Nor widows' sighs, nor orphans' tears,
> Wont at such times each heart to pierce,
> Attend the progress of his hearse.

12. The famous general was John Churchill, first Duke of Marlborough (1650–1722), greatly admired for his victories but hated by those who opposed his wars and his self-enrichment from those wars. 'Elegy' in the title would be a local irony (and the only one in the poem) were it not turned into an oxymoron by 'satirical' (see Chapter 21).

But what of that? his friends may say,
He had those honours in his day.
True to his profit and his pride,
He made them weep before he died.
    Come hither, all ye empty things!
Ye bubbles raised by breath of kings
Who float upon the tide of state;
Come hither, and behold your fate!
Let Pride be taught by this rebuke,
How very mean a thing's a duke;
From all his ill-got honours flung,
Turn'd to that dirt from whence he sprung.

Like Cummings's poem, this powerful indictment never says the opposite of what it means to convey; but you can see in what way invective differs from sarcasm. Sarcasm insinuates—leaves the judgment unspoken; invective speaks it out, loud and clear, impatient of detours.

(8) To conclude, let us inquire in what way or ways raw propositions are energized by the trope of irony; in plainer English, what makes irony potentially so interesting to us?

For one thing, our *grasp* of the true minus that has been deceptively advanced as a plus (or the opposite) is in itself a pleasure. Understanding, discovery, unmasking, exposing—these are pleasures, small or great, depending on the situation—pleasures probably anchored in a self-congratulatory sense of achievement or superiority.

I have also mentioned the teasing of the intellect caused by an indirect approach to situations and concepts.

But irony possesses a more important and vital force. Imagine walking on a busy street, one side of which is lined with lovely houses and gardens, while the other is a fetid slum. Our walk enables us to capture both realities at the same time. Something of this kind is essentially what irony gives us: we see both sides at once, the high and the low, the should-be and the what-is, the dream and the reality, the desired and the dreaded, and so on. The down side of this double vision may not be pleasant—but poems and novels, like many of the motion pictures you see, deal with down and up alike. Irony is *rich* in the sense that it delivers a double vision in a single expressive act. Instead of 'This man is ignoble,' the ironist says, 'Such a noble man!' or else, even more pregnantly, has the man himself boast of his noble mind. On a lowly humorous level, the top-hatted gentleman slipping on a banana peel exhibits at the same time high decorum and vulgar pratfall.

The force we are talking about is well exemplified by Swift's ironically titled *Modest Proposal* (which is neither modest nor a proposal). One side of the street shows a self-satisfied, high-minded and scientifically oriented gentleman outlining an efficient set of recommendations on what to do with the excess of babies in the land, while simultaneously, on the other pavement, we descry a furious Swift attacking Ireland's oppressors who have starved the country.

Similar observations can be applied to the other texts we have considered in the present chapter and elsewhere in this book. You might recall in this connection how, in Chapter 11, we spoke of Eddie Guest's 'flatness' and contrasted it with a dense, complex poem by Milton. Now again we can speak of a special density, complexity, or richness created by the double vision of irony.

I have devoted a full though brief chapter to the topic of irony because it is so fascinating and widespread a tactic, but also because our century has shown a special predilection for it. Nevertheless, it remains but one out of a multitude of possible rhetorical figures, and in our next chapter we need to pass some of these in quick review.

Chapter 21

Infinite Resources

'Infinite' is a lot. But the truth is that no limit has been, or can be, set on what writers (and speakers) can do to and with language in order to persuade or simply impress other people. The Greeks and the Romans, and then a band of scholars in the Renaissance, analyzed how lawyers, politicians, poets and other specialists of tongue and quill manipulate language to attain their ends, and came up with long yet always open-ended lists of devices under the heading of *rhetoric,* that is to say effective speech, or, simply, eloquence: the very thing we have called *energized propositions* in these pages. As a result, you can, if you wish, pepper your readings of a poem with resounding Greek terms like antimetabole and brachylogia and hysteron proteron and apophasis and ecphrone-sis and polyptoton and what-have-you—some of which are called figures of words, others figures of thought, with further distinc-tions and sub-distinctions to make the pedantic heart rejoice.[1] I will spare you most of this impressive terminology, as I did before in discussing sound and rhythm—even though it often com-presses into one word what takes up several in English; but it should be observed that a few of these technical terms have made their way into our everyday or near-everyday language; among them, metaphor and symbol, hyperbole, antithesis, apostrophe, and even oxymoron.

---

1.   If you detect a note of sarcasm in this sentence, you have put your finger on a figure of thought. The heart rejoicing is, instead, a figure of speech, namely a synecdoche. 'Trope', for our purposes, is a synonym for *any* figure.

The reason why analyses of eloquence can go on practically *ad infinitum* is that it takes very little to energize an unaffected expository text of the kind you are reading in this very sentence. We saw at the beginning of Chapter 11 that many a raw proposition possesses what we can now call a pre-rhetorical energy of its own; but whether its power to excite us be small or great, the merest nudge—an exclamation point, a repetition, a nice metaphor—will add something, however minor, to that power; and no matter *how* minor, a student of rhetoric has detected it and given it a name.

Let me repeat that rhetoric is a fountain from which all people can drink. It is not held in reserve for poets. Indeed, the Greeks and Romans who wrote on these matters (from Aristotle onward) were more concerned with practical eloquence—winning a case before a set of judges or talking the citizens into declaring a war— than in the innocent eloquence of the poet, whose success consists, as we have seen, not in persuading a judge or urging a war, but in thrilling his audience—whatever else he may achieve on the side, or wish he could achieve. Very few are the drops of the fountain of rhetoric that flow entirely, or almost entirely, for the poet and no one else: the rhetoric of 'limited quanta', rhythm and rhyme—and the cup is full. Everything else is available to all comers. I made a point of this in my discussion of synecdoches, symbols, metaphors, similes, irony, etc. All these are rhetorical devices—resources—weapons in the arsenal—colors on the palette—energizers of propositions (choose your metaphor!) that are given to all the world to use and abuse.[2]

Another point worth reaffirming is that while some rhetorical strategies may function chiefly or exclusively as intensifiers of a proposition, most of the time 'applying a rhetorical device to a proposition' (which is a mechanical way of putting our creative act) endows the latter with a halo of implied propositions that carry emotional charges of their own. It may be that in Pope's

> Shut, shut the door, good John! fatigu'd, I said,

the repetition is nothing more than an intensifier—'I want you very much to shut the door' (the poet is not asking John to close

---

2.   I omit from this discussion the considerable rhetorical resources available to those who choose visual or auditory media of communication— with advertisers at the head of the list.

the door twice!)—but we have seen already that figures like metaphors and symbols can accomplish far more than simply 'turn up the heat'; for, as I have stressed repeatedly, any work applied to a raw, pre-poetic proposition will cause an alteration of meaning, however subtle or minute. I will have occasion in what follows to present additional evidence for this concept.

Of course, power of any kind has to register; it has to be felt before it can succeed as power. In other words, a rhetorical turn must *strike* the reader as an augmentation of normal, plain discourse. If I speak about the success of a rhetorical maneuver, I must always be understood to imply a very substantial public— sometimes an entire culture—whose receptivities, which we can compare to antennas, are sufficiently alike to make generalizations possible.

We can count, for instance, on a largely uniform receptivity to *repetition*, of which we have just seen a typical poetic instance, and which is perhaps the all-around favorite rhetorical move.[3] No rhetorical maneuver is more elementary, more deeply rooted in our animal and infantile natures, and more vital to eloquence, whether practical or disinterested. Not surprisingly, repetition is also the trope most subdivided into types, each bearing its own name, by the Greek analysts and their progeny. We have dealt already with repetition as the defining element of both rhythm and rhyme; but now we look for repetition of words, as in Pope's line or Donne's 'arise, arise' (Chapters 12 and 13), repetition of phrases, clauses, 'related signs', blocks of text—anything that goes into the building of a text.

Repetitions can be effectively scattered throughout a text. You should return to Cummings's 'my sweet old etcetera' for a fine example—fine because the obstinate repetition of 'etcetera' does more than merely augment and intensify: it yields a conceptual richness of sarcastic innuendo.

In Chapter 16 we looked at a passage from Eliot's *Murder in the Cathedral*, which is singularly rich in scattered repetitions:

3.   Assuming that dead metaphors, which constitute a great part of our languages, are excluded from the count—the purely imaginary count, of course. Music, incidentally, relies even more pervasively on repetition.

You know and do not know, what it is to act or suffer.
You know and do not know, that acting is suffering,
And suffering action. Neither does the actor suffer
Nor the patient act. But both are fixed
In an eternal action, an eternal patience
To which all must consent that it may be willed
And which all must suffer that they may will it,
That the pattern may subsist, that the wheel may turn and still
Be forever still.

The device shown in the first two lines is called *anaphora*: the repetition of words or phrases (often incantatory) at the beginning of each clause—a childlike but often powerful energizer of thought. Here is an ampler instance:

The shapes arise!
Shapes of factories, arsenals, foundries, markets,
Shapes of the two-threaded tracks of railroads,
Shapes of the sleepers of bridges, vast frameworks, girders, arches,
Shapes of the fleets of barges, tows, lake and canal craft, river craft,
    (etc.)[4]

Another familiar kind of repetition is that of the *refrain*, so well known that no example is needed here. The point to remember is that larger units than words, phrases or clauses are often effectively repeated. Do such blocks have to be repeated *verbatim*? Not so. Repetition need not be perfect and literal in order to register on the mind *as* repetition; and this is especially true of such larger units, where recurrence is often partial. We even have the term 'incremental repetition' to denote the partial or approximate repetitions in many ballads that move the narrative intriguingly forward up to its climax.

Approximate repetition registers on the mind in shorter units as well, just as approximate rhyme does. A trope esoterically known as *polyptoton* refers to one such type, exemplified by a couple of lines from Act I, Scene i of Shakespeare's *Troilus and Cressida*:

The Greeks are strong, and skilful to their strength,
Fierce to their skill, and to their fierceness valiant.

---

4.   From section 9 of Walt Whitman's 'Song of the Broad-Axe' (1856). A sleeper is a heavy horizontal beam.

The device of repetition is also effective when applied to *rhetorical questions*. In Herbert's 'The Collar', for instance, sheer repetition of questions powerfully augments the anguish the poet expresses:

> Is the year only lost to me?
> Have I no bays to crown it,
> No flowers, no garlands gay? all blasted?
> All wasted?

The questions are 'rhetorical' in that the answer to them is so obvious (in context) that they register on the mind as vehement statements. Much more could be said about repetition, but it is not the purpose of this chapter to exhaust either the subject of tropes or the reader.[5]

'Edward' is a famous old anonymous Scottish ballad that features the rhetoric of *climactic structure*. The poem is a mini-drama concerning a mother and her son, building to its climax through the aforementioned incremental repetition, namely of questions and answers framed in parallel but advancing with each stanza. Here is the opening stanza—in plain English, however, rather than the original Scottish:

> 'Why does your brand so drop with blood,
>   Edward, Edward?
> Why does your brand so drop with blood.
>   And why so sad go ye, O?'
> 'O I have killed my hawk so good,
>   Mother, mother,
> O I have killed my hawk so good,
>   And I had no more but he, O.'

In the next stanza—composed in the same dialogue form—the mother objects that 'Your hawk's blood was never so red,' and the son replies that it was his steed he killed. When this fails to satisfy the mother again, he admits that he killed his father. Well now, what penance will he suffer for this, she asks. He will 'fare over the sea' in a boat. But what about his towers and hall? (For Edward, it must be understood, is a nobleman.) He will let them fall down. And what will he leave his children and wife? Let them

5. My exploitation of two senses of the word 'exhaust' is a special kind of pun (see below) called *antanaclasis*.

go begging through the world! Now comes the seventh and last
stanza—always in the same form:

> 'And what will you leave to your own mother dear,
>   Edward, Edward?
> And what will you leave to your own mother dear.
>   My dear son, now tell me O?'
> 'The curse of hell from me shall ye bear,
>   Mother, mother,
> The curse of hell from me shall ye bear,
>   Such counsels you gave me, O.'[6]

Needless to say, climactic structure does not depend on incre-
mental repetition. In Pope's *Essay on Man*, it happens to emerge
out of ordinary repetition:

> All Nature is but art, unknown to thee;
> All chance, direction, which thou canst not see;
> All discord, harmony not understood;
> All partial evil, universal good:
> And, spite of pride, in erring reason's spite,
> One truth is clear, WHATEVER IS, IS RIGHT.

Climactic structure becomes completely independent of repeti-
tion in 'The Collar' (see the full text in Chapter 6).

The climax of 'Edward' illustrates a related but separate rhetor-
ical move, that of *surprise*—keeping something hidden in our
sleeve, and then springing it on a listener. Children and even our
friend Fido respond excitely to surprise, but in the following
poem by James Wright (1927–1980) we find a deeply mature
application of this figure:

> Over my head, I see the bronze butterfly,
> Asleep on the black trunk,
> Blowing like a leaf in green shadow.
> Down the ravine behind the empty house,
> The cowbells follow one another
> Into the distances of the afternoon.

6.   'Brand' in the first stanza means sword. Note the pungent local irony
of 'dear' in the climactic stanza. Scholars began to collect these folk ballads
(the best of them obviously composed by very gifted poets) in the eighteenth
century. Having been sung from memory or unpublished manuscripts for
centuries, many of them survive in several variants.

To my right,
In a field of sunlight between two pines,
The droppings of last year's horses
Blaze up into golden stones.
I lean back, as the evening darkens and comes on.
A chicken hawk floats over, looking for home.
I have wasted my life.[7]

The poet has been careful to write a poem that lounges metrically in free verse as it depicts a lounger in his hammock. A couple of unobtrusive metaphors and similes blend in with a serenely tropeless description. All the more startling the last line, which lands us in a far different country of the mind at the snap of a finger.[8]

Pope surprises us rather differently when, in *The Rape of the Lock*, he describes his coquettish Belinda at her dressing table:

Here files of pins extend their shining rows,
Puffs, powders, patches, Bibles, billet-doux.[9]

A given passage in a text, or an entire text, can do several effective things at the same time, to which analysis responds by attaching two or more labels to what is happening. We have seen climax coupled to surprise. Pope's couplet just cited is both surprising and sarcastic. Next we can twin surprise with *anticlimax*, the sudden humorous demotion at a point where something higher rather than something lower was expected. Take, for instance, the stanza in Byron's *Don Juan* where the poet begins with a tragic

7.   'Lying in a Hammock at William Duffy's Farm in Pine Island, Minnesota', in *The Branch Will Not Break* (Middletown, CT: Wesleyan University Press, 1963).

8.   The reader is expected, naturally, to supply the conceptual bridge between lines 1-12 and the final line. Doing so eliminates the surprise, to be sure. That is why these mental acts remain as mute helpers outside the poem as such. If the poet himself had supplied the bridging implied proposition or propositions, he would probably have poisoned his poem, for we do not like to be blabbed at.

9.   Canto I, lines 137-38. Elegant ladies adorned their cheeks with little patches that mimicked beauty-spots. A billet-doux is a tender note—a brief love letter. There are scholars who believe that Pope meant to write 'bibelots' (knick-knacks), not 'Bibles'; but even if he did (and most scholars doubt it), the mistake stands, the word has been read as 'Bibles' for over two centuries, and we learn that good art is sometimes inadvertent.

account of castaways from a shipwreck, but ends on a gag:

> Famine, despair, cold, thirst, and heat, had done
> Their work on them by turns, and thinn'd them to
> Such things a mother had not known her son
> Amidst the skeletons of that gaunt crew;
> By night chill'd, by day scorch'd, thus one by one
> They perish'd, until wither'd to these few,
> But chiefly by a species of self-slaughter,
> In washing down Pedrillo with salt water.[10]

Here, without question, we get surprise and anticlimax in a single burst.

Quoting Byron's stanza just after Pope's couplet may alert us to the principle that not only metaphors but *all* rhetorical maneuvers can be either flashy or genuinely brilliant. They are brilliant when they convey striking implied propositions. The rhetoric of Pope's line, for instance, is not 'just fun'—it tells us, without telling us, something significant about Belinda, and beyond that, something very significant about high society in Pope's time. It seems to me, on the other hand, that Byron, in this instance, has nothing to offer more interesting than a quick laugh.

Climactic structure, anticlimax and other maneuvers could be subsumed under a still larger category that could be called the rhetoric of *strategic location*, which covers any segment of a text that acquires part of its power from the sheer fact of its placement in relation to the position of other segments. A poem like 'Edward' could easily have *begun* with a curse on the mother rather than ending with it. But locating the curse at the end was, of course, the more energetic move. Similarly, in Reed's 'Naming of Parts' (quoted in Chapter 6) we discovered that the mere act of juxtaposing two contrasting elements conveyed rich implications.

At several points in this volume we have examined instances of the rhetoric of *typography* and *layout*, by which I mean the energy the poet can infuse into his text by capitals, lower cases, italics, and so on, and also by singularities in the visual display of his lines, including the extreme case of emblem poetry.[11]

10. Canto II, Stanza 102. Pedrillo is young Don Juan's hapless tutor. The reader must be perfectly familiar with the speech level and connotations of 'washing down' in order to register the anticlimax.

11. You will recall that emblem poems crudely imitate the shape of

Proceeding: Pope's 'All partial evil, universal good' is an instance of one of his favorite devices, namely *balance*; partial and evil in one pan of the scale, universal and good in the other. Next to balance, we place *antithesis*, of which the line just quoted is in fact an example, antithesis being a balance of opposites rather than likes. In the following lines about aging flirts and coquettes we get both:

> See how the world its veterans rewards!
> A youth of frolics, an old age of cards;
> Fair to no purpose, artful to no end,
> Young without lovers, old without a friend;
> A fop their passion, but their prize a sot;
> Alive, ridiculous, and dead, forgot.[12]

And, once again, we note climactic structure giving form to this set of balanced and antithetical clauses.

A very frequent rhetorical resource is *personification*, where something that is not living is turned into a living and acting personage. In the morality plays of the Middle Ages, abstractions such as Riches or Gluttony were embodied by actors, put into costume and given roles in the drama. The perfectly sound premise was that live beings (human, animal, divine, etc.) are more exciting than concepts conveyed by collector words. This premise naturally carries over to verbal rather than stage representations of human beings. Today, the general opinion (it might change) is that our eighteenth-century poets were rather too fond of this device, not realizing that most of their personified abstractions remained more abstraction than person. We say, in effect, that putting capital initials on a vast concept may not be enough to bring the latter to life. Consider, for instance, a long didactic poem called 'The Vanity of Human Wishes', where Samuel Johnson (1709–84) informed his readers in a series of couplets that even the virtuous youth who dedicates his life to learning is not immune to grief:

---

objects in their layout on the page, for example, an altar or a DNA molecule. Nowadays such works are called 'concrete' poetry.

12. Lines 243-48 of Alexander Pope's 'Epistle II. To a Lady. Of the Character of Women' (1735). The 'prize' in line 247 is the husband whom the flirt finally lands.

> Should Reason guide thee with her brightest ray,
> And pour on misty Doubt resistless day;
> Should no false kindness lure to loose delight,
> Nor praise relax, nor difficulty fright;
> Should tempting Novelty thy cell refrain,
> And Sloth effuse her opiate fumes in vain;
> Should Beauty blunt on fops her fatal dart,
> Nor claim the triumph of a letter'd heart;
> Should no disease thy torpid veins invade,
> Nor Melancholy's phantoms haunt thy shade;
> Yet hope not life from grief or danger free,
> Nor think the doom of man reversed for thee.[13]

In the age we call Neoclassical, this elementary dramatizing of virtues and vices was thought to impart grandeur to what might otherwise have sounded low. Instead of an unshaved undergraduate jumping out of bed in a messy room, we view a malicious goddess called Sloth spreading 'opiate fumes in vain'. For better or for worse, our taste today favors the unshaved undergraduate, not to mention his dubious underwear.

However, the personification of abstractions has not absolutely disappeared from poetry. (I doubt that *any* rhetorical maneuver ever becomes truly extinct.) It has lost its pre-eminent role, yet it has remained quite serviceable, as we see, for instance, in Philip Larkin's rich personification of work as a toad—where Sam Johnson would perhaps have turned it into a spirit of divine retribution:

> Why should I let the toad *work*
>   Squat on my life?
> Can't I use my wit as a pitchfork
>   And drive the brute off?
>
> Six days of the week it soils
>   With its sickening poison—

13. Lines 145-56 of the 368-line poem published in 1749. The third line of this selection probably alludes to seductive wenches or wicked friends. Two lines farther we find new-fangled notions avoiding the student's little room. More seductive wenches appear another two lines down, but they trouble only fops, not our studious hero, who has a 'letter'd heart' (note the synecdoche) not given to idle follies. Repetition, balance and climax are also evident in this passage.

Just for paying a few bills!
That's out of proportion.[14]

If abstractions can speak, think, feel and act, so *a fortiori* can objects, plants, animals and so on. We might call this the rhetoric of *humanization*. 'I am a little snail' in Chapter 12 provides a palpable instance. And here is Tennyson giving human speech and action to a rivulet:

> I come from haunts of coot and hern,
>   I make a sudden sally,
> And sparkle out among the fern,
>   To bicker down a valley.
>
> By thirty hills I hurry down,
>   Or slip between the ridges,
> By twenty thorps, a little town,
>   And half a hundred bridges.
>
> Till last by Philip's farm I flow
>   To join the brimming river,
> For men may come and men may go,
>   But I go on for ever.[15]

And in 'The Bed' A.D. Hope (b. 1907) turns a mere object into a feeling creature :

> The doctor loves the patient,
> The patient loves his bed;
> A fine place to be born in,
> The best place to be dead.
>
> The doctor loves the patient
> Because he means to die;
> The patient loves the patient bed
> That shares his agony.
>
> The bed adores the doctor,
> His cool and skilful touch
> Soon brings another patient
> Who loves her just as much.[16]

14. Opening stanzas of 'Toads' (1955), taken from Larkin's *Collected Poems* (New York: Farrar & Giroux, 1989). Note the approximate rhymes.

15. There are six more stanzas, all lodged in various parts of a longer narrative poem called 'The Brook' (1855).

16. In *Collected Poems 1936–1965* (New York: Viking Press, 1963). Note the

Tennyson's 'The Brook' exhibits another widely used figure, namely that of *hyperbole*—and here we can safely use the Greek word for exaggeration, since English has altogether adopted it. In the arts (but not in public affairs) the hyperbole is an open, innocent lie that gives dramatic emphasis to raw propositions referring to great quantity or size.[17] The classic instance occurs in Andrew Marvell's 'To his Coy Mistress':

> An hundred years should go to praise
> Thine eyes, and on thy forehead gaze;
> Two hundred to adore each breast,
> But thirty thousand to the rest.[18]

The expression 'the rest' allows us to recall the figure *innuendo*, which was discussed in our chapter on *irony*, another major trope that must be listed here.

While hyperbole is a much-favored tool or weapon in the poetic arsenal, so is its opposite, *understatement*. How is it, you might ask, that opposite rhetorical maneuvers can be equally effective? The answer takes us back to one of our earliest points, namely that what we desire, in art, is to be moved (at our preferred level of intelligence)—and it seems that we are not too finicky about the 'color' of our emotions, accepting (within the limits we have discussed) all kinds of contraries, the bright and the dark. Rhetoric naturally reflects this situation.

You will remember Frank O'Hara's 'Poem', quoted in Chapter 12, with its typically modern jaunty understatements regarding death. An earlier instance on the same topic is John Crowe Ransom's 'Bells for John Whiteside's Daughter', from which I quote the first and last of its five stanzas:

> There was such speed in her little body,
> And such lightness in her footfall,
> It is no wonder her brown study
> Astonishes us all.
>
> . . . .

disparity between tone and theme that we discussed in Chapter 12, section (3). Antanaclasis reappears in 'The patient loves the patient bed'.

17. It is equally innocent, I hope, in the title of this chapter.

18. Lines 13-16 of the 46-line poem published in 1681, three years after Marvell's death.

> But now go the bells, and we are ready,
> In one house we are sternly stopped
> To say we are vexed at her brown study
> Lying so primly propped.[19]

Compare this sedate approach to King Lear's hyperboles in the presence of his murdered daughter:

> Howl, howl, howl! O! you are men of stones;
> Had I your tongues and eyes, I'd use them so
> That heaven's vault should crack.[20]

Two extremes indeed. And both at home in the canon.

A special name, *litotes*, is given to the type of understatement in which something positive is suggested by denying its contrary negative, with the effect of reinforcing the positive because it lets us see, by implication and yet transparently, that the speaker is making an effort to be restrained, modest or virtuously sparing of his listener's feelings. Here Sophocles' *Antigone* is helpful again. The queen of Thebes knows that she is about to receive dreadful intelligence from a messenger:

> As I came out to offer up my prayer
> To Pallas, and was drawing back the bar
> To open wide the door, upon my ears
> There broke a wail that told of household woes.
> Stricken with terror in my handmaids' arms
> I fell and fainted. But repeat your tale
> To one who is not ignorant of woe.[21]

The restraint of the last line preserves the queen's dignity even as it solicits from the messenger, the assembled Thebans, and, in a leap from the text, from us readers or spectators, the recognition that her knowledge of grief is immense.

Returning to Lear: of course, *exclamation* is a figure, since, even more than repetition, it is the basic and original intensifier of a raw proposition. Not unrelated to exclamation is *apostrophe*, a

---

19. First published in 1924. In *Selected Poems* (New York: Alfred A. Knopf, 3rd rev. and enlarged edn, 1969). The comma after 'we are ready' is likely to be a misprint for a period.

20. Act V, Scene iii. *King Lear* was published in 1608.

21. Lines 1184-90 in the Storr translation, slightly modified. See Chapter 16.

vehement direct address to someone or something. Because apostrophe has a distinctly oratorical lilt, it has largely faded from view in our age of dejected understatement.

Naturally, it was much in favor in the Neoclassical age, when, as we have seen more than once, poets took a rather loftily Roman view of themselves. Glancing at a series of poems by the typical eighteenth-century bard William Collins (1721–59), we find an 'Ode to Pity' where this respectable virtue is apostrophized as

> O thou, the friend of man assign'd;

an 'Ode to Fear':

> Ah Fear! Ah frantic Fear!
> I see, I see thee near,

along with:

> O thou whose spirit most possest
> The sacred seat of Shakespeare's breast;[22]

followed by an 'Ode to Simplicity', which begins:

> O thou by Nature taught,
> To breathe her genuine thought;

and, to conclude, an 'Ode to Evening' with the lines

> O Nymph reserv'd, while now the bright-hair'd sun
> Sits in yon western tent, (etc.)

Fortunately, in contrast with this ludicrous series, we know of many fine apostrophes in our tradition, like Wordsworth's

> Milton! thou shouldst be living at this hour.

Besides, as I suggested before, no rhetorical gesture ever dies. In the twentieth century we hear Theodore Roethke's

> O my bones,
> Beware those perpetual beginnings,[23]

and, in a poem by Allen Ginsberg we glanced at in Chapter 5:

---

22. A lamentable instance, in addition, of an absurd metaphor grafted on a synecdoche.

23. From 'What Can I Tell My Bones?' (1957). In *The Collected Poems of Theodore Roethke* (Garden City, NY: Anchor Press, 1975).

America when will we end the human war?

While apostrophe has nevertheless lost much ground in our times, the serious employment of *solecism* is practically a monopoly of ours—using bad English on purpose: incorrect grammar, punctuation, capitalization, diction—anything that can reinforce an emotion and/or suggest interesting thoughts. We have seen that the pioneering E.E. Cummings made effective use of this rhetorical maneuver, beginning with the immodest humility of using the lower case for his name (a practice I have cheerfully betrayed in these pages). Only in a democratic age of large, encouraged freedoms and affection for the underdog could this sort of rhetoric flourish:

> Henry's pelt was put on sundry walls
> where it did much resemble Henry and
> them persons was delighted.
> Especially his long & glowing tail
> by all them was admired, and visitors.
> They whistled: This is *it*.[24]

In the past, grammatical audacity seldom went beyond the decorous *ellipsis*: suppressing from a phrase or clause one or more words that pedestrian prose requires. In the following passage from Shakespeare's *Richard III*, we get not only ellipsis but also *interruption* (*aposiopesis*):

MESSENGER
My lord, the army of great Buckingham—

KING RICHARD
Out on ye, owls! nothing but songs of death?

where, after interrupting the Messenger, a more prose-bound King Richard would have cried, 'Do you have nothing but songs of death?' This leads us to the more famous ellipsis later in the play, when the harried Richard twice cries out:

A horse! A horse! my kingdom for a horse![25]

24. John Berryman (1914–72), *77 Dream Songs* (New York: Farrar, Straus & Giroux, 1964), first stanza of number 16.
25. Act IV, Scene iv, and Act V, Scene iv. The play was first printed in 1597, but had been written several years earlier.

We would hardly expect him, under the circumstances, to shout, 'I would give my kingdom for a horse!'

Interruptions are dramatic and almost certain to be loaded with meaning and emotion. This is obviously true in poems like 'my sweet old etcetera' (you might read part of it once more on pp. 317-18); but also more subtly in another one of Robert Browning's famous portraits of Italians of the Renaissance. Here the poet has a rather less than saintly bishop soliloquizing on his deathbed in the presence of several young men. He begins as follows:

> Vanity, saith the preacher, vanity!
> Draw round my bed: is Anselm keeping back?
> Nephews—sons mine…Ah God, I know not! Well—

Are the youths his nephews or are they his sons? True to the custom of his age, the bishop has been passing them off as nephews. Now, however, that he is dying, he finally calls them his sons. But the double interruption in the third line shows us what it costs him to speak the truth. He hates to confess his sins, and perhaps he hates the idea that such a confession means that his death is truly at hand; but he longs to have a magnificent tomb erected for him, and for that he needs sons, not nephews. Hence the unfinished phrases and clauses.

Later in the poem, the bishop brings out, with equal reluctance, a yet more reprehensible confession. Long ago there was a fire in the church. The bishop took advantage of it to make a bulky precious stone disappear. (Browning does not allow us to accuse him definitely of having *set* the fire.) He is longing to have it used for his tomb, but of course he hates to admit the theft, and at the same time he is afraid that his sons will cheat him of it. Three interruptions, one of them significantly the same as at the beginning of the poem, mark these strong meanings:

> Go dig
> The white-grape vineyard where the oil-press stood,
> Drop water gently till the surface sink,
> And if ye find…Ah God, I know not, I!…
> Bedded in store of rotten fig-leaves soft,
> And corded up in a tight olive-frail,
> Some lump, ah God, of *lapis lazuli*,
> Big as a Jew's head cut off at the nape,
> Blue as a vein o'er the Madonna's breast…

> Sons, all I bequeathed you, villas, all,
> That brave Frascati villa with its bath,
> So, let the blue lump poise between my knees,

And so on.[26]

Our next rhetorical device is that of *altered word order* or *hyperbaton*. Despite their many experiments and audacities, most of our living poets use a straighforward word order most of the time. Even our difficult poetry is likely to be written in the way English is normally spoken, for in modern contexts hyperbaton often feels like an obsolete 'poeticism', unless it reproduces the innocuous rearrangements we all continue to make in our everyday lives ('Gone are the days!' and the like). But our poetic ancestors routinely altered prose word order. Here, in addition to the extremely common 'I know not' that Browning's bishop utters, are a few instances lifted from Chapter 13:

> To your scatter'd bodies go.

> Grand go the Years in the Crescent above them.

> Of all its wreathed pearls her hair she frees.

> The rest to some faint meaning make pretense.

For one reason or another, altered word order often imparted to readers the sense of elevation, the ennobling of common speech, that was the hallmark of 'Poesy', along with the other dignifying tropes I have mentioned before. On a more down-to-earth level, the possibility of playing with word order gave poets additional flexibility in obtaining a desired rhyme or rhythm—in ages when these two elements were of central importance to poetry.

Another elevating trope favored by our ancestors in the craft was *periphrasis* (better known in English as *circumlocution*, grounded in Latin instead of Greek) that is to say a roundabout way of describing something. Call to mind again the lines of Thomas Gray's ode on Eton College quoted in Chapters 12 and 13, with their 'rolling circle' for 'hoop' and similar enhancements. Here is Milton's lofty way of saying that it took Satan and the other fallen angels nine days and nights to fall from heaven to hell:

26. Lines 1-3 and 36-47 of 'The Bishop Orders his Tomb at Saint Praxed's Church, Rome 15—', published in 1949. A frail is a basket.

> Nine times the space that measures day and night
> To mortal men, he with his horrid crew
> Lay vanquished rolling in the fiery gulf.[27]

I should also mention Pope's well-known periphrastic 'finny tribe' for fish, and Tennyson's 'manly growth' for moustache, both of which strike modern readers as funny, though not meant to be. The Tennysonian example, furthermore, illustrates the fact that the figure of periphrasis is often used to create yet another trope, the *euphemism*. In a poem about King Arthur and his knights, 'moustache' seemed unacceptably modern and vulgar. Nowadays, euphemism thrives not in poetry but in everyday speech, as when we 'obey the call of nature' or 'pass away'.

Like the other tropes that have gone out of fashion without disappearing, circumlocution puts in an occasional appearance in the poetry written since World War I. Robinson Jeffers, for instance (1887–1962) used it with deep meaning in describing the killing of a wounded hawk:

> We had fed him six weeks, I gave him freedom,
> He wandered over the foreland hill and returned in the
> evening, asking for death,
> Not like a beggar, still eyed with the old
> Implacable arrogance. I gave him the lead gift in the twilight.[28]

We could also consider 'the lead gift' an instance of *paradox*, another trope with a Greek name long since assimilated into English. In a paradoxical utterance the speaker or writer teases us by playing with a seeming contradiction or impossibility that, upon examination, is revealed as a meaningfully complex, logical and possible statement. The sudden revelation of this reversal operates as a tiny drama in our minds; hence the proposition comes alive. But paradox is also conceptually fruitful, for, like irony, it manages in a compressed space to display two sides of an idea, a scene, a character. Yes, we realize, the fatal bullet *is* a gift!

A similar combination of drama and intriguing thought occurs in the paradox of a baby winning a war. Impossible? Not so, says the poet:

27. *Paradise Lost*, Book I, lines 50-52.
28. From 'Hurt Hawks' (1928). In *The Collected Poems of Robinson Jeffers* (ed. T. Hunt; Palo Alto: Stanford University Press, 1988).

> This little Babe, so few days old,
> Is come to rifle Satan's fold;
> All hell doth at his presence quake,
> Though he himself for cold do shake;
> For in this weak unarmèd wise
> The gates of hell he will surprise.[29]

Remember, in this connection, the paradoxes we inspected in Dante's *Paradiso* (Chapter 14) and Eliot's *Murder in the Cathedral* (Chapter 16). And here is John Donne, speaking to God:

> Take me to You, imprison me, for I,
> Except You enthrall me, never shall be free,
> Nor ever chaste, except You ravish me.[30]

The *oxymoron* is simply a compressed paradox, as, for example, in Shakespeare's *Love's Labour's Lost*, when one of the characters chides Love as follows:

> This wimpled, whining, purblind, wayward boy,
> This signior junior, giant-dwarf, dan Cupid.[31]

For our next and final trope, consider the following exchange which occurs a little later in the same play:

> PRINCESS
> Was that the king, that spurr'd his horse so hard
> Against the steep up-rising of the hill?

> FORESTER
> I know not; but I think it was not he.

> PRINCESS
> Whoe'er a' was, a' show'd a mounting mind.[32]

29. The first of four stanzas by Robert Southwell (1561–95).

30. The conclusion of Holy Sonnet 14, published posthumously in 1633. Incidentally, these lines allow us to revive for a moment the important fifth practical pointer of Chapter 9. Both 'enthrall' and 'ravish' have double meanings that were already current in Donne's time. Shall we allow the *other* possible meaning of each word to affect the poet's primary propositions? Or shall we exclude them? For this particular reader, incorporating them dilutes the force of the primary, hard-hitting paradox: for the Christian, being imprisoned by God is true freedom, being 'raped' by God is true innocence.

31. Act III, Scene i. The play was published in 1598. 'Wimpled' = blindfolded; 'dan' = don.

32. Act IV, Scene i. The 'a = he.

'A mounting mind' is one of Shakespere's countless and not always applauded puns. The *pun* is probably as old as mankind, and I doubt that anybody can be found who refuses to slip it now and then into a discourse.[33] In our discussion of metaphor, I observed a degree of laziness in man's construction of language. One consequence is that most of the words of, I presume, all human languages carry more than one meaning. A pun is created—or detected by us—when this 'more than one meaning' is activated by the context; that is to say when we decide *not* to exclude the other possible meaning or meanings.[34]

Mostly we think of the pun as a humorous device; but if we summon Hopkins's

> Because the Holy Ghost over the bent
> Word broods with warm breast and with ah! bright wings,

(see Chapter 9) it becomes clear that this trope can be given a highly serious significance. When this occurs, we sometimes avoid the word 'pun' because of its comic connotation and speak of *ambiguity*.

Rhetoric is not, in sober truth, a subject of infinite extension; but the present chapter could unquestionably be doubled or quadrupled in length without much effort, for there are handbooks with alphabetical lists that can be harvested by anyone who can read. Let it be enough for our purposes if we come away with a sense of no little amazement at what people have squeezed out of language beyond mere basic communication. At the same time, we should keep in mind that some very good poets prefer to squeeze lightly. We have seen that superb poetry can be written without memorable metaphors, symbols and synecdoches. This can be extended to any or all of the other means of giving high color to one's utterances. And yet, I doubt whether a connoisseur of rhetoric could go far into any fine 'simple' poem without detecting, sooner rather than later, some not-so-simple enhancement beyond plain communication, and even beyond rhythm, rhyme and our old friend the limited quantum—something eloquent, in short, that invites our admiration.

---

33. The word 'Overture' at the start of this book is a certifiable pun.

34. Donne's 'enthrall' and 'ravish' can thus be called potential or excluded puns.

Chapter 22

Epilogue: Touching Genius

I want to summon one last time the concept of off-stage illumination that we discussed in Chapter 8:

> If a poem both puzzles and delights you, tantalizing you with the notion that you have not taken true possession of it yet, a fascinating search may begin, of the sort I mentioned in connection with 'The Sick Rose'... This search for off-stage light will, or should, begin with the artist's other works. That is where you are most likely to find hints regarding his fundamental concerns, or even direct answers to your questions. Other important off-stage sources of light may be the poet's life and beliefs as far as we know them through letters, reports by family and friends, documents of all sorts; then the historical situation (politics, economics, social realities, etc.) in which the poem is embedded; a political, social or metaphysical ideology underlying this situation; the artistic tradition in which the poet was or is writing; his direct literary debts (the sources); and even the circumstances of public reception, publishing methods, patronage and the like. Any of these, or all, may suggest credible meanings (and the satisfaction that ensues) when the poem does not radiate them sufficiently on its own.

In short, off-stage illumination can be brought in from an impressive number of sources. But only the biographical source will be considered in what follows: 'the poet's life and beliefs as far as we know them through letters, reports by family and friends, documents of all sorts' and, I should now add, the accounts given by biographers and editors—people who have done the digging for us and whose help we gratefully exploit, inasmuch as we can hardly be expected to do all the research in person for all the works of art that interest and yet in part elude us.[1] So then, leaving aside the other possible sources of off-stage light mentioned in the quotation, we dwell for a moment on the possibility that our comprehension of a poem, or any other work of art, may occasionally be enhanced by means of biographical materials, with the almost certain consequence that our enjoyment—otherwise said: the success—of the poem will increase accordingly.

You will recall that we spread some of this biographical light in attempting to explicate Sylvia Plath's 'The Hanging Man', W.H. Auden's 'A Misunderstanding', and the fragment from one of Ezra Pound's Cantos. If you will glance again at the latter (p. 141), you will notice that the foreign idioms Pound uses, and his allusions to 'the Romagnolo' and 'San Giorgio', can be looked up in various reference works that have nothing to do with the poet; but for Dr Wallushnig and Virginia Marotti purely biographical information would have to be accessed if we felt unable to take adequate possession of the Canto without knowing who these people were and what role they played in the poet's life.

Now, however, that we have thoroughly viewed and reviewed this concept, we can draw a line under it and start a fresh page, on which we note that most of us welcome and cherish biographical information even when we do not feel that we need it in order to take satisfying possession of a given work of art. We welcome and cherish it when it 'adds something' to an already satisfying grasp of the work, but also, more broadly, when it opens a window for us on to the figure of the artist as such, that is to say without specifically addressing and affecting the poem, the painting, the musical score that gratifies us.

When we first hear the voice of Milton's protagonist in the dramatic poem *Samson Agonistes* (1671), the biblical hero is lamenting his blindness:

> O dark, dark, dark, amid the blaze of noon,
> Irrecoverably dark, total Eclipse
> Without all hope of day!

---

1.   Not to complicate matters, I am going to assume throughout this chapter that we trust the accuracy of the biographical information we have acquired.

O first created Beam, and thou great Word,
Let there be light, and light was over all;
Why am I thus bereav'd thy prime decree?[2]

Do we need to know, in order either to understand or to admire these lines, that Milton was himself blind? And is it necessary to realize that his blindness would naturally make the subject of Samson particularly attractive to him as a poet? Of course not. But does not the knowledge instill a broader knowledge and satisfaction when we reread the lines? For most of us it does. Now, it may happen that as we read or reread these lines (which stand, of course, for all works of art) the thought of Milton's blindness fails to occur to us. We know all about it, but the cell in our brain where this knowledge is housed happens to be asleep. Let it sleep in peace. The lines are magnificent enough on their own. However, when the knowledge is awake and impregnates our experience, something I would like to call a *plenitude* of feeling supersedes and improves the purely aesthetic thrill afforded by the lines as such.

Samson's and Milton's blindness are obviously connected. But why does it make news that a request for a grant of arms and crest (namely, a bird flapping at a spear), preserved to this day in the London College of Arms in Queen Victoria Street, might be in Shakespeare's own hand? If it is in fact, will we be able to untangle one of those notorious knots in Shakespeare's plays? Hardly. And yet—a document written by Shakespeare himself! The thrill of it is evident. And it is our worship of the poet that makes us seek it out. Does a scholar discover an affidavit in the archives written by Henry Chettle or Barnabe Barnes, two irretrievably obscure contemporaries of Shakespeare? No one cares.

Now imagine yourself raptly listening to Beethoven's Ninth Symphony, but without knowing much about the composer except, perhaps, that he was an unkempt curmudgeon and deaf. Suppose now that the concert has moved you to read a biography of the composer. You are told that the symphony's premiere took place in Vienna in 1824. It appears that, exceptionally, the composer was escorted to the podium and placed next to the conductor.

---

2. Lines 80-85; the 'of' after 'bereaved' could be omitted in seventeenth century English.

At the close of the performance an incident occurred which must have brought tears to many an eye in the room. The master, though placed in the midst of this confluence of music, heard nothing of it at all and was not even sensible of the applause of the audience at the end of his great work, but continued standing with his back to the audience, and beating the time, till Fraulein Ungher, who had sung the contralto part, turned him, or induced him to turn round and face the people, who were still clapping their hands, and giving way to the greatest demonstration of pleasure. His turning round, and the sudden conviction thereby forced on everybody that he had not done so before because he could not hear what was going on, acted like an electric shock on all present, and a volcanic explosion of sympathy and admiration followed, which was repeated again and again, and seemed as if it would never end.[3]

I submit that this life-event—this gossipy anecdote, if you wish— throws no light whatsoever on the Ninth Symphony. It does not make the music better for us, nor does it give us some new insight into its structure, instrumentation, etc. The music is not better, but the total experience is. It fills more space in our soul, so to speak, than the music alone.

The examples I have given here suggest that our ever-so-human curiosity has taken us outside the precincts of the strictly aesthetic 'laws' we have considered throughout this book; and standing outside, we take hold of the final vital principle in our study of the fundamentals of the aesthetic life: *The experience of art embedded in the humanity that created it is more gratifying than the experience of art alone.* Or: *Aesthetic pleasure tends to propel us beyond aesthetic pleasure.* There is, in other words, an inner energy, or dynamic, in the emotion generated by a fine work of art that tends to make us seek the broader satisfaction of an acquaintance with the human being to whom we have owed that purely aesthetic emotion, and the events and realities of his life into which the artistic work is implanted, even when the work of art is aesthetically 'perfect' in itself. This is the satisfaction I have called plenitude.

Of course, most of us are intensely curious about all kinds of extraordinary people, living or dead, famous or infamous. Publishers are happy feeding this hunger and cashing in on it. Grisly

---

3. In John N. Burk, *The Life and Works of Beethoven* (New York: The Modern Library [Random House], 1946), p. 226.

tyrants, Mafia gangsters, scheming businessmen who defraud the public; movie stars and astronauts; celebrated chefs; operatic divas; luminous scientists; saints on their way to heaven; painters and novelists—anyone whose contribution to society lifted him or her above the average awakes in the public an avid curiosity. Here, however, we are not discussing the knowledge and wisdom we acquire by reading biographies, but what this learning contributes to our experience of art. Art is a gift we receive from 'out there'. One loves a gift in and for itself. And yet a disembodied gift, a gift severed from the giver, is less fulfilling that one whose giver we know.

And so we take the gift as Beethoven accepted Handel's music, 'kneeling at his tomb' (the biographers tell us) with passionate gratitude. Who was this Handel whose music fills us with joy? What was he like? When did he write the oratorio we are hearing this moment? Under what circumstances? How did people like it? No theory of art can dispel this curiosity, without which we would be less than wholly human. Did the deeply spiritual painter mistreat his students? Did the poet write his melancholy ode at the time he knew he was dying? Was it a busy king who found time to compose that charming flute concerto? Can it be that the great novelist wrote his masterpiece in jail? To be sure, we cannot always satisfy this curiosity. A plain lack of time or opportunity can stand in our way; or else the artist has left few traces; or yet the work we love is anonymous—the artist has disappeared from view forever. Often, therefore, we remain content with the autonomous aesthetic pleasure afforded by the disembodied work of art. But whenever we can insert the work of art into the life of the artist, we breathe a richer air.

However, we should not sentimentalize our desire to be in touch with genius. Beethoven's biographers inform us that he was so disgruntled with the receipts for the Ninth on opening night that afterwards, in a tavern, he wrathfully accused the conductor and one of the sponsors of having cheated him. There are nice geniuses and others not so nice. Beethoven was among the not so nice. The biographical circumstances we seek are not required to be morally uplifting. Plenitude is not all roses.

Indeed—and here I return to a topic very briefly brought up in Chapter 11—the extra-aesthetic information we acquire may make the artist so hateful in our eyes as a human being that our hatred spills over all his works and poisons them for us. Perhaps we had loved his simple poems about Nature. Suddenly we discover that he was a monster or that he held monstrous views (in our eyes). And we find that we can no longer stomach his delicate poems about the leaves and lakes and lilies. It is pointless for a theorist to demand that we separate our loathing for the man from our feelings about his work. That the phenomenon of spillover does sometimes occur is simply another one of the facts of our aesthetic life. To which we can add a related fact, namely that the overflow of our hatred from the artist to his art is much more likely to take place when the artist is close to us in time and place than when he is a faraway historical figure.

This then is the exception to the gratifying plenitude that comes to us when we immerse the work of art into the life that made and surrounds it. Even wisdom, it seems, can taste sour.

Mediocre and bad works of art seldom motivate us to inquire into the lives of their makers. But what happens if we come into endearing information about someone we consider a bad artist? How likely is that information to overflow as well, and cause us to admire what we would otherwise despise? Not very likely. And yet, in extreme situations, where we discover the profoundest and most vital of bonds between ourselves and the artist, his badness as artist may well disappear for us. Away from the extreme, the spillover ceases. If, for instance, we feel that 'Departed Friends' is wretched doggerel, the discovery (I am inventing) that Edgar Guest was blind, deaf and lame when he wrote it, or that reciting it to a tribe of Indians who were about to scalp him saved his life and got him appointed chief medicine man—a story of this kind, however satisfying and enriching to our intellect, will not redeem the poem. Doggerel remains doggerel with the information, as works of genius remain works of genius without it. Even when the life story behind a work of art truly moves us and we would love to admire it (think, for instance, of the bereaved American pioneer whose 'Twas midnight and he sat alone' I quoted in Chapter 11), even then we rarely succeed in fooling our deepest selves into relishing a work we would normally dismiss.

Genius! What is genius? A word. Simply another one of those verbal medals we like to pin on anyone we greatly admire. To be sure, if we use the word at all, we go on to admit different degrees of applicability, just as we distinguished between major and minor classics, and just as some medals speak of nobler deeds than others. Yet even a minor artistic genius is a person who handled the materials and resources of his art significantly better than most of his rivals, even though the latter shared with him the artistic tradition, access to the materials and resources, and, of course, the historical moment in which he lived. Our verbal accolade expresses this recognition in two simple syllables. If, in the grips of one or another egalitarian ideology, we were to deny the distinction between talent and mediocrity, and lose interest in the lives of those who have made the coarse raw materials of art shine, the resulting dullness would cover only ourselves in a mantle of ash.

INDEX OF QUOTED TEXTS

An asterisk following a page number indicates that the selection is quoted in full.